ORGANIZATIONAL PARADOXES

The basic premise of *Organizational Paradoxes* is as relevant today as when it was first published fourteen years ago – to help individuals in organizations make sense of the things happening around them and within them. The themes of power, paranoia, work disorders, leadership and followership, alienation, folie à deux, and the vicissitudes of the career life cycle remain central concerns. Presented in the form of case vignettes of people in boundary situations or coping with major life changes, Kets de Vries illustrates the various strata of working life.

Organizational Paradoxes takes the reader on a journey into the individual's personal 'underworld'. Its primary objective remains to help the reader understand the inner theatre of leaders and followers. It looks at the deep structure of the executive's world, and tries to extricate some of the wishes, fears and anxieties prevalent in the world of organizations. This is not, however, a 'quick-fix' solution for the executive keen to improve his working life. By urging the reader to practise the self-observation that leads to self-understanding, Kets de Vries reveals that this is an essential quality of leadership.

Professor Manfred F. R. Kets de Vries is a practising psycho-analyst and clinical professor of management and leadership at the European Institute of Business Administration (INSEAD) in Fontainebleau, France. He holds the Raoul de Vitry d'Avaucourt Chair of Human Resource Management. He is the author or co-author of ten books.

ORGANIZATIONAL PARADOXES

Clinical approaches to management

Second edition

Manfred F. R. Kets de Vries

London and New York

First published 1980
by Tavistock Publications Ltd

Second edition published 1995
by Routledge
11 New Fetter Lane, London EC4P 4EE

Simultaneously published in the USA and Canada
by Routledge
29 West 35th Street, New York, NY 10001

Typeset in Palatino by
Michael Mepham, Frome, Somerset
Printed and bound in Great Britain by
Mackays of Chatham PLC, Chatham, Kent

British Library Cataloguing in Publication Data
A catalogue record for this book is
available from the British Library

Library of Congress Cataloging in Publication Data
Kets de Vries, Manfred F. R.
Organizational paradoxes: clinical
approaches to management /
Manfred Kets de Vries.
p. cm.
Includes bibliographical references and index.
1. Organizational behavior.
2. Management. 3. Psychology.
Industrial. I. Title.
HD58.7.K47   1994
658—dc20   94–15858
                                                  CIP

ISBN 0–415–11072–6(hbk)
ISBN 0–415–11073–4(pbk)

*To Elisabet, Florian,
Henriette and Jonas*

CONTENTS

FIGURES AND TABLES

FIGURES

TABLES

PREFACE TO THE
FIRST EDITION

It has been many years since I learned about Muhammad Tughluq. One cannot remain unaffected by his life story. This sultan of Delhi who ascended the throne in 1325 was known for his eccentric rule and ferocious temperament. His actions made him a man of extremes. What made him particularly notorious was laying Delhi in ruins, forcing its inhabitants to leave the city as punishment for having incurred his wrath. Angered, he had ordered them to move a forty-day's journey away, to Daulatabad, a city which he felt should be his new capital. According to the legend, a search by his slaves unearthed two people who had remained in the city after his deadline for departure had passed: a cripple and a blind man. These two were brought before Muhammad Tughluq, who ordered the cripple to be flung from a mangonel and the blind man to be dragged to his new capital. Only the blind man's leg arrived. Shortly afterwards, one night, the sultan mounted the roof of his palace, which now overlooked a completely dead city, and remarked that his mind was tranquil and his wrath appeased.

Many years later on a visit to Delhi I found myself face to face with the ruins of the ghost city created by Muhammad Tughluq, once more reminded of the pathology of leadership and the abuse of power. I was fascinated by the story not only as a historical curiosity but also by the parallels which could be drawn with contemporary leadership behaviour. The story became a stimulus for further reflection on the enigmatic nature of power and leadership. I felt an urge for a greater understanding of these processes. The story also raised questions about the nature of man, and human motivation. Dealing with this material in an organizational setting I came across related topics such as organizational alienation, work disorders, and organizational stress. Eventually, these reflections led to thoughts about the concept of the career life cycle, particularly as experienced by the middle-aged and aging executive.

These seemingly disjointed topics acquired a unifying rationale. My objective became to contribute to the development of a theory of organizational functioning viewed from the perspective of a clinician. This orientation combines the applied areas of diagnosis, 'treatment', and prevention with some basic research. For some time I had been disenchanted with prevailing simplistic notions of executive behaviour which I often encountered in organizational literature. It struck me how far removed such a view of people seemed to be from what I actually experienced in my consulting work. In contrast, using the tools of the clinician, particularly psychoanalytical concepts, I felt much closer in touch with the reality of organizational processes. These conceptual notions became even more alive when I became formally involved with psychoanalytical training at the Canadian Institute of Psychoanalysis. A more complex, but at the same time more authentic and realistic description of managerial behaviour emerged.

Fortunately, in this process of maturation and reorientation I did not stand alone. I am in great intellectual and emotional debt to a number of people who helped me by deepening my understanding of human behaviour. Professor Erik Erikson's writings, applying clinical insights to the study of society, have been of great influence. His lectures at Harvard University, which I followed for many years, were a source of great intellectual excitement and influenced my way of thinking considerably.

A debt of a very different nature I owe to Dr Maurice Dongier, chairman of psychiatry at McGill University and director of the Allan Memorial Institute in Montreal. Engaged in the 'impossible profession', he has helped me understand the nature of empathy. Generativity became more of a reality under his tutorship. For this, and more, I am extremely grateful.

Professor Sudhir Kakar of the Centre for the Study of Developing Societies in New Delhi has been not only a very patient tutor but also an extremely close friend over the years. He helped me in my initial steps on the clinical road, always able to split fact from fantasy and at the same time creating a new inner reality. Notwithstanding great geographical distance we have been able to meet and I hope will continue to do so in the future.

The debt I owe to Professor Abraham Zaleznik of the Harvard

Business School is difficult to express in words. A gifted teacher, a great conceptualizer, and an excellent clinician, he has been one of the pioneers in the application of psychoanalytical concepts to the study of management. He awakened my interest in this orientation. Over the years, first when I was his student, later his research collaborator, and finally co-author of our book *Power and the Corporate Mind*, he has taught me a great deal about human behaviour and became a determining factor in my choice of career. For his contribution to the broadening of my horizon, introducing me to a world beyond the apparent, I wish to thank him deeply.

My association with the Faculty of Management at McGill University has been very beneficial, providing me with an excellent research climate and a very collegial atmosphere. I particularly appreciated the encouragement I received for my work from the former Dean, Stanley Shapiro, and his successor, Laurent Picard.

In the process of rewriting and editing this book a number of people were especially helpful with their critical comments. I would like to extend my appreciation to Professors Roger Bennett, Gerry Gorn, Roger Gosselin, Henry Mintzberg, James Waters, and Danny Miller, all of McGill University, Faculty of Management. In addition, I would like to thank Jack Ondrack and John Wynne for their very useful comments. I am also very grateful to Lawrence Nadler, not only for his detailed comments about the various chapters, but also for the opportunity he has given me to test some of my ideas in his company. His contributions helped me to remain closely tuned to the concerns of the business practitioner.

Portions of this book have appeared in a modified form in a number of articles: 'The Entrepreneurial Personality: A Person at the Crossroads', *Journal of Management Studies*, 1977, 14 (1); 'Crisis Leadership and the Paranoid Potential: An Organizational Perspective', *Bulletin of the Menninger Clinic*, 1977, 41 (4); 'Defective Adaptation to Work: An Approach to Conceptualization', *Bulletin of the Menninger Clinic*, 1978, 42 (1); 'Folie à Deux: Acting Out Your Subordinates' Fantasies', *Human Relations*, 1978, 31 (10); 'The Mid-Career Conundrum', *Organizational Dynamics*, Autumn 1978 and 'Is There Life After Retirement?', *California Management Review*, Fall 1979. The editors of these journals are thanked for permission to reprint.

The author and publishers would like to thank the English and American publishers of W. H. Auden for permission to reprint the extract from 'The Quest' on page 13. The poem is reprinted by permission of Faber and Faber Ltd from *Collected Poems* of W. H. Auden and by permission of Random House Inc. from *W. H. Auden: Collected Poems*, edited by Edward Mendelson.

The typing of the manuscript was tirelessly done by Cheryl Kelahear who kept her good cheer in what eventually must have been a very tiresome, repetitive effort. In addition, I am grateful for the assistance of Pina Vicario and for the editorial contribution of Ken Norris.

Finally, I would like to thank my wife Elisabet not only for her patience, encouragement, and support during the years I worked on the book, but also for being among the best of colleagues. Her clarifying and editorial comments have been invaluable. There are times when words seem inadequate and this is one.

PREFACE TO THE
SECOND EDITION

The world has changed significantly since *Organizational Paradoxes* was first published more than fourteen years ago. Who could have predicted the astonishing developments which have occurred over the last decade? We have seen the end of communism in Eastern Europe, the fall of the Berlin wall and the reunification of Germany, the demise of the old Soviet Union, the bloody break-up of Yugoslavia, the end of apartheid in South Africa, 'closet' capitalistic developments in China, spectacular economic developments in the countries of the Pacific rim, dramatic changes in the political fabric of Japan and Italy, and a handshake on the lawn of the White House between the prime minister of Israel and the head of the Palestinian Liberation Organization. Anyone foreseeing all this ten years ago would have been declared out of their mind.

The Chinese curse, 'May you live in interesting times', seems to have become almost too real. These rapid changes in our environment have created an enormous amount of anxiety about the future and have resulted in great fear of the unknown. These feelings of anxiety tend to have a regressive impact on people, arousing a sense of helplessness and dependency reactions. The most natural corollary to these psychological processes is a fascination with powerful individuals and a deep yearning for leadership. In such situations of change and transformation people search for leaders who will help them to deal with these feelings. Leaders are the ones expected to demonstrate some sort of stability, to offer some form of guidance, in a highly uncertain world.

The English word leader comes from the Anglo-Saxon root *laedare*, meaning to take people on a journey, and the notion of a joint journey is a very appropriate metaphor of leadership. Leaders are the people who show us the direction in which we are supposed

xiii

to go, who provide us with a road map for our actions. Such people help us to master uncertainties, create order out of chaos, and know how to create a sense of excitement about the future. Effective leaders know how to rally people behind their ideas. They provide us with a persuasive and durable sense of purpose and direction, rooted deeply in human values.

It is interesting to ask why certain people possess leadership abilities while others do not. What enables some individuals to recognize the dissatisfaction with the *status quo* among the various constituencies in their respective societies, and present new alternatives, while others miss the boat? What makes such people realize that the old ways of functioning are no longer viable? What makes them sensitive to the wind of change? Can it be ascribed to chance or is there more to it? Is there something unique in their personality make-up that makes them catalysts for change?

Clinical detective work on people with leadership qualities has unravelled a picture of individuals in search of some kind of congruence between the driving forces in their own intra-psychic world and what is happening in the outside environment. These people are different from more common mortals in that they are able to find a match between their own needs and the transformations taking place in the external world. They have a sense of timing, they recognize opportunities, and have a great talent for enthusing others and aligning them behind their ideas. In all their actions they realize (whether consciously or unconsciously) that there is such a thing as a historical moment, a window of opportunity. With their compelling need to act in a certain way, leaders like Gorbachev, Yeltsin, Mandela, De Klerk, Deng Xiaoping, Kohl, Rabin and Arafat have become household names.

Unfortunately, truly transformational leadership is an exceedingly scarce commodity. Inspiring leaders who have the ability to create a sustained, shared road map of the future are hard to come by. The current nightmare in Bosnia is a terrible reminder of the failure of leadership in the Western world. It demonstrates the devastating effects of an absence of effective leadership. The break-up of the former Yugoslavia has made us realize that there are times when boundaries have to be set, when decisions have to be made, and that certain situations necessitate strong action. These are the processes that leaders are expected to put into effect.

It is easy to forget that inaction is also a form of action. If no action is taken in response to events, there is always the danger that familiar scenarios will repeat themselves. For example, intervention from other powers to prevent Hitler's annexation of Austria, or to block Germany's claim on Czechoslovakia's Sudetenland, or support for Czechoslovak resistance to German invasion, would have gone a long way toward preventing the suffering that occurred in the years to follow. Just as Chamberlain failed to deal with Hitler and made the kind of compromises that proved to be exceedingly costly, so are world leaders compromising over the tragic events in Bosnia. The catastrophe that has taken place in the former Yugoslavia over the past two years could have been prevented if the leadership of the international community had been stronger in its convictions, rallied its constituencies around them, set boundaries, and intervened to block military aggression.

The crisis of leadership is not only a reflection of the mediocrity of many who rise to positions of power, but also a reflection of the unwillingness of many leaders to transcend their own personal agendas to create a better world. Too many leaders become addicted to the power associated with their position and start to act in a very destructive manner. Too many are tempted to appeal to people's most base and primitive motives rather than their more positive and elevated ones. And as the atrocities in Bosnia illustrate, the aggressive potential dormant in all of us can easily be awoken. Power can be used for constructive purposes, but, unfortunately and all too often, for destructive ones as well.

Bosnia is only one example of the crisis of leadership in the Western world. Many other examples can be offered. That the seventh annual report of *The Index of Social Health* (which attempts to monitor the well-being of US society by examining statistics from US Census Bureau reports on sixteen major social problems) shows a twenty-year low, is another illustration of the failure of leadership. The confidence index in a poll taken of 1,200 US citizens on how they evaluate national performance in areas that shape the quality of life (education, health care, safety, occupation and living standards) was thirty-four out of a hundred, indicating the respondents' pessimism about the nation's well-being and the future.[1] That loss of confidence in the future has hit an all time low can again be seen as an indictment of current US leadership.

Effective leadership implies finding individuals who are receptive to the needs of their followers, who are cognizant of the sensitive nature of the leader–follower relationship. These people are characteristically deeply reflective, thoughtful, and explicit about their core values and beliefs. Such individuals know how to arouse people's hopes and aspirations, transform personal needs into political demands, liberate human energy and inspire people to action. They can balance their personal convictions and values with a sense of flexibility in execution. They recognize when to be playful and when to draw boundaries. In acting the way they do, they transcend the narrow, parochial personal concerns of themselves and their followers. In the process they raise people to the highest level of personal motivation and human morality. These are the kinds of people we need in our rapidly changing world.

The need for inspiring leadership in this age of transformation and change, however, is not the preserve of national politics. On a much smaller scale, organizations are also experiencing some of the same needs. The environment in which most organizations operate is becoming exceedingly complex. Apart from the dramatic political transformations taking place in the world of business, organizations are more susceptible to international competition and technological change. The communication and technology revolution of the last two decades has been formidable and is having an enormous impact on the way businesses organize themselves. Moreover, the world is becoming increasingly a global market place, a development which creates a host of other issues.

Bearing in mind that the average age of the world's largest corporations seems to be no more than forty years, a glance at today's *Fortune* 500 and that of twenty years ago is a sobering exercise. More than one third of the companies that were on the original list no longer exist. Although a number of variables play a role in organizational decline, a critial one seems to be the leadership factor. Reviewing the history of a failing corporation, we repeatedly see the extent to which its fall is influenced by the leadership factor. Conversely, in excellent organizations we find leaders who are able to tame the pull of excessive narcissism, leaders who are able to empower their subordinates, leaders who create the kind of culture of trust that makes for a learning organization, and leaders who are able to articulate a sustained, shared image of the future.

Unfortunately, the kind of leader who has the vision to guide organizational participants through the kind of turbulence they are likely to face in the future is rare. Rare too is the leader who is able to create the kind of corporate culture that is conducive to learning and personal growth. Life in organizations frequently has a negative quality. All too often, in too many organizations, credit goes up, and garbage goes down. Organizational participants end up feeling frustrated, abused and exploited.

Many executives are unable to handle the psychological pressures of leadership. Power turns into a drug, and goes to their heads. In the process, the organizations they create turn into abominations. Feelings of alienation and dissociation are very familiar to many executives in such abusive work environments. Organizational talent is frequently under-utilized or misdirected. This causes a considerable amount of stress and is an enormous waste of resources.

Moreover, the crisis of leadership is exacerbated by the prevailing model of rational action in decision making. Economic man, that lightning assessor of the pleasures and pains of living in an optimizing world, is a model of human functioning which has been the mainstay of economic theory for too long. Subscribing to such a paradigm does not make for a model of realistic action. On the contrary, it makes for a very artificial, two-dimensional world. Astute observers of organizational life have sensed all along that a model of rational action only gets them so far. It leaves too many organizational phenomena unexplained. They recognize that rationality has its limits. They realize that other dimensions of human functioning have to be taken into consideration. The challenge for the realistic executive is to find a balance between the striving for rationality on the one hand, and the underlying irrationality of human existence on the other. This is not easy. The idea that many human processes operate beyond our direct awareness is very hard to take. It raises doubts about the autonomous functioning of the individual and the amount of control we have over our environment. Just as Galileo questioned the centrality of humankind in the cosmos and Darwin the centrality of humankind in the animal kingdom, Freud questioned the amount of awareness individuals have of their own actions. Each of these giants from the world of ideas met an enormous amount of resistance. It is hard for us to give up the notion that we are in complete control of our environment, that part of our functioning is outside our awareness. Some of the more elusive processes which are beyond direct awareness, however, have to be taken into consideration if we really want to understand human functioning.

The search for alternative ways of looking at organizational life has been stimulated by the realization that a great many screws are

xvii

loose at the top of quite a few organizations. From the organizational 'soap operas' portrayed in the popular press, it is clear that corporate executives are not always rational beings; on the contrary, their emotions, wishes, fantasies and defences have a direct influence on the way they run their organizations. Even stock markets have recognized the 'CEO effect', implying that the leader's role in an organization may have a discounting or upgrading effect on the value of the company's shares.

In order to understand why corporate leaders act the way they do, and why the model of rational behaviour and action does not work, we have to return to the personal struggles and psychological pressures on leadership. Clinical insights can help to make sense out of what may otherwise be perceived as inexplicable phenomena.

Freud's genius was to make people realize that there is a continuity between childhood and adulthood, waking life and sleeping life, and mental health and pathology. In his struggles with the 'demon of irrationality' he helped people understand that even the most irrational forms of behaviour have a rationale, that certain behaviour patterns are outside our conscious control, and, moreover, that we have a tendency to repeat earlier established patterns of functioning. Freud shed light on the fact that many people are stuck in certain types of behaviour. He pointed out how these impasses can lead to dysfunctional action. But his insights have also made us realize that mental health is basically *having a choice*, having the capacity to expand one's zone of discretion by better understanding these elusive processes and finding a way to break out of our self-imposed prisons. Sadly, many people become prisoners of their own neuroses, and remain trapped in vicious circles of dysfunctioning.

Since Freud's original contributions, psychoanalytic theory has evolved and has become increasingly complex, integrating concepts taken from drive psychology with neurology, ethology, information theory, cognition, child development, family systems theory, ego psychology, self-psychology, and object relations theory. These developments have made psychoanalytic theory more of a general psychology.

When I wrote *Organizational Paradoxes* in the late 1970s, I was struggling to integrate many of these emerging ideas of clinical theory. I was looking for concepts which might help me to better understand the world around me. At the time I was starting out on a personal psychoanalytic journey and also training to become a psychoanalyst. Learning from one's patients is an excellent way to see what clinical insights can accomplish in the way of change. My clinical work as a psychoanalyst and psychotherapist has helped me to sort out the useful from the less useful conceptualizations and improved my understanding of the more elusive processes in organizations. Theory, closely tied in with the practice of everyday living, can be highly effective. As the French psychiatrist Charcot used to say: 'La theorie c'est bon, mais ça n'empêche pas d'exister!' In addition, a leadership seminar I give once a year at INSEAD has been a marvellous 'laboratory', illustrating the infinite variety of styles leaders may adopt. Asking a group of leaders to tell their life stories and helping them make sense out of them is a great way to better understand the vicissitudes of human existence.

Organizational Paradoxes was originally written as an effort to humanize the organization, to recognize the role of the individual in the various dramas that make up organizational life. At the time, my main objective in writing the book was to make people realize that too many models of organizational functioning are highly unrealistic and superficial, that too many models take the obvious for granted, while ignoring the deeper significance of individual action. And the central theme of the book was the leader–follower interface in its many shapes and forms.

In the years since the first publication, however, things have changed. People have become more aware of the fact that organizations are not rational institutions where people optimize, but that a large 'irrational' component is intrinsic to this particular world. People have come to realize that it is vital to pay attention to the quirks and irrational processes that are part and parcel of individual behaviour. Students of organizations now acknowledge that much organizational behaviour expresses the unconscious conflicts, fears and yearnings of each organizational participant. An increasing number of organizational scholars have come to realize that executives are highly susceptible to unconscious and irrational processes. Given what we now know about human behaviour, the kind of models that take rational action for granted are increasingly dismissed as impractical to the understanding of organizational phenomena, and ineffective in enabling intervention and organizational transformation.

There has also been a growing realization of the effects of stress on the job. Stress-related diseases are increasing, and can frequently be traced to the vicissitudes of organizational life. Confronted with health statistics, students of organizations have begun to ask themselves about the negative effects of organizations on people and whether the drive for success may be taking too much of a toll on executives and their families. The International Labor Organization report – that in the US, 45 per cent of salaried workers state that they experience excessive stress and that 15 per cent have at some point suffered a nervous breakdown – is a real cause for alarm. Moreover, the estimate that 12 per cent of reduced output is related to stress disorders, and that 60–90 per cent of health care costs are related to stress, is not good news. According to the American Psychological Association, stress is costing organizations in the US an estimated $150 billion a year in diminished productivity, absenteeism and medical expenses. Claims for work-related mental stress now account for 14 per cent of all work-related stress claims filed under worker compensation. When a healthy male child has a one-in-five chance of developing coronary disease before the age of 60 (25 per cent of these coronaries being fatal), and a direct relationship with the nature of work can be demonstrated, some explanations are called for. [2] The paradigm of the economic man is not going to provide answers to these devastating statistics.

So what is the clinical paradigm all about? What are some of its more salient elements? First, there is the notion of determinism, implying that all behaviour is motivated, and that even highly irrational behaviour has a rationale. Puzzling as such behaviour may be, it is up to the observer to interpret it, to decode its meaning. Here an assortment of clinical concepts such as transference, counter transference, defence mechanisms, and character types can be helpful. Second, as I said earlier, many of our wishes and fantasies are outside our conscious awareness. All of us have blind spots – aspects of character, defensive patterns, wishes or fantasies of which we are not completely aware. Turning our attention to these elements of our personality may help expand the terrain of the unknown. Finally, previously internalized 'scripts', learned through contacts with our principal care takers and other influential people during the susceptible period of childhood, are the mainstays of our intra-psychic world and very much influence our ways of behaving and acting. These intra-psychic scripts determine our behaviour patterns and form the foundation of our core values and belief systems. Because of these scripts we are never completely free; our preconceptions, dictated by the past, determine the way we experience the world around us. These scripts create a sense of continuity between past, present and future. They may be the cause of repetition compulsion, a tendency to repeat patterns of behaviour, but understanding these scripts will make us more aware of the extent to which our future behaviour is determined by our past. It also will help us expand our zone of discretion in all our activities.

It has been satisfying to see, since the original publication of this book, that an increasing number of organizational scholars have realized the usefulness of the clinical approach to management. Many people have grasped that an understanding of unconscious processes can be of great help in deciphering what otherwise would be incomprehensible organizational phenomena. An indication that the clinical paradigm has moved more onto central stage is reflected in the increase in books and articles dealing with the subject. I have tried to make my own contributions to this change of attitude in books such as *Power and the Corporate Mind*, *The Irrational Executive*, *The Neurotic Organization*, *Unstable at the Top*, *Prisoners of Leadership*, *Organizations on the Couch*, and *Leaders, Fools, and Imposters*.

Since *Organizational Paradoxes* first appeared, I have been involved in the founding of the International Society for the Psychoanalytic Study of Organizations, the specific purpose of which is to help people understand the value of clinical concepts in making sense of organizational functioning. The success of this organization, indicated by its ever increasing membership, reflects the need of many organizational students to better understand the interface between people and organizations.

The basic premise of *Organizational Paradoxes* remains that of helping individuals in organizations to make sense out of the things happening around them. This is as relevant today as when the book was first published. The themes of power, paranoia, work disorders, leadership and followership, alienation, folie à deux, and the vicissitudes of the career life cycle remain central concerns. In order to illustrate these various themes, I presented in the first edition of the book a number of case vignettes of people who found themselves in boundary situations, who were trying to cope with major life changes. As William James once said, 'To study the abnormal is the best way of understanding the normal'. Reading the book once more, I believe that most of these original examples retain their value in illustrating various human foibles.

Organizational Paradoxes, now as before, takes the reader on a journey into the individual's personal 'underworld'. Its primary objective remains to help the reader understand the inner theatre of leaders and followers. It looks at the deep structure of the executive's world, and tries to extricate some of the wishes, fears and anxieties prevalent in the world of organizations.

Naturally, the ideal laboratory for examining what takes place in the mind of others lies within one's own mind. The Socratic philosophy that the unreflective life is not worth living is very much the leitmotif for this book. Self-understanding is the antecedent of effective action. The saying 'Know thyself' was written in the temple of ancient Delphi. A person who fails to realize how his or her actions affect the lives of others can become a danger to his or her organization. Effective executives monitor the impact they have on others. They know how to balance action with reflection; they realize that the capacity for self-observation is an essential quality of leadership. My hope is that the kind of material presented in this book will help people to realize their potential for meaningful action, and accept the responsibility for such action, while at the same time recognizing their limitations.

At the present time we find an abundance of self-help books telling people what to do to become a more effective executive. They seem to occupy a permanent position on the non-fiction best seller lists. Extreme hyperbole, promising magical, instant change, is used to bring these books to the attention of readers. Ironically, what makes these self-help books so ineffective is that in many instances people do not even know what their problems are. The popularity of such books again illustrates humankind's pursuit of the irrational.

This book does not provide magical answers. It differs in that it tries to point out that many psychological problems are extremely insidious and not susceptible to quick-fix solutions. The alternative, although more realistic, is also much more difficult. The process of self-discovery can be a lengthy and difficult journey. Looking deep into oneself is not always pleasant and may arouse a host of resistances. Moreover, the confrontation with the self and the acquisition of psychological intelligence takes time. Insights have to be metabolized, resistances have to be worked through. As painful experience has shown, change involves a lot of hard work. There is no such thing as a magical solution. However, setting this reflective process into motion will add an additional dimension to the reader's understanding of organizational phenomena. Doing so will have a preventive effect, and will eventually lead to more effective action.

Anton Chekhov wrote in one of his letters: 'When a man does not understand a thing, he feels discord with himself: he seeks causes for his dissonance not in himself, as he should, but outside himself, and the result is war with something he does not understand.'

My hope is that in this book I can help the reader to prevent, in a small way, this 'war with something he does not understand', that this book will provide readers with insight to make them more sensible and sensitive students of organizational phenomena, and in the process designers of more creative and humane organizations.

Manfred F. R. Kets de Vries
Paris, France

1

INTRODUCTION

That reason may not force us to commit
That sin of the high-minded sublimation,
Which damns the soul by praising it.[1]

W. H. Auden

There is a story about a wily bandit who was finally captured by
the king's troopers. The king, a man fond of games and riddles,
made the bandit a proposition. He told the bandit that he was
allowed to make one statement. If that statement contained the
truth he would be shot, if it contained a lie, hanged. The bandit,
after some thought, said: 'I am going to be hanged'.

This is where this puzzling story ends. The reaction of the king
and the fate of the bandit remain unknown. But whatever the king's
actions this logical paradox resulted in an impasse. The tables had
been turned and the king was placed in what can be described as
a double-bind situation. Whatever he did would be wrong. A
situation was created without objective reality or obvious answer.

Admittedly, we might brush this anecdote aside as some kind
of joke, it merely being a logical paradox which does not warrant
further thought. Yet, organizational life is a territory full of comparable dilemmas – of course not of such an extreme nature – which
arise inadvertently in the course of day-to-day activities. Executives will be confronted with many paradoxical encounters which
at first glance might seem irrational and lack obvious answers. But
there is some kind of logic behind these behaviour patterns which
warrants further investigation. We cannot just ignore these paradoxes met in interpersonal relationships. They raise important
questions about human motivation, individual and organizational
action, the nature of decision making, and the problem of change.

1

Executives are discovering that the pursuit of the ideal of the rational decision maker might be an illusion, that the traditional models of choice and organization may be insufficient in giving guidance through the maze of paradoxes which make up organizational life. Executives are realizing that there are limits to rationality. Other factors seem to be involved in human interaction, decision making and motivation, which have received insufficient attention.

I am not just referring to the often-suggested contradiction between management as an art placed in contrast to management as a science. Calling the unexplainable and the confusing an art does not bring us much further. It only gives these enigmas another name. Instead of leaving these puzzling issues unresolved, I would welcome a greater understanding of irrational behaviour patterns in organizations and would like to add another dimension to the explanation of human behaviour and individual and organizational action. I am referring to the need for a different level of organizational and individual analysis which goes beyond mere description; which is more orientated towards explanation and focuses on the psychodynamic forces at work in human interaction and motivation. This twilight zone where we find the boundaries of rationality and irrationality needs further exploration if we want to possess a better understanding of intra-personal interpersonal and organizational processes and the strategy-making process.

Although there are many executives who are aware of the emotional costs of organizational life, these insights are usually repressed, suppressed, or dismissed as unfit to the particular atmosphere of action which characterizes organizations. Time spent on these thoughts is perceived as a side-tracking effort to the real business of management and as deviating from the organization's main objectives. The consequence of this attitude is that ritualistic activities and rationalization of behaviour seem to be the norm and have become the more acceptable ways of dealing with the routines of organizational life.

It is obvious that the present state of emotional impoverishment and lack of insight about human action in organizations needs more attention. The situation indicates that a major educational effort might be needed to renew the executive's acquaintance with the unusual and, in a conventional sense, the unacceptable, thereby moving away from simplistic theories of human motivation and management to more realistic ones. This reorientation might turn into a journey into the self, not only establishing greater awareness of the reasons for individual and organizational action but also recognizing the emotional costs of corporate life. Such a search might also lead to the realization of the limitations of rationality in organizational life, the relationship between reality and fantasy in individual and organizational action, and the nature of the differences between manifest and latent thought processes and communication patterns. Another consequence might be that we will pay more attention to self-observation, self-analysis, and the development of empathy. In the management of human interaction we have to retrace the steps which make us act as we do, reflect on their origin, and recognize our possibilities and limitations.

The capacity for this type of learning is present in each executive. Pressures toward conformity in organizations have led to neglect and inattention to insights about dependency, affection, aggression, shame, and guilt. But this dormant capacity can easily be revived if sufficient effort is made and some of the pathways to understanding are shown.

There are, however, exceptions. Although adaptation is more the rule, rigidity which accompanies neuroticism is ever present. There are people who will reject any insight because of the benefits of 'secondary gain', the almost imperceptible advantages associated with human suffering, processes which tend to support the *status quo*. Also, confrontation with the real, often repressed reasons for individual action can be an extremely painful experience, which makes it more comfortable to distance oneself from these insights and leave things as they are. In these instances of compulsions and other forms of neurotic behaviour more drastic efforts for change might be needed. I am referring particularly to more intensive psychotherapeutical interventions. Most executives, however, do not fall into this category and have ample resources at their disposal facilitating change, adaptation, and personal growth.

In this book I will try to convert rational concern with organizational structure and decision making into the problem of people in situations of conflict, constrained on one side by environmental realities and on the other side by conscious and unconscious motivations. In paying attention to what are superficially perceived as irrational and unconscious processes, I am thus advocating a more clinically orientated approach to organizational diagnosis. A more complex, but, at the same time, more realistic view of men and women in organizations will emerge, in contrast to the mechanical, one-dimensional people presented by many organizational theorists, human resource specialists and industrial psychologists.

In the search for supporting disciplines I have discovered that psychoanalytically orientated concepts can be of great help. They will add another dimension to organizational studies otherwise looked at from a purely descriptive angle. A psychoanalytical orientation, with its concern about empathy and with its specific ability to distinguish between illness and health, can contribute substantially in conceptualizing about the nature of work, the etiology of individual and organizational stress, the vicissitudes of power and leadership, human motivation, and the effects of career. In addition, apart from using concepts derived from psychoanalytic psychology, I will also draw upon developments in other fields such as social psychology, sociology, economics, anthropology and, naturally, management theory.

An important further source of material for this book has been the observations of executives in action, clinically orientated interviews in organizations, and educational dialogues. The data obtained through these processes has been invaluable and these interactions have been the catalyst for many of the hypotheses presented in this book. These encounters have supported the notion of transference, countertransference and resistance, and particularly the importance of empathy in organizations.

We know that human development and organizational change pose constant conundrums to the executive. Management can be compared to a balancing act, the elements being in this instance the basic human drives of love and aggression transformed into feelings and attitudes such as dependency and control, conflict and compromise, hostility and compassion. It will become clear in the discussion of the various themes of this book that the executive's ability to work and thereby his or her effectiveness in organizations is largely determined by adaptive capacity. These forces of maturation which combat neurotic suffering will eventually make for the creation of new individual and organizational equilibria.

2

THE OBLOMOV THREAT

> My view of life is utterly meaningless. I suppose an evil spirit
> has set a pair of spectacles on my nose, of which one lens is a
> tremendous magnifying glass, the other an equally powerful
> reducing glass. . .[1]
>
> S. Kierkegaard

The casual observer, reconsidering the media's reports on the
developments in the White House during the final days of the
Nixon presidency, may have been reminded of a Greek tragedy,
the only difference being that, in this instance, the drama of the 'rise
and fall' of a man who, at that time, was one of the most powerful
people in the world, was not fiction at all but frightening reality.
The dramatis personae seemed locked in, unable to escape the final
act; eventually neither denial of complicity with the Watergate
scandal nor diversionary activities, such as accusing supposed
enemies of persecutory actions, sufficed to turn the tide of public
opinion and prevent legal action. In the end we were faced with
the spectacle of an immobilized president, seemingly confused,
suffering the pangs of depression, work inhibition and impaired
action. The organizational and politically alarming consequences
of a paralyzed president troubled by work inhibition were only
mitigated by the efforts of his latter-day palace guards as represented by Haig and Kissinger. These two men kept the office of the
president functioning by assuming a caretaker position, taking
responsibility for the day-to-day decision-making process.

One of the underlying, powerful messages of Greek tragedies
has been to warn the spectator of the danger of hubris, the sinful-
ness and arrogance of power. This message has not lost its impact
in a contemporary setting, and the case of Richard Nixon has been

5

a strong reminder. 'After the fall' – like the ending of a Greek tragedy – confronted us with the wretched spectacle of a bitter, stooped, aged, disgraced man walking on the beach, pathetically shaking hands with passers-by. We can speculate that, in this instance, the increasing strain due to the never-ending stream of disclosures of new illegalities, in addition to the inevitable lurking threat of conviction, may have been responsible for Nixon's final inability to function, his state of apathy, confusion and general emotional disarray, accentuated by a physical ailment in the form of phlebitis.

A less dramatic but still very disconcerting example of impaired work performance – one of a lasting duration – can be found in literature as told in the story of Oblomov by the nineteenth-century Russian novelist Goncharov.[2] This tragedy of passivity, apathy, and impaired work performance described a kind of indolence of a more permanent nature. The influence of this novel has been considerable, not only in Russia but in many other countries as well – so much so that the accusation of being an Oblomov has become well-understood in most European countries and is associated with behaviour patterns such as inertia and laziness.

Oblomov became an example of arrested character development, an individual completely incapable of going beyond a functionally vegetative state, unable to comprehend adequately the realities of life. Sapped by passivity and apathy, life became too straining; but so was suicide. With increasing frequency the hero of the novel was replacing real action with daydreams and fantasies, leaving the care of everyday reality to his servant. And although the story may be interpreted as a tragi-comedy when it deals with Oblomov's inability to get out of bed, the reader cannot shake off a sense of impending doom and futility.

One example is the incident in which Oblomov reflects on the strange, incomprehensible state of inner paralysis which troubles him. He comments on all his unfolded plans and ideas:

> Where has it all gone to? Why has it all burnt out? I can't understand it! I had no storms, no shocks of any kind; I did not lose anything; I have nothing on my conscience – it is clear as glass; no blow of any kind has shattered my ambitions, and God only knows why my life is such a waste!
> ...From the moment I became aware of myself I felt that I was already withering... Yes, I am like an old worn-out coat, and

it isn't because of the climate or of work, but because for twelve years a fire has been shut up within me which could not find an outlet, it merely ravaged its prison and died down...[3]

These are the upsetting reflections of a man in a far-reaching state of depression, a man who is dealing with basic existential questions about the futility of life and feelings of annihilation. These statements also portray a sense of depersonalization, a sense of estrangement with the world of reality, and resemble a regressive search for a paradise forever lost. We are face to face with a man who has basically given up any action and who lacks the fighting spirit necessary to deal with the vicissitudes of life. For Oblomov, there is no rage, no excitation; he seems already dead although he is still alive, locked into his increasingly autistic world.

The novel had and still has a shocking impact since 'Oblomov-ism' evokes the threat of a kind of living death present in each of us. The sense of inertia as portrayed by Goncharov remains dormant for most people. But anyone who has been exposed to patterns of childrearing that have incorporated elements of 'the Protestant Ethic' may experience a great sense of discomfort in reading about the situation portrayed by Goncharov.

One of the inescapable by-products of growing up and adapting to societal demands is the constant reminder – initially by external but increasingly by internal forces (reinforced by the developing conscience) – of the things we 'should' or 'ought' to do. Unfortunately, this internalization of industriousness is not necessarily conflict-free, but may turn into a battle of wills with authority figures and may be accompanied by powerful aggressive feelings. The degree of internalization and the strategies for living which evolve out of this interaction process are manifold. One of the possible outcomes, being content with the line of the least resistance, lapsing into indolence and passivity, and substituting daydreams and fantasies for real action, can be perceived as a danger since it reawakens painful memories centred around prohibitions, demands and controls. That is one of the reasons why the figure of Oblomov is so disturbing. He symbolizes human stagnation and apathy, tendencies which are present in each of us, and are conducive to seriously impaired work performance.

ATTITUDES TOWARD WORK

The examples of defective adaptation to work are numerous although seldom of such spectacular dimensions as with Nixon or Oblomov. Most people at one point in their life have experienced impasses in their work capacity, usually of a more temporary nature, and in that period may have realized the importance of work for their emotional and physical well-being. This insight may seem obvious, but whatever the exact nature of the experience, man's attitudes toward work have continued to be of an ambivalent nature.

The view of work as man's 'link to reality' was introduced by Freud and studies concerned with the detrimental effects of unemployment have confirmed many of his theories. Freud transformed existing ideas about work by complementing Marx's conceptions and transcending the mere focus on material needs, tying work in with an individual's emotional state, and viewing it as a way of satisfying one's sense of self-esteem.

Other psychologists, for example Hendrick, have suggested the existence of an 'instinct of workmanship' whereby a work principle was postulated as an innate drive of man.[4] White, from a more human developmental point of view, introduced the idea of 'effectance motivation'.[5] Work viewed as a product of feelings of efficacy became for him the outcome of an individual's ability to influence and master his or her environment.

Presently, it has become a platitude to argue that providing for purely material needs is only one of the dimensions of work; apart from money many other factors have to be taken into consideration to make an individual interested in his job. The popularity in industry of concepts such as job enrichment or enlargement, work restructuring, human resources accounting, management by objectives, organizational development, quality circles, bench marking and re-engineering – all endeavours to make work more challenging and less monotonous – illustrates this point. We are realizing the diversity of the problems associated with work. Apart from output problems (quantitative or qualitative) there exist also accident proneness, absenteeism, strikes, sickness or industrial fatigue and labour turnover. All these examples can be considered as problems of adapting to the work environment.

8

A SENSE OF INADEQUACY

Freud, in his role as a clinician, made a pioneering effort to deal with the problems of work inhibition. In his study dealing with inhibitions, symptoms, and anxiety he tries, for example, to discern patterns in work impairment. He commented that:

> In inhibition in work – a thing which we so often have to deal with as an isolated symptom in our therapeutic work – the subject feels a decrease in his pleasure in it or becomes less able to do it well or he has certain reactions to it, like fatigue, giddiness or sickness, if he is obliged to go on with it. If he is a hysteric he will have to give up his work owing to the appearance of organic and functional paralysis which make it impossible for him to carry it on. If he is an obsessional neurotic he will be perpetually distracted from his work or lose time over it through the introduction of delays and repetitions.[6]

In describing the reactions of various psychiatric stereotypes of work, Freud laid the groundwork for a better understanding of the problem of work impairment. His point of view has been elaborated by later writers. A more contemporary clinician, Erik Erikson, continued Freud's endeavours but placed greater emphasis on the social context and introduced as one of his conceptualized eight stages of a human's life the polarity of industry versus inferiority. He views this stage, characterized by exposure to the peer group, the period of 'entrance into life' otherwise described as latency, as crucial in the development of later attitudes toward work. For Erikson, a sense of industry 'involved doing things beside and with others' and implies 'a first sense of division of labour and differential opportunity'.[7] It is the period during which play becomes a guiding force and a building block for adaptive behaviour. But adaptation to the world of work is not the only outcome; a sense of inadequacy and inferiority due to frustrations in interactions with peers may evolve as well, a situation which may prevent being at ease in any interpersonal encounter. Despair and impaired development occur when family life has been inadequate in preparing the child for school life and thus the earlier promises of childhood are not sustained. The final result of these developmental processes can lead to frustrations and disappointments in dealing with the work environment when maturity is reached and contribute to job dissatisfaction, stress reactions and career stagnation.

AGGRESSION AS A DOUBLE BIND

The search for explanations of work adaptation problems makes us realize that such incidents as accident-proneness, impaired work performance, and absenteeism are the end-results of a more deeply rooted psychological drama centred around an individual's problems in coping with conflicting wishes, emotions, and motives. The ability to cope with one's immediate surroundings, dealing with the hazards and uncertainties of working life while fulfilling one's aspirations, places high demands on the most essential defences needed for one's self preservation. The management and control of aggression in this emotional defensive process, as a derivative of the preservation of the self, is closely tied in with the enhancement or impairment of self-esteem. An individual's particular way of coping with aggression in the process of human development, apart from transforming affectionate attitudes, becomes an important factor in later attitudes toward work.

The management and control of aggression, however, has a Janus face; aggression can be directed outward or inward. We are all familiar with the many forms which outward-directed aggression can take. The daily politics of organizational life with its built-in competitiveness give frequent examples of projecting and directing aggressiveness toward others. The self-destructive aspects of inward-directed aggression, however, have remained a more puzzling issue because of their apparent contradiction with the human need for self-preservation.

The basis for the psychodynamic understanding of the relationship between self-destruction or inward-directed aggression and self-preservation has been laid by Freud in his classic work, *Mourning and Melancholia*.[8] He explains the self-destructive elements present in grief as a reaction to narcissistic identification. This identification process implies that we view other individuals as mirrors of the self; the attractive aspects of others will be incorporated and attached with feelings of love and affection while unattractive aspects will be expelled. In the case of loss of the loved person a depletion of the self occurs, and due to the emotional attachments developed in the original identification process, remorse and self-reproach about the loss follow.

The notion that inward-directed aggression is linked with human narcissistic needs (the latter a term describing an archaic love of self, being the basis of self-preservation and experienced gradually during the course of human development as a sense of self-esteem) has been furthered by Rochlin, who supports the contention that an injury to narcissism will always provoke aggression.[9] This loss of self-esteem may be caused by our own self doubts and demands or by devaluation and abuse from others. He argues that the outlet may be twofold: aggression may be projected onto others (we may blame them) or we may turn it to ourselves, causing both social and inner conflicts. Inward-directed aggression, the manifestation of self-reproaches and self-attacks, seems a consequence of injured narcissism which, on its part, can be considered a result of defects in the developmental process.

The complexity of the management of aggression is illustrated by the defence mechanism, 'identification with the aggressor' meaning the impersonation of the perceived aggressor – represented by an authority figure.[10] In this form of identification a transformation process takes place whereby the role of the passive, helpless victim is replaced by acting the role of the one in control, a defence which becomes important in warding off the dangers of everyday life; moreover it enhances self-esteem due to the illusion of merger with the powerful figure. But the mere choice of this defensive strategy may indicate emotional instability, facilitates the occurrence of impaired self-esteem, and arouses guilt due to feelings of impotence toward the aggressor. The end result reminds us of Sartre's play *No Exit*: the individual is locked in, seems to have no outlet for his aggression, and the manifestation of inner doubt, anxiety, and guilt tells a tale of inward-directed aggression.

The channelling of aggression becomes extremely important for the way a person deals with organizational life. If aggression is too much inhibited and inward-directed the result may be immobilization and the incapacity to engage in any form of self-assertion. In addition, apart from paralyzing thoughts about shame and guilt, psychosomatic disorders may occur. The organizational consequences of uncontrollable outward-directed aggression are obvious. Survival and adaptation to organizational life seem to be determined to some extent by the balance between inward- and outward-directed aggression. As much as limited restraints on outward-directed aggression seem advisable in the early stages of life to facilitate the development of skills, adulthood has its own demands and requires both a moderate dose of inward-directed aggression to modify human narcissistic needs and to further social adaptation (a role taken up by the conscience with all its sanctions and prohibitions), and a degree of outward-directed aggression. The genesis of work adaptation problems can be traced back to a disequilibrium in this balance between assertiveness and self control.

In view of the described relationship between aggression and narcissism we will now try to discern patterns in work adaptation problems. That various forms of work problems are highly interdependent, not mutually exclusive, and can occur concurrently is self-evident. Moreover, in the effort to discern patterns we may occasionally oversimplify or create artificial boundaries.

THE NARCISSISTIC POSITION

One way of describing work problems caused by inward-directed aggression is by the designation, 'the narcissistic position'. Defective narcissistic development is at the core of this form of work inhibition and in the context of work problems narcissism assumes a double meaning. While early in the process of human development narcissism can be considered a necessary ingredient for self preservation, at a later stage of life extended, unmodified narcissistic fantasies may be the root cause of serious work disorders.[11]

We have observed that, in the process of human development, the child gradually has to face up to the fact of external constraining forces, painful as this understanding might be. Slowly the realization breaks through that human interactions are not always gratifying but can also be the cause of feelings of deprivation and frustration. Prolonged injuries to a person's sense of self-esteem and the impotence experienced in not living up to expectations make for situations where self-esteem is injured or impaired. One of the outcomes of excessive deprivation may be a regressive retreat to a kind of self-contained primary state of existence. This extreme form of reaction is usually characterized by a loss of interest in the outside world, apathy, and inertia.

The role of the ego ideal

In examining a cluster of related work problems, the narcissistic position is probably the most complex cause to deal with, due to

12

the great diversity in possible manifestations. But whatever its final representation it is defective narcissistic development which remains at the core. Prolonged experiences of deprivation may result in unrealistic incorporation and identification with reference figures – those people with whom a person is intimately engaged – and contribute to a defective sense of self-esteem. In those instances we observe how fantasies centred around grandiosity gain in importance and even take over, counteracting the experience of helplessness and loss; eventually these fantasies may totally replace reality. An unrealistic development of the ego ideal (that part of the powerful agency of inner surveillance, the conscience, which serves as a guide for the development of one's identity, and what one aspires to become in a career sense) may result. Unrealistic demands from the ego ideal make only omnipotence and omniscience states to which one can aspire and inevitably disappointment will follow. The individual seems to be caught between the need to strive for perfection to placate his ego ideal and his inner doubts about his ability to accomplish these goals.

The poet Auden describes this conflict very well:

His peasant parents killed themselves with toil
To let their darling leave a stingy soil
For any of these smart professions which
   encourage shallow breathing, and grow rich.
The pressure of their fond ambition made
Their shy and country-loving child afraid.
No sensible career was good enough,
Only a hero could deserve such love.

So here he was without maps or supplies
A hundred miles from any decent town;

The desert glared into his blood-shot eyes;
The silence roared displeasure: looking down,
He saw the shadow of an Average Man,
Attempting the Exceptional, and ran.[12]

Effectively the individual plagued by work problems of a narcissistic nature is running away from things by not running at all but by surrendering. The wish to be exceptional and the impossibility of achieving perfection turns any work effort *a priori* into a meaningless endeavour. What we can observe is that frequently disturbed work capacity evolves as a consequence of an emotional over-investment in what can be described as a 'grandiose self'. This sense of aggrandizement was noticed by Helen Tartakoff in her therapeutic work and subsequently she introduced the notion of the existence of a 'Nobel Prize complex' exemplified by individuals with highly ambitious goals. She came to believe that the recurring problems around productive work were a consequence of the 'all or nothing' attitude which characterizes the aspirations of these persons. Her comments about this narcissistic form of work inhibition were:

> The 'Dream of Glory' which these patients entertain has been reinforced by goals in our social structure. It is, in fact, the personal expression of the American Dream – a narcissistic fantasy which has become institutionalized. The unconscious determinants of the Dream have remained repressed; therefore, feelings of depletion, precipitated by a realistic or fantasized disappointment, be it on the level of love or work, lead quickly to a sense of failure, often accompanied by depression and psychosomatic symptoms. . .[13]

She continued by saying:

> one is reminded of an addiction which is characterized by an insatiable desire to recover an infantile state of gratification which can never be fulfilled in reality. Disillusionment in such instances may not occur until middle age, when recognition and reward in an ascending scale are no longer forthcoming. . .[14]

The main theme in the 'narcissistic position' seems to be the predominance of inward-directed aggression which, as we have indicated before, can be viewed as a defensive means of coping with injured narcissism. Feelings of self-deprecation and inadequacy are the usual outcomes. Due to the 'all or nothing' attitudes which surround this type of person's aspirations, the relationships with the work environment become extremely fragile. Any disturbance of these fantasies from within the organization may break 'the spell' and lead to states of apathy, passivity, work inhibition, and stress reactions of a recurring nature. Moreover, a sense of depersonalization sets in. In a way we are reminded of the novel *The Stranger* by Camus. For 'the stranger' there was no feeling, no emotion, only a sense of numbness. The death of his mother, a murder, the love of a girl, all did not really matter but just passed by, leaving the stranger standing at the side as a disinterested spectator.

The instalment plan approach

Since the desired perfection of living up to a grandiose self image becomes an impossible state to achieve, criticism, ostracism and punishment are feared; this fear, in turn, assumes forms of social anxiety. These individuals seem to live in a continuous state of preparedness; they disseminate an uneasiness about the future and a sense of impending doom, emotions which become particularly aroused in social situations. There exists an aura of tension around such people, a sense of anxiety and guilt due to an unforgiving harsh conscience.

Freud, in an article about people whom he called 'the exceptions', mentions the instances of 'criminals out of a sense of guilt', those individuals who, paradoxically enough, seem to be in search of punishment.[15] And the concept of 'criminal out of a sense of guilt' is very much applicable to the work situation. The mere fact of being at work can be perceived as a form of exposure, making oneself vulnerable, and may turn into a danger. Good illustrations of these dynamics are stage fright and fear of examinations. Failures at work become identified with a loss of love and the accompanied danger of humiliation. The threat of punishment may become so overwhelming that these individuals – not necessarily at a conscious level – engage in a kind of pay-off system. In a symbolic sense their conscience requires a sacrifice as a way of expiating their feelings of guilt. Regular, self-induced punishment to release tension – like paying off on an instalment plan basis – seems preferable to the continuous threatening alternative of a sudden, unexpected, much less controllable request for complete redemption. Among this group we find those individuals who engage in unacceptable practices in the work situation and thus continually provoke criticism. This narcissistic form of work inhibition characterizes people who are unable to finish their organizational tasks, seem incapable or unwilling to follow up on their promises, make obvious errors, and tend to forget things. An appearance of passivity surrounds their actions.

The need of some individuals to engage in incessant, frantic work activity which is sometimes described as 'Sunday neurosis' (people who become upset when they do not work, Sunday being

15

a typical example) is closely linked to this form of work inhibition. Although this behaviour pattern at first glance seems far removed from the previous one, it is merely another way of expressing inward-directed aggression. The individuals go through robot-like movements, substituting means for ends, form for substance, and resemble the mythological figure Sisyphus who likewise was engaged in endless, impossible tasks without any real purpose. This pattern seems at first glance a form of self-punishment but actually is more than that and can also be considered a way of coping with, and warding off, a sense of self-fragmentation, implying lack of coherency in self images. In as much as inactivity may cause depressive reactions stemming from anxiety about adequacy, self-worth, and general fragmentation of the self, hyperactivity becomes a way of warding off this danger by placating the conscience through the 'sacrifice' of work without concern for its meaningfulness. Psychological detective work will unravel, however, the influence of the parents (or caretakers) in developing this conscience. In many instances of 'workaholism' these people have become the 'proxies' of their parents, sent on a mission to succeed where their parents failed. Tangible achievements are continually needed to placate these internalized parents.

The symptoms of disturbed work capacity become a manifestation of an excessive emotional investment of the grandiose self. Overwork and other forms of frantic activity turn into a means of preventing an emerging emotional breakdown and a dangerously increasing fragmentation of the self by giving some form of structure to an individual's general living environment. These symptom patterns demonstrate that the ability to work necessitates an integration and moderation of existing grandiose fantasies with realistic ambitions and action patterns.

THE RIVALROUS POSITION

The rivalrous form of work problems can be considered as having evolved out of the narcissistic position. Inward-directed aggression, again, is central, in this case as one of the possible strategies to use in dealing with the question of rivalry.

In his review of the human life cycle Erikson discusses the polarity 'initiative versus guilt', a dilemma which occurs during what psychoanalysts call the Oedipal stage of development in the life of a child, the time when the child is around five years of age.

It is a period when a child's environment is broadening from the dyadic relationship (mother–child) to a triadic relationship (the increasing importance of father and siblings). Erikson comments that:

> The danger of this stage is a sense of guilt over the goals contemplated and the acts initiated in one's exuberant enjoyment of new locomotor and mental power: acts of aggressive manipulation and coercion which soon go far beyond the executive capacity of organism and mind and therefore call for an energetic halt on one's contemplated initiative. While autonomy concentrates on keeping potential rivals out, and therefore can lead to jealous rage most often directed against encroachments by younger siblings, initiative brings with it anticipatory rivalry with those who have been there first and may, therefore, occupy with their superior equipment the field toward which one's initiative is directed. Infantile jealousy and rivalry, those often embittered and yet essentially futile attempts at demarcating a sphere of unquestioned privilege, now comes to a climax in a final contest for favoured position with the mother; the usual failure leads to resignation, guilt, and anxiety. . .[16]

The continuation of conflict around rivalry, the persistence in adult life of ghosts of the past, the competition for being the 'favoured one' may lead to inhibited aggression, anxiety, and guilt over self-assertion and may eventually re-emerge as problems in the work situation. These developments may have been strengthened by an originally precocious, premature specialization of talents which may have prevented any sense of initiative to experiment. The threat of not living up to these originally excessive promises may be one of the underlying causes for this sense of inhibition.

The duality of simultaneous fear of failure and fear of success is closely related to the rivalrous position in work problems. While the fear of failure, evoking memories of humiliation and defeat, does not need much explanation, the same cannot be said about the fear of success. Freud once wrote about 'those wrecked by success', those people who get sick when a deeply rooted and long-cherished wish comes to fulfilment. He gives the example of a professor who cherished the wish to succeed his original teacher. When this wish came true and the individual eventually replaced his teacher and became his successor, a depressive reaction soon followed; he engaged in accusations of a self-deprecatory nature and was unable to work.[17] Even Oblomov is affected by the fear of success, as his love affair with the girl Olga (whom he almost marries) indicates. In this particular example we notice how, after his proposal and her acceptance, Oblomov's state of exultation quickly fades; his energies seem drained and he begins to avoid Olga. This phenomenon is sometimes called success or promotion depression.

The problem with fixation on the archaic need for success, limitless achievement, and societal acclaim is that this fixation not only arouses primitive emotions centred around annihilation and loss of self (in the unconscious, success symbolically may be equated with the need to undergo a personality transformation: to lose one's original identity) but also is associated with fear of retaliation from one with whom the individual is unconsciously competing. Success and competitiveness make one stand out and may arouse the envy of others. Maslow introduced in this context the idea of the 'Jonah Complex', the fear of one's own greatness.[18] The Prometheus myth and the Don Juan legend moralize about the dangers of incurring the wrath of the gods. The mere existence of the goddess Nemesis, the enemy of too much success and happiness, who symbolizes jealousy, is illustrative. Nemesis represents the universal fear that too much success causes *koros* (self-satisfaction) which leads to *hubris* or excessive pride, which in turn cannot be tolerated and will evoke punishment. The story of Polycrates, tyrant of Sumos, is a good illustration of this fear. To forestall the jealousy of the gods and terrified by his unheard-of luck, he threw a priceless ring into the sea. But the ring returned in the belly of a fish served to Polycrates. He then knew that Nemesis had refused his sacrifice and misfortune would come his way.

People in the grip of the 'rivalrous position' seem to be haunted by an 'evil eye', are competing with ghosts of the past and regularly appear immobilized. What we notice is that the potential rivalry with work associates has an impact far beyond the reality of the situation. Superiors, subordinates, and peers arouse strong aggressive feelings which are inward-directed. The 'whale' of a conscience these people possess contributes to a state of work paralysis. The legacy of memories about conflictive competitiveness in the original family environment prevents an attitude of conflict-free behaviour to present-day reality.

THE DEPENDENT POSITION

In the 'dependent position', as in the previously described forms of work problems, we find again the presence of inward-directed aggression, only, in this instance, coupled with reactions of a dependent nature. Also this time we have to study the process of human development and the various ways of dealing with frustration and dissatisfaction in human interaction to find explanations. Identification and the internalization of values of those people to whom one is close become an important part of this process. But crises in interpersonal human encounters are not infrequent and may cause disruptions and deviations from original perceptions. Only under optimal conditions of 'good enough' care will disappointment with idealized figures or role models occur gradually without traumatic incidents. Situations of consistency in childrearing, of mutual give and take, will contribute to a sense of realism in the internalization of values and to the absence of excessive discrepancies between a person's fantasies and the existing realities. In the case of traumatic loss, prolonged depriving experiences, or other forms of excessive disruption of relationships with parental figures, severe, as opposed to gradual, disappointment sets in and the desired internalization process can become disrupted. What, in ordinary circumstances, would have matured into the capacity for adaptation, into a greater sense of mastery and control over the environment, and would have contributed to a feeling of independence, changes into something which might be described as a 'search for the lost object' and indicates a depressive disposition. A rather undefined sense of loss, of longing, remains, continues to dominate psychic structure, and repeatedly causes dependency reactions when these feeling are rearoused. To the same degree that the excessive use of shame as a controlling device leads to a pervasive sense of doubt, the heightening of conscience may give rise to a deep and lasting sense of guilt in interpersonal relationships. Dependent behaviour with the purpose of alleviating these feelings and finding support for one's actions becomes a way of life.

Various childhood studies indicate how impaired development of this type may lead to situations of apathy in adult life, difficulties in taking initiative, and problems in personal control and human relations.[19] Apathy becomes a way of withdrawing from stimuli when other efforts to reduce tension are chronically frustrated. The manifestation of helplessness and dependency seems to be a result of a state of chronic tension between highly charged narcissistic aspirations and the sense of impotence encountered in attempting to live up to these expectations.

Robert White, in his very perceptive longitudinal study of three lives, illustrates this process when he deals with a temporary crisis of dependency and work inhibition in one of his subjects.[20] In the case example, White indicates how the businessman Joseph Kidd's precocious early development with its stress on appearances – being a 'beautiful child' – predisposed him to both helplessness and self-consciousness and made for a childhood devastated by conflicting demands and feelings of inferiority. A serious emotional crisis in young adulthood during his student years was the consequence. Highly dependent on the esteem of others to maintain his psychological equilibrium, Kidd manifested all the symptoms of the dependent position. He commented later:

> I often think about how I look and what impression I am making upon others; my feelings are easily hurt by ridicule or the slightest remarks of others; when I enter a room I often become self-conscious and feel that the eyes of others are upon me. I often interpret the remarks of others in a personal way; I pay a good deal of attention to my appearance; clothes, hats, shoes, neckties. . .
>
> I had lost all the ability to concentrate, remember, think, and correlate. I just couldn't study because when I did I became all nerved up and jumpy. . .[21]

Joseph Kidd eventually managed to work himself out of his psychological impasse. In this case it was through his stay in the army where he found an opportunity to pick up the thread of his development, prematurely broken off at adolescence. Working together, and testing his abilities, with a peer group became important in helping him finally to acquire a feeling of competence, making him aware of his ability to get things through his own efforts. This period became a moratorium allowing him to develop a clear sense of identity and to arrive at a sense of self-respect and self-confidence. Others, however, are not fortunate enough to have sufficient emotional resources at their disposal and for them the 'dependent position' may be a recurring problem.

The 'dependent position' is not only characterized by a sense of longing but also has another facet. In a symbolic sense the notion of work becomes equated with a sense of independence and being in control, perceptions and feelings which cause a fear of being a target and being victimized. The previous comments about the 'instalment plan' approach to psychological punishment are again appropriate. Working as a form of independence is a threat since it may arouse the attention of others and with attention may come disapproval. We are also reminded of the fear of success associated with the 'rivalrous position'. Therefore, the way of avoiding disapproval is through self-recrimination; this, in turn, serves both as an invitation for positive reassurance and as a means of warding off imagined dangers. A combination of the fear of victimization and disapproval causes postponement or avoidance of responsibility. The individual, not wanting to be taken seriously, takes refuge in helplessness, ignorance, idleness, and seemingly playful, irresponsible acts. Accident proneness, i. e. the remarkable susceptibility of some individuals to accidents, can be explained through the 'dependent position' as can alcoholism and drug addiction. The same is valid for hypochondriacal reactions.

People who fall into the 'dependent position' will continue to make excessive demands on others and tend to become angry and anxious when their demands are not met. They are like a sponge; whatever you do, they will never be satisfied. The casual observer usually only becomes concerned when a state of depression has been reached. Naturally, the other end of the spectrum, excessively independent behaviour, has its own problems; for example, inability or difficulty in establishing close relationships. The implications for collaboration and team work in organizations are obvious in these cases. Yet, given the culture of the work environment with its emphasis on activity, decision making, and assertiveness, excessive dependency and the 'dependency position' is viewed as a more serious problem.

THE REBELLIOUS POSITION

We have seen in the previous discussion that inward-directed aggression is a main element in work problems. Many of the work problems we observe in everyday life can be viewed as reactions of a depressive nature. Notwithstanding the predominant role played by inward-directed aggression in work problems, a form of work problem can be discerned which is linked to outward-directed aggression. The combination of outward-directed aggression and a sense of independence (as another influencing personality variable) may cause work problems of a rebellious nature.

Camus once summarized the problem of rebelliousness by saying, 'I rebel – therefore we exist'[22] and added, 'the rebel. . . from his very first step, refuses to allow anyone to touch what he is. He is fighting for the integrity of one part of his being. He does not try, primarily, to conquer, but simply to impose.'[23] Camus' description illustrates the difference between 'the rebellious position' and other forms of work problems; it portrays a notion of activity in contrast to the previously described, more passive forms of work disorder. In this type of work problem the extreme case of complete work paralysis is rather uncommon; the individual will usually retain the ability to function. Unfortunately, it is exactly his or her way of functioning that has become the very problem. The provocative manner which characterizes his or her work behaviour becomes a cause of irritation and annoyance and may result in discharge or demotion.

'The rebellious position' is often typical of 'job hoppers', those individuals who seem incapable of holding onto a job for a prolonged period of time. These people continually get in trouble with their superiors and seem to be caught in an endless cycle of being hired and fired. Their life in organizations possesses all the characteristics of a self-fulfilling prophecy where the worst is expected and subsequently occurs.

In a symbolic sense, for individuals prone to 'the rebellious position', work resembles a duty, a demand imposed by authority figures and therefore the opposite of pleasure, which is one explanation for their unwilling or provocative manner of participation in work activities. Although not necessarily consciously, work assumes the form of a symbolic struggle for obedience and control.

We can again look at childhood to explain the origins of the highly charged emotional feelings surrounding work. We discover that these individuals portray a lack of identification with parental authority. This may be the outcome of a situation where parents frustrated their children through an attitude of rejection but did not instigate and force conformity by over-controlling. A combination of rejection and low control makes motivation for compliance weak, undermines the development of internal constraints, foresight, and realizing the consequence of one's actions. Parents become perceived as confusing and inconsistent; there is no mak-

22

ing sense out of them. They become fragmented, not really integrated figures, obstacles which have to be overcome. The patterns developed in family interactions become transferred to other authority figures and will eventually determine the nature of interpersonal relationships. Lack of identification may turn into a compensatory reaction as reflected in rebelliousness. The outcome resembles a kind of sado-masochistic transference to authority figures with all its destructive overtones. We are implying in this instance that aggression is not only outward-directed but has, in addition, an inward-directed component in 'the rebellious position'. Provocative behaviour, with its invitation to disaster, contains a masochistic element from the point of view of career progression in organizations.

Although this pattern of behaviour occasionally may be viewed as a sign of real independence, in most instances the description 'pseudo-independence' is probably more accurate, because this 'independence' marks highly charged emotions centring around a desire to rebel. What is missing in these cases is a sense of playfulness in human relationships which is a vital element in the development of adaptive behaviour and the prevention of defensive rigidity.

The classic entrepreneur, the individual who jumps from one new undertaking to another, has some of the characteristics of 'the rebellious position', only in this instance the destructive 'roller coaster ride' of disappointments and frustrations in work relationships is taking a more constructive turn because of the choice to become one's own person, a decision which usually comes only belatedly to those characterized by 'the rebellious position'. But in contrast with the entrepreneur, who eventually masters his conflicts about control and rejection by being in control of his or her own structured situation (the enterprise), most people who fall into 'the rebellious position' do not show the foresight of the entrepreneur by making a career choice which excludes dealing with authority figures. Instead, these individuals usually drift through organizational life troubled by frustrations and disappointments. It seems that the influence of a lower degree of control in childhood differentiates these people from entrepreneurs where half-hearted compliance to overcontrol was more of an issue.[24]

HOMO FABER AND HOMO LUDENS

The previous comments on work problems in organizations indicate that we can get more insight into the incidence of symptoms by studying the way an individual passes through the human life cycle. The failure of an individual to function in an organizational setting seems to a large extent a legacy of frustrating interpersonal experiences at earlier stages of life. What we observe as symptoms in organizations are basically the outcomes of defensive reactions of individuals needed for the preservation of the self. The avoidance of feelings of self-fragmentation, of a sense of nothingness, lead to rigidity and prevent adaptive behaviour. Adaptability, with its implicit playfulness, acceptance of the unexpected, and ease of action has become too risky. Instead we are confronted with ritualistic behaviour which can be interpreted as a way of controlling inward- and outward-directed aggression and also as a means of ensuring selected outlets for aggression. Konrad Lorenz' comments, based on his ethological studies, are appropriate in the context:

> for a living being lacking insight into the relation between causes and effects it must be extremely useful to cling to a behaviour pattern which has once or many times proved to achieve its aim, and to have done so without danger. If one does not know which details of the whole performance are essential for its success as well as for its safety, it is best to cling to them all with slavish exactitude. . .[25]

This description is very applicable to individuals prone to work problems and explains the persistence of the 'Oblomov threat'. Man prefers known dangers over the unknown, even if the former means illness. Insight is feared; it deviates from established patterns, disrupts the homeostatic state, and only causes disturbing thoughts. Defensive strategies are devised to circumvent these unknown situations. But these defences are certainly not impregnable. Symptoms become indications that all is not well. Unfortunately, to put an end to self-fulfilling prophecies, to re-evaluate, and, more importantly, to stop repetitive patterns is a difficult endeavour, a painful journey of personal insight. But although we cling to the known with incredible tenacity, we also will 'search for a cure' given sufficient pain and discomfort. And although it may take time to overcome the need to believe in

24

'instant solutions', and realize instead that there are only arduous roads to change, change is possible. If childhood did not provide for a base of security as a building block for adaptability of behaviour, adulthood can, but with much greater effort and discomfort. It necessitates a journey of critical re-evaluation of action patterns, and the re-examination and redefinition of behaviour, an effort which may increase self-awareness and insight and prevent the 'Oblomov threat'.

These steps are not easy to take since they imply a direct confrontation with the self, an integration of feeling and thinking, and a determination of one's role in organizations. They also imply a degree of realism which may be uncomfortable given one's aspirations. Direct confrontation with the self also involves honesty about one's feelings and one's belief systems. While physiological changes are the predictable natural marking points in childhood, adulthood, while providing less dramatic opportunities for change, does not exclude change, such as adaptation to organizational life. A weakening of the defensive structures of personality is only one step and one which, by itself, would leave a person wide open to emotional disarray. More is needed to eliminate anxiety about change and replace rigidity in behaviour with greater adaptability, implicit acceptance of confrontation, and self-evaluation. What might be needed is a form of 'regression in service of the ego' or regressive adaptation, implying the reintroduction in adulthood of the play element which was so important in childhood. This play element once made for a sense of efficacy, added to feelings of security, and is the antithesis of rigidity in behaviour. The cultural historian Johan Huizinga's advocacy of the need for a play element in culture,[26] the reunion of *homo faber* with *homo ludens* has not lost its significance. Play prevents repetition compulsion, and that is what the 'Oblomov threat' is all about, the problem of getting 'stuck' to dysfunctional behaviour patterns in organizations. Adaptability in behaviour makes for relaxed, more open interpersonal relations in organizations, prevents symptom formation, forestalls work problems, and wards off the 'Oblomov threat'.

3

THE ORGANIZATION OF EMPTINESS

The gods were bored, and so they created man. Adam was bored because he was alone, and so Eve was created. Thus boredom entered the world, and increased in proportion to the increase of population. Adam was bored alone; then Adam and Eve were bored together; then Adam and Eve and Cain and Abel were bored *en famille*; then the population of the world increased, and the people were bored *en masse*. To divert themselves they conceived the idea of constructing a tower high enough to reach the heavens. This idea is itself as boring as the tower was high, and constitutes a terrible proof of how boredom gained the upper hand. . .[1]

S. Kierkegaard

Defective adaptation to work can take many other forms. The nature and intensity of organizational experiences become indicative of these potential work problems. Commonly overheard complaints in organizational life have been lamentations about boredom, alienation, and the quality of working life. Boredom, particularly, has been used to describe vague, rather undefined feelings, centred around life's meaninglessness, futility, absurdity, and purposelessness, going, therefore, beyond just narrow concerns about the working environment. Such feelings confront us with an image of people being cast adrift, being afloat, searching through life like eternal wanderers. Being bored has also been looked at as the experience of inner impoverishment, an attempt to describe the inability to participate fully in life, a state of living without enjoyment.

One of the functions of work has been to give some form of structure to a person's being and thereby enable him or her to cope with this feeling of boredom. Work, like birth and death, offers at least some degree of certainty among the many undependable aspects of life's existence. Many philosophers, psychologists, and sociologists have recognized this function of work. Take, for example, Schopenhauer, who once said:

> Work, worry, toil and trouble are indeed the lot of almost all men their whole life long. And yet if every desire were satisfied as soon as it arose how could men occupy their lives, how would they pass the time? Imagine this race transported to a Utopia where everything grows of its own accord and turkeys fly around ready-roasted, were lovers find one another without any delay and keep another without any difficulty: in such a place some men would die of boredom and hang themselves, some would fight and kill one another, and thus they would create for themselves more suffering than nature inflicts on them as it is. . .[2]

Existential philosophers such as Heidegger, Jaspers, Marcel, and Sartre dwelt on the pervasive influence of the experience of emptiness and nothingness which in their constructs was facilitated by modern industrial society. In their statements man's struggle in dealing with anxiety, despair, and the dread of aloneness became a central theme. This notion can be found in the work of many writers. Beckett's characters, in his play *Waiting for Godot*, symbolize life's emptiness. Similar views are portrayed in Camus' novel, *The Stranger*, or Kafka's writings such as *The Trial*, *The Castle*, and *Metamorphosis*. When Eliot's hero J. Alfred Prufrock says: 'I have measured out my life with coffee spoons'[3] or Brecht comments: 'if you cram a ship's hold full of human bodies, so it almost bursts – there will be such loneliness in that ship that they'll all freeze to death'[4] then we get an inkling of what is meant. These lines contain a sense of extreme hopelessness and despair and describe a dissociation from one's own feeling in spite of apparent normality and ability to function.

Work can be viewed as one of the ways of coping with the feeling of boredom, emptiness, loneliness, and nothingness. The process of work itself can also lead to a new experience of boredom, may contribute to work futility, and raise more questions about the significance of one's existence. With the advent of modern industrial society this adverse effect of work has been popularized and has led to the introduction of concepts such as nihilism, anomie, and alienation. We can look at these terms as attempts to conceptualize the experience of boredom and related questions dealing with the meaningfulness of life.

Many critics of contemporary culture have argued that man's feelings of boredom, futility, meaninglessness, and also loneliness have intensified in the midst of bureaucratic, highly impersonal mass society. The organizational sub-groupings required for the functioning of the large, modern corporation or bureaucratic institution may have fostered cooperative work structures, but these more or less forced associations have seemed to be without avail in countering depressive feelings.

The concept of 'alienation' began to capture the imagination as a mental device for analyzing modes of human unhappiness and frustration, and as a way of embracing these notions of boredom, meaninglessness, and inner emptiness. Not only was it meant to describe distance from nature, loss of religion and community sense, but also to be a term to capture the dysfunctional effects of monotonous, highly atomistic jobs. Alienation portrayed a sense of cultural discontinuity, dehumanization, and depersonalization. Critics of society warned about the alienating influences of industrialization, globalization, urbanization, automation, technological change, specialization, and bureaucratization. The argument arose that originally meaningful work relationships had changed into mere associations between exchangeable objects making for a world ruled by efficiency experts, systems analysts, and conforming organization people, at the price of individuality and humanity. One student of alienation, after doing a content analysis of popular fiction comparing the 1900s with the 1950s, came to the conclusion that themes of self-alienation increased in both frequency and intensity during those fifty years.[5]

These feelings of alienation have always been associated with work. Organizations have been looked at as major culprits in the causation of this form of alienation. Lack of job involvement, decline in productivity, and stress symptoms became viewed as the inevitable outcomes.

A reaction to this trend has been contemporary interest in quality of working life. Here, organizational specialists have become concerned with the question of how to humanize work and how to arrive at criteria required to improve the general working environment.[6] This involves such principles of humanization of work as security, equity, individuation, and work place democracy, or criteria such as autonomy, feedback, multiple skills, safe and healthy working conditions, and opportunities for continued growth and security. We can view this present concern not only as a search for congruence between the needs of individuals belonging to organizations and organizational goals, but also as a way of influencing effectiveness and efficiency of organizational functioning.

Much has been said about the alienating influence of organizations, of the various working conditions adversely affecting an individual's life; very little, on the other hand, has been said about the role of the individual in this process. We should not forget, however, that organizations are created by individuals. It is people who are more or less responsible for the design and functioning of these very organizations. Not only is it necessary to look at alienating working conditions, but also at the state of mind of individuals who work in these organizations. While, for very good reasons, much attention has been given to the former (whereby the source of alienation is found to be based on environmental conditions and social structure), the contribution of the individual to this alienation process has usually been de-emphasized.

Alienation seems to be an interactive process of both alienating structural conditions and a peculiar intra-psychic reaction experienced by many individuals populating organizations. I will not argue one in favour of the other, or what started the process of alienation in the first place. I will only explore a specific personality constellation more susceptible to the experience of alienation and will suggest that this type of person is more inclined to stress the alienating aspects of work. I believe that by pursuing this particular point of view we will arrive at a greater understanding of what originates inside an individual (feelings which will persist no matter how enlightened the organization is in its policies), and what is caused by outside conditions. In using this approach the concept of quality of working life might become more meaningful. A dimension of reality will be added to change strategies aimed at enhancing the working environment.

Each of us may use work in one way or another to give meaning and structure to our lives. It is when work becomes mechanical, when we experience a sense of detachment, when there is no pleasure associated with our efforts, that questions begin to arise about boredom, meaningfulness, nothingness, and futility, or, in a more general sense, alienation.

THE ENCOUNTER WITH MEANINGLESSNESS

Alienation has meant a great number of different things to different people at different times, depending on the individual's background, and whether the approach is that of the philosopher, economist, sociologist, psychologist, or anthropologist. In a very broad sense alienation refers to a process of estrangement from oneself, others, objects, values, and the world. Historically, conditions in the environment contributing to this state have assumed a central position in these analyses. Thus we can make a distinction between the structuralist point of view of alienation, taken by those students of the topic interested in finding specific conditions of the environment contributing to this process, and a more individualistic orientation. The latter group looks at alienation from a more personal perspective – in the sense of what it means to the individual.

Hegel, Feuerbach, and Marx were the first writers really interested in the topic. But while Hegel and Feuerbach looked more at the metaphysical aspects of alienation or *Entfremdung*, and viewed it as a general human condition, Marx popularized the concept by referring to the worker who, in the absence of ownership of the means of production, becomes disconnected and loses control over the fruits of his labour. Apart from referring to estrangement from the process and product of labour, Marx also mentioned estrangement from others and self-estrangement.[7]

Nihilism, originally a philosophical movement associated with atheism, incorporated aspects of alienation. In some ways it became the ideological framework surrounding the experience of nothingness. Writers such as Nietzsche and Sartre advocated the association of nihilism with a mood of despair and moral scepticism over the emptiness or triviality of human existence. Gradually, the originally attributed cause of nihilism, atheism, became replaced with new causations such as industrialization, social pressures, and, more generally, the stress of life.

The structural point of view of alienation became more deeply entrenched through Durkheim's introduction to the concept of anomie.[8] This term was meant to describe a state of deregulation of the social forces working in society contributing to a condition of relative normlessness. Social change leading to industrialization contributed to this condition. Tonnies' classical study *Gemeinschaft und Gesellschaft* had set the stage for this notion by placing in juxtaposition traditional and industrial society.[9] This theme was picked up by Merton who described anomie as: 'a breakdown in the cultural structure, occurring particularly when there is an acute disjunction between the cultural norms and goals and the socially structured capacities of members of the groups to act in accord with them.'[10]

These writers pursue the ideal of integrated man in a cohesive society because, in their view, man needs continuity, consistency, and confirmation. If these needs are lacking, culture shock, disintegration, anomie, and alienation follow.

In discussions of nihilism and anomie disintegration of social structure is key, with a sense of estrangement being the consequence, making for a close association and even overlap with alienation. This is particularly true if we adopt Etzioni's conception of alienation.[11] In his opinion it is an estrangement to be understood as the result of social arrangements which deny fulfilment of basic needs such as affection and recognition. Although his emphasis is on structural factors he touches upon individual needs.

Seeman's view of alienation is more balanced in combining individualistic and structural elements.[12] To him alienation becomes a sense of powerlessness, meaninglessness, normlessness, cultural estrangement, self-estrangement, and social isolation. A similar position is taken by Eric and Marie Josephson who noted that:

> 'alienation' has been used by philosophers, psychologists, and sociologists to refer to an extraordinary variety of psychosocial disorders, including loss of self, anxiety states, anomie, despair, depersonalization, rootlessness, apathy, social disorganization, loneliness, atomization, powerlessness, meaninglessness, isolation, pessimism, and the loss of beliefs or values.[13]

We will concentrate on alienation viewed as a personal experience. Alienation, in the sense of self-estrangement and estrangement from others, then becomes a description of a personal crisis. Kierkegaard calls it 'the sickness unto death', this sense of nothingness which becomes 'the disrelationship in a relation which relates itself to itself'.[14] Horney compares this feeling of alienation from the actual self as 'the remoteness of the neurotic from his own feelings, wishes, beliefs, and energies. It is the loss of the feeling of being an active determining force in one's own life. It is the loss of feeling...

31

as an organic whole.'[15] Fromm views it as 'a mode of expression in which the person experiences himself as alien. . . The alienated person is out of touch with himself as he is out of touch with any other person'.[16] Moreover, he says that:

> The alienated person. . . cannot be healthy. Since he experiences himself as a thing, an investment, to be manipulated by himself and by others, he is lacking in a sense of self. This lack of self creates deep anxiety. The anxiety engendered by confronting him with the abyss of nothingness is more terrifying than even the tortures of hell. In the vision of hell, I am punished and tortured – in the vision of nothingness I am driven to the border of madness – because I cannot say 'I' anymore.[17]

A personal account of this experience is given by the poet Rilke in a semi-autobiographical journal during his stay in Paris:

> It is ridiculous. Here I sit in my little room, I, Brigge, who have grown to be twenty-eight years old and whom no one knows.
> I sit here and am nothing. . .
> Is it possible, it thinks, that one has not yet seen, known and said anything real or important?. . .
> Yes, it is possible.
> Is it possible that despite discoveries and progress, despite culture, religion and world-wisdom, one has remained on the surface of life?. . .
> Yes, it is possible.
> Is it possible that the whole history of the world has been misunderstood? Is it possible that the past is false, because one has always spoken of its masses just as though one were telling of a coming together of many human beings, instead of speaking of the individual around whom they stood because he was a stranger and was dying?
> Yes, it is possible. . .
> Is it possible that all these people know with perfect accuracy a past that has never existed? Is it possible that all realities are nothing to them; that their life is running down, unconnected with anything, like a clock in any empty room?
> Yes, it is possible.[18]

The experience described is not an uncommon one. Each of us, at one time or another, may have had similar thoughts. What is interesting is why some people seem more troubled by this experience than others. Why are they so different?

We realize now that the togetherness supposedly found in organizational life has been of little help in preventing feelings of alienation. Although organizations have become more pervasive than ever people feel no less alone, or less troubled by questions about the meaningfulness of life's existence. Organizational life, with its concentrations of people, does not necessarily lessen loneliness and alleviate the sense of alienation. In spite of all the advancements in mass communication and transportation, facilitating contacts, individuals seem less and less able to engage in true interpersonal encounters, unable to communicate satisfactorily with their immediate environment. The personal experience of estrangement from oneself and others is the unfortunate outcome.

ALIENATED MAN

Some people are deeply concerned that life is slipping away. No cure seems effective enough in halting this process. Even desperate steps such as changing jobs, locations, friends, interests, husbands, or wives are of no avail; the sense of meaninglessness continues. Nothing seems to help. Instead, these people find themselves in the role of spectators observing their life as a play from a distance. There is an absence of real permanent identification with other people or ideas due to a rather undefined sense of self; what remains is a retreat into nothingness, a dread of the void, an absence of realness.

In psychiatric literature we can find a description of two specific character disorders which show strong resemblances with alienated man: schizoid and avoidant. The first disorder is defined in the following way:

> The essential feature of this disorder is a pervasive pattern of indifference to social relationships and a restricted range of emotional experience and expression, beginning by early adulthood and present in a variety of contexts. People with this disorder neither desire nor enjoy close relationships, including being part of a family. They prefer to be 'loners', and have no close friends or confidants (or only one) other than first-degree relatives. They almost always choose solitary activities and indicate little if any desire to have sexual

experiences with another person. Such people are indifferent to the praise and criticism of others. They claim that they rarely experience strong emotions such as anger and joy, and in fact display a constricted affect. They appear cold and aloof.[19]

In the case of the avoidant personality disorder:

The essential feature of this disorder is a pervasive pattern of social discomfort, fear of negative evaluation, and timidity, beginning by early adulthood and present in a variety of contexts. Most people are somewhat concerned about how others assess them, but those with this disorder are easily hurt by criticism and are devastated by the slightest hint of disapproval. They generally are unwilling to enter into relationships unless given an unusually strong guarantee of uncritical acceptance; consequently, they often have no close friends or confidants (or only one) other than first-degree relatives. Social or occupational activities that involve significant interpersonal contact tend to be avoided. . . Unlike people with Schizoid Personality Disorder, who are socially isolated, but have no desire for social relations, those with Avoidant Personality Disorder yearn for affection and acceptance. They are distressed by their lack of ability to relate comfortably to others.[20]

These clinical descriptions may seem unrelated to the person we are trying to identify in organizations. But what we should realize is that illness is a question of degree. Many individuals may have 'schizoid' and 'avoidant' tendencies but are able to function in a very acceptable way. Indeed, some students of this disorder argue that this schizoid condition (here the avoidant personality disorder can be viewed as a less dramatic variant of the schizoid) might be a rather common phenomenon in contemporary society. Actually, to some extent, we all possess schizoid characteristics.[21] The difference with the more serious disturbances found in borderline cases is the degree of awareness and psychological insight which alienated man with the schizoid condition has about his problems. The seriously schizoid person may not even realize that something is wrong and seems untroubled by his behaviour. In contrast an individual who possesses some schizoid inclinations may, at times, admit to himself that he actually feels nothing, that he cannot come close to people, that everything seems unreal and meaningless, that life passes by as a film reel with him playing the role of disinterested spectator. Referring to the schizoid condition we are apparently dealing with a person who is:

> detached, cold, peculiar, suspicious, arrogant, condescending, and cocky. Thus the interpersonal world will not be able to interact with ease with a schizoid person. A state of tension, distance, mistrust, and mis-interpretation is likely to occur. . . he will continue to envision his being with others as a chronic, unspoken, moderate state of danger or surrounding hostility, from which he has to continue to defend himself. . .[22]

A closely related description of this type of persona has been made by Deutsch. She introduced the 'as if' personality. These individuals may give the impression of complete normality but there is a staged quality to their behaviour. They suffer from a sense of depersonalization and derealization and complain that 'the world seems strange, objects shadowy, human beings and events theatrical and unreal.'[23] We are observing individuals who look at their behaviour as a collection of roles. Deutsch comments on the extreme suggestibility and weakness of moral attitudes which these people possess. Although outwardly they seem to have the faculty for handling complete and sensitive emotional experiences, in actuality they act out a simulation of affectivity. Deep down inside there is a lack of warmth and emptiness in emotional relationships.

Guntrip mentions as the most prominent behavioural expression of the schizoid condition that 'in and out' programme, the individual who is 'always breaking away from what [he or she] is at the same time holding on to'.[24] We are reminded of the parable of Schopenhauer's hedgehogs who tried so desperately to be close, but because of their quills had to remain at a distance. And that is what the schizoid condition is all about, it is a double bind, a situation made up of a fear of isolation and a simultaneous fear of bondage. We are dealing with a type of person who cannot really stand alone, but at the same time cannot give up his independence.

These individuals find it much easier to cope with cold, hostile interpersonal relationships than with warm, affectionate ones. They are quick to blame others if hindrances are put in their way. Hostile relationships are preferred since they make the process of scapegoating easier. What counts in these instances is taking the initiative and feeling in control of the situation. This is not the case when dealing with warm, affectionate relationships; then the feeling is of being at the mercy of others. Real relationships are sensed as being too dangerous to enter into. Consequently, though there may be great longings for other persons, these feelings are not expressed, but turned into abstractions such as love for mankind, religious and ideological beliefs, and even such work-orientated attitudes as devotion to organizational goals. Affection is expressed from a distance: the actual presence of the other person usually causes emotional withdrawal. Therefore, relationships possess a pseudo-affective quality; they are emotionally shallow with strong mechanical, machine-like features. The most persistent relationships are emotionally neutral, often intellectual. And because of the intense fear to commit oneself to anybody, indecision becomes a fairly common schizoid behaviour pattern.

Guntrip says of this behaviour: 'Schizoid aloofness is the fear of loving lest one's love or need of love should destroy.'[25] Laing comments that this person's 'isolation is not entirely for his own self's sake. It is also out of concern for others.'[26] The schizoid's need for affection is actually so strong that there exists a strong fear for personal destructiveness if expressed. Consequently, self-protection (the anxiety over being rebutted in his or her demands) and protection of others (the unconscious anxiety that affection might destroy) result in this state of detachment. But behind this aloof, cold mask of people with the schizoid condition lies hidden inner despair and loneliness.[27]

We notice that, in contrast with the depressed individual who directs his aggression at himself and feels guilty, a person with a serious schizoid condition withdraws from the situation altogether and becomes troubled by having no feelings. If anything is felt it is a sense of futility, the experience of being cut off, and the sentiment that the present and future are meaningless. The need to get away from people occurs concurrently.

Johnson relates the schizoid condition to the experience of self-alienation and inauthenticity. He remarks that 'the exquisitely schizoidal person becomes, as it were, an amateur sociologist studying his own operations. He looks on himself as a collection of roles rather than a self.'[28]

According to Guntrip these people:

Live far below their real potentialities and life seems dull and unsatisfying. If we could pursue this problem into a mass study of human beings in their everyday existence, we would probably be shocked at the enormous number of people who cannot live life to the full, and not through any lack of means or opportunity, but through a lack of emotional capacity to give themselves to anything fully. Here is a cause of boredoms, discontents, dissatisfactions, which are often disguised as economic and social but which no economic or political means can cure. The person with schizoid tendencies usually feels that he is 'missing the bus' and life is passing him by, and it eases his mind superficially if he can find a scapegoat.[29]

What these various descriptions of the schizoid condition suggest, in light of the complaints about the dehumanizing alienating aspects of work and the quality of working life, is that many of these concerns may be caused by a group of individuals who are desperately trying to make sense out of an experience of depersonalization and derealization. The original of this *Weltanschauung* can be found in developmental problems of early life. The inner sense of non-involvement, observation at a distance without feeling, is displaced on external targets such as deficiencies in the work environment or unfair labour practices. In making this statement, however, I do not underestimate the presence of dehumanizing aspects of work; I only argue that this is not the only factor.

What becomes frightening is that, in spite of all these complaints, these individuals are remarkably adaptive to a dehumanizing working environment. Actually, in many instances, they are the very ones instrumental in creating exactly this type of environment. This can be viewed as an effort to find some form of structure in coping with the schizoid condition. Because of the protean nature of their activities, which can be attributed to a lack of real, meaningful identification with anything, resulting in a low emotional investment in love or work, they bear a large degree of responsibility in creating an extremely shallow work environment and society. It leads to the experience of inauthenticity and insincerity, existing in a world in which actually nothing really matters.

THE STRUCTURING OF NOTHINGNESS

While we can blame modern society in many ways for the apparent prominence of alienation and the possible increase in the schizoid condition, we suggest, based on observations in organizations, that a considerable number of individuals distinguished by the schizoid condition are populating organizations. We could argue that these individuals have a substantial responsibility in the design of the infra- and suprastructure of the modern organization. It reflects their way of coping with the schizoid condition.

At the danger of oversimplification we will now distinguish between two styles of coping with the schizoid condition. Naturally, these two styles are not mutually exclusive. Since they derive from the same basic personality constellation they have many patterns in common, the most common quality being the mechanical nature of dealing with their environment. This quality is coupled with the tendency of blaming others or the 'system' when things do not work out. There is a difference, however: one group of individuals directs its emotional energy more to people, while the other group focuses on ideas, tasks and 'things'.

In suggesting this typology I do not deprecate the importance and usefulness of these individuals to organizations. They can make great organizational contributions. But I do note how frequently we can detect behind great organizational dedication and involvement signs of callousness and zealous devotion to ideas and goals with very little consideration for the impact of their actions on other people's feelings and lives.

The social sensor

A prominent feature of this group of people is their compulsive sociability, but this is an activity which serves as a disguise for a strong sense of detachment. This compulsive sociability becomes part of a forced, exhausting act which fails to hide its lack of real meaning. What we observe in the action of these people is a great capacity for mimicry. There is a chameleon-like quality to their behaviour given their ability to pick up signals from the outside world and adjust their behaviour accordingly. Their loss of a true sense of self, of a deep-seated sense of identity, drives these people to change their role according to the requirements of the situation. We are reminded of Thomas Mann's *Felix Krull*, the confidence man, the impostor, who assumed different roles depending on the occasion, appearing as it were magically transformed while changing clothes. The story tells how Felix Krull's childhood games of dressing as the Kaiser, a prince, or a violinist continued through adulthood demonstrating an inability to present a true self.[30] These people, good impersonators as they are, will produce the feelings which often go with their roles. But in interpersonal encounters we are often left with a notion of pseudo-sincerity and pseudo-authenticity.

Deutsch talks about the 'automaton-like identification' of these people with others and stresses the pseudo-affective nature of their behaviour patterns.[31] Fromm calls this behaviour the 'marketing orientation', individuals characterized by a marked superficiality in human relations. When dealing with these people one has a subtle, almost unnoticeable sense of being manipulated, a sense that for them the surface feature is what counts, and that

> no specific and permanent kind of relatedness is developed, but that the very changeability of attitudes is the only permanent quality of such orientation. . . Not one particular attitude is predominant, but the emptiness which can be filled most quickly with the desired quality.[32]

Here, we can find the individual who fits very well into the large organization. I am referring to that person who is highly mobile because of an ability to play-act the expected role and identify and please superiors; but behind this façade of easy-goingness, active busyness and success are hidden feelings of emptiness and meaninglessness. Such individuals might be the centre of action in public, while in private they are often depressed and troubled with questions about the reasons for existence.

We have all met these people in organizations. Their career orientation often gives them away. Among them we find most prominently the salesperson, the marketing person, and not infrequently the human relations expert. The mask of extroversion becomes not only a disguise for their sense of detachment, but also a desperate effort to make up for the sense of being cut off from the world of outer reality. What remains is the experience of being alone even in the midst of a crowd.

The systems person

These individuals deal with their problems in establishing real affective relationships with other people by avoiding personal associations altogether. They devote themselves to abstractions, tasks, ideas, and things. Feelings are superfluous; what counts, warrants complete obedience, and assumes final responsibility is 'the system'. These people concern themselves with work of an impersonal nature; their contacts with other persons are depersonalized, mechanical, and frequently intellectual. Doing the right and necessary thing is predominantly on their mind. Attachment to procedures, organizational strategies and goals, and, occasionally, complete devotion to a vision of a future scenario for the organization become their way of coping with the experience of inner emptiness. The systems person organizes his or her emptiness, while professing great sincerity and involvement, by carrying out automatically a fixed routine or through zealous advocacy of abstractions, thereby abolishing relationships with real people.

A compulsive, driven quality is noticeable in the systems person's organizational zeal; in reaching his or her goal no means are spared. Guntrip even warns that 'the schizoid intellectual wielding unlimited political power is perhaps the most dangerous type of leader. He is a devourer of the human rights of all whom he can rule.'[33] He gives as an example the SS leader, Himmler.

Obviously, in organizations, the most typical individuals who fall into this category are bureaucrats. They are the persons often caricatured as possessing excessive aloofness, ritualistic attachment to routines and procedures, and resistance to change. Relationships between individuals may become depersonalized through rules and regulations, thereby preventing the danger of coming close and getting emotionally involved.

As another example of this category we can take the organizational 'whizz kid'. No means are off limit to pursue his or her particular view of the future of the organization. But in his or her actions little or no consideration is given to how these changes will affect other peoples's lives. And although some of the ideas may be sound and timely, it is the manner of implementation which distinguishes the style of these people. The devastating effect their actions often can have on organizational morale and the damage they can do to other people's lives seem to be of no importance.

THE PURSUIT OF THE POSSIBLE

In the light of the previous discussion the schizoid condition poses a conundrum. This type of person adopts a particular way of coping with his personal experience of boredom, nothingness, and meaninglessness, consequently contributing to the creation of de-humanizing, alienating working conditions. In addition, given their character structure, persons of this type are also prone not to find fault in themselves, but to blame others for feelings of unhappiness, dissatisfaction, and meaninglessness. They may also blame 'the system' for these wrongdoings. We are looking at a person who bears a strong responsibility in causing alienation (meant in a structural sense as a deterioration of quality of working life) while, at the same time, blaming alienation as the cause of their personal unhappiness. What we observe is a breakdown between inner and outer world, a lack of symbolic integration of what originates inside the person and what is caused by the reality of the external situation. This lack of integration will make any effort for change highly problematic.

Whatever we do in the way of changing structural conditions to enhance quality of working life, there is no way of satisfying these people completely. Because of the emptiness of their inner experiences no measure is ever sufficient. Mere satisfaction of the structural conditions of the working environment is certainly not enough. The organizational theorist and psychoanalyst Jaques touched upon this basic truth when he said that 'effective social change is likely to require analysis of the common anxieties and unconscious collusions underlying the social defenses determining phantasy social relationships.'[34] It is important that practitioners and researchers dealing with the quality of working life recognize this prerequisite for change.

What the occurrence of the schizoid condition in organizations implies is that many advocates of the improvement of quality of working life are bound to be disappointed, setting and propagating too high expectations for change. In most instances the effects of their actions involving job and organization redesign will be very moderate and often much less than expected. Although this realization may be discouraging, the positive side is that it will make for more realistic goal setting.

Given the deep-seated nature of the schizoid condition, more draconian measures are needed than merely changing some vari-

41

ables in the working environment. The creation of autonomous work groups, of career development programmes, of quality circles, of safer and healthier working conditions, may not be enough. We are referring to a restructuring of the person's relationships outside work and particularly the re-evaluation of affective contacts. What basically has to change is the nature of human interactions. A willingness is needed to accept close, affectionate relationships. The road to the establishment of meaningful relationships, however, will be an arduous one, necessitating a continuous critical evaluation of actions and the development of a less fragmented sense of self through a gradual attainment and restoration of competence in interpersonal encounters. Disclosure, the expression of affection, and the tolerance of closeness will be critical factors. In spite of the obstacles, the end result, the fading out of meaninglessness, may be very well worth it. Usually this route will be taken only by that individual who experiences sufficient discomfort in dealing with his day-to-day existence.

The previous statements are not meant to be interpreted in such a way that, given the human condition with its solidly established behaviour patterns, effort to improve quality of working life and the creation of more meaningful organizations and work conditions are meaningless. I am only warning not to oversimplify the issues and expect miracles. The schizoid condition is a well-entrenched pattern in society which will not disappear overnight.

What I am advocating is the pursuit of the possible, which implies the incorporation in any plan for change of a basic understanding of the meaning of social structure in organizations to the individual and, particularly, the recognition of the schizoid condition in organizations. Only then can we make a significant contribution to effect change. Fairy tales have their purpose, everybody likes to 'live happily ever after'; however, we should not forget that that is exactly the point where fairy tales usually stop. We have to start from there and accept and deal with schizoid behaviour patterns if we want to make a realistic contribution to improve life in organizations. To get people who suffer from the schizoid condition involved is no easy task and quite a challenge, but if we know what we are up against we can take more appropriate measures and behave accordingly. Changing the conditions of working life is one step; fostering warm, truly mutual and trusting interpersonal relations is another. Only then can we prevent boredom and create a more meaningful society.

The task of the organizational leader becomes now how to make organizational structure and job content as meaningful and realistic as possible so that it will lead to career involvement and a sense of pleasure in one's activities. In this process the executive inevitably will be exposed to the problems of power and ambiguity.

4

POWER AND HELPLESSNESS

Somewhere in the world there is defeat for everyone. Some are destroyed by defeat, and some made small and mean by victory. Greatness lives in one who triumphs equally over defeat and victory . . .[1]

J. Steinbeck

These were wise words of council which Merlin the wizard gave to King Arthur. But even King Arthur had a hard time living up to these lofty standards of perfection. We can thus imagine how difficult it would be – outside the domain of legend and fairy tale – to find mere mortals able to pursue these ideals. Usually setbacks are dealt with very differently. Helplessness is a more common reaction when the pursuit of power fails. In these instances the individual's perception is that the environment is uncertain, unpredictable, and uncontrollable. A sufficient number of these experiences can affect the health of the people populating organizations. Stress reactions might eventually emerge as symbolic expressions of experienced disappointment, anger, and helplessness.

In psychiatric literature we can find the notion of a 'giving-up-given-up complex'.[2] This complex can be defined in the following way:

The giving up part of the complex indicates the inability of the individual to let go or give up wished for gratification which has been lost (helplessness). The given up part of the complex indicates the resolution phase of the complex which follows the recognition and tolerance of the loss of gratification and a final recognition that the old wished for gratification is not to be achieved.[3]

Two researchers in psychosomatic medicine, Engel and Schmale, indicate that psychic giving up as an antecedent condition is related to the etiology of stress reactions. Situations leading to the experience of powerlessness and helplessness will increase susceptibility to this emotional state and seem to have a stress-inducing impact. These feelings of distress can be attributed to failures and deficiencies in coping with environmental demands as well as the experience of personal failure and inadequacy which the individual sees as being permanent. Lack of control over changes in the environment, real or fantasized dangers, humiliations, or loss of status are some examples. Five factors seem to facilitate the manifestation of this complex:

1 the giving up affects of helplessness or hopelessness;
2 a depreciated image of oneself;
3 a loss of gratification from relationships or roles in life;
4 a disruption of the sense of continuity between past, present and future;
5 a reactivation of memories of earlier periods of giving up.[4]

The description indicates a relationship between the experience of deprivation, feelings of being let down or left out, a sense of futility, loss of satisfaction, helplessness, powerlessness, and illness. Apparently, the psychic injury which these experiences cause might reopen old wounds. Notions of giving up or having given up occur, and the concurrent disequilibrium of defensive structure seems to facilitate the incidence of stress reactions and has been found to be work-related.[5] Support for the relationship between helplessness and stress has also been given by Seligman in his theory of helplessness. He postulated that depression and anxiety are related to uncontrollability and unpredictability, implying that the experience of helplessness reduces the ability to cope with stress and, in his opinion, is a major factor in the etiology of illness.[6]

THE EFFECT OF STRUCTURE

In organizations there is ample opportunity for the observation of the giving-up-given-up complex. Disappointments, frustrations, and deprivations seem to be inevitable elements of an executive's life. At one time or another every executive is faced with situations conducive to a state of helplessness. Of course there are variations. The degree of intensity will vary. Some individuals possess a greater tolerance to deal with these experiences than others. But whatever the exact nature of the experience managers will resort to some form of adjustment, prevention, or flight to cope with these situations, thereby setting a defensive process into motion.

Some individuals fail to adapt because of personal or organizational reasons. Instead, an overwhelming sense of being locked in arises; no escape seems possible from a very unsatisfactory state of affairs. Coping mechanisms seem to fail. It has become increasingly apparent that, if this happens, organizational life might become experienced as uncontrollable and unpredictable, can be extremely anxiety-provoking, may contribute to a state of helplessness and hopelessness and, eventually, lead to illness.

The nature of organizational structure and patterns of decision making can add to this experience – flat, 'organic' organization structures (characterized by few authority levels) and empowerment have become key concerns. These concerns can be taken as a representation of man's rejection of excessive obedience to the authority associated with tall, pyramidal, 'mechanistic' organization structures, having bureaucratic overtones, where strictly defined duties, responsibilities and authority stand central. To many people the term 'bureaucracy' has become a dirty word evoking memories of red tape, anonymity, rigidity, frustration, helplessness, resistance to change. Bureaucratic/mechanistic organizations are all too often a reminder of Chaplin's film *Modern Times* or Orwell's novel *1984*, representing dehumanizing and depersonalizing types of work. Others associate tall organizations and bureaucracy with the government and think of civil servants supposedly bilking the tax payers.

Although informal structures also arise in these mechanistic organizations, the relief which these informal groupings of people might provide as an outlet for pent-up emotions is often insufficient in counteracting the experienced rigidity. Thus, other forms of organization are being considered and preferred. We are now, therefore, much more enamoured of 'organic' boundary-less organizations, networking systems, empowered management and leaders as cheerleaders and coaches. These organizations are associated with greater participation, adaptiveness, flexible leadership and innovation, supposedly possessing a much better utilization of human potential, thus making for a learning organization.

Unfortunately, there is a price to be paid for the lack of structure in these apparently less rigidly designed organizations. In organic

46

organizations, matrix structures, adhocracies and virtual organizations, roles, patterns of responsibility and authority are usually
less clearly defined than in the more mechanistic organizations. A
highly ambiguous and uncertain organizational environment may
be created in which boundaries delineating interpersonal relationships are extremely hard to determine. The result might be the
executive's experience of helplessness in determining his or her
role in the organization, which can make for a setting conducive to
the giving-up-given-up complex. Concurrent with the existing
ambiguity and uncertainty in role and performance evaluation and
the prevailing helplessness, we can find frequently in these organizations a high incidence of stress symptoms.

I am not defending one organizational type above the other, nor
implying that stress reactions are less prevalent in the more bureaucratic organizations. Each organizational type creates its own
problems. Very little effort is needed to notice the incidence of
stress in bureaucracy. The existence of the term bureaupathology
is indicative, bringing to mind the dysfunctional effects of these
institutions on their employees. Bureaucratic organizations might
make for more structure and therefore greater certainty in roles,
authority, and responsibility; frequently, however, they also imply
greater rigidity and greater resistance to change. The reaction of the
executive to such a state of affairs again can lead to the perception
of helplessness and hopelessness associated with an inability to
influence the environment in any way.

Whatever organizational design innovations may have been
made, we can find that most organization charts still resemble
pyramidical structures: broad-based at the bottom, with very little
room at the top. Another obvious organizational characteristic
worth mentioning in this context is that organizations have limited
resources at their disposal; reward systems have to be set up
accordingly. To become president, or even vice-president for that
matter, is not everybody's destiny. Actually, organizational life
implies that only a very few ever will reach a top management
position, a situation which leads to a serious organizational dilemma. While Western society instills the vast majority of
executives at earlier periods of their lives with the 'Protestant Ethic'
(implying among other things the desire for upward career mobility), the strong drive for career advancement and the need to live
up to the expectations set on the 'career clock' inevitably invite
disappointment.

Until more imaginative organizations are created the design of contemporary organizations makes it impossible for most executives to reach the top of the organizational pyramid. Somehow this fact of organizational life has to be communicated to its organizational participants. Although most executives have an adequate perception of reality and, at a rational level, realize that most of them will not rise to the top executive ranks, it is a different matter to apply this situation to themselves. This news, in most instances, is not very welcome and, not only that, can be extremely painful. Often this information is viewed as a depletion of their power base, as a direct threat to self-esteem, and reactions may follow of anger, hostility, and, eventually, helplessness. Ultimately susceptibility to stress symptoms may increase.

INTERPERSONAL DYNAMICS

Understandably, most senior executives are quite reluctant to tell their subordinates that they have attained a plateau in their career and that originally set expectations on the 'career clock' are not going to be met, or at least not in the present organization. Not only can this reluctance be explained by rational concerns over the effects of such statements on motivation and morale, but other more irrational reasons can be found. Frequently the executive is not even aware of these reasons and uses various forms of rationalization as explanation. What we can observe is that, although life in organizations is often portrayed as a jungle, a pitiless race to the top, what actually happens frequently is quite different. Ruthlessness is not the major problem. What can become a problem is the general unwillingness of most executives to make harsh decisions when needed; for example, when a subordinate does not live up to the standards set for performance.

Most people have a great need to be loved. To confront others with noticeable inadequacies and imperfections is far from achieving that need. Instead, executives use circular routes, disguise or withhold information, are not really honest in giving feedback, and become apologetic and evasive during performance-appraisal sessions. Executives deny their aggressive feelings and hostility toward their subordinates for not living up to the standards they have set for them, and at the same time, feel guilty over the anger which the behaviour of their subordinates provokes. As an added factor we can also mention the lingering feelings of anxiety (usually repressed) about retaliatory activities if anger and hostility of subordinates is aroused. Questions might arise about what will happen if roles are reversed. Will these people remember? Moreover, there may also be the thought on the executive's part that he might be 'done unto' as he himself is 'doing to others', a notion which has an additional restraining effect. Therefore, decisions are frequently postponed or disguised in ambiguous statements. In some instances executives retain the same job titles but, little by little, responsibilities are taken away; *de facto* demotions become disguised in impressive but meaningless re-definitions of the job or through lateral transfers; promotions stand for empty titles void of real responsibility and authority; roles, responsibility, and authority become unclearly defined. Firing becomes the measure of the last resort.

These are all examples of different ways of keeping the person in question and his or her immediate environment under the illusion that nothing has actually happened, that everything has basically remained the same and things are going well. But how long can this person maintain this illusion? There comes a time when it will no longer be possible to rationalize and deny what is happening. If the executive possesses a sufficient capacity for reality testing, eventually this bubble has to burst. The executive has to come to grips with his present career state. But in the meantime he or she might be plagued by doubt concerning the lack of authenticity and sincerity of his or her present existence.

The government is an example where the avoidance of real confrontation about performance often has gone to an extreme. One of the main criteria of business organizations, profitability, is not necessarily operative in the government. In the absence of this form of accountability, given human nature, abuse is invited. In the government automatic pay increase just by remaining on the job has frequently become the accepted rule.[7] The near impossibility of firing government workers – an excessive number of rules leading to a state of rigidity and inflexibility – is another indication of ambivalence in this matter. A point may have been reached where it has become very difficult to act differently. When mediocrity becomes the norm and warrants support, ambiguity becomes less of a concern. And in large organizations in the private sector similar trends are discernible. In these instances, however, there is always a counter force in the form of the need for continued profitability.

Clearly, there may be a group of people who like to coast along, who are basically underachievers. To these individuals automatic merit raises may seem attractive. They may search specifically for these types of situations. In the US Federal Government there is even the notion of 'turkey farms', places where executives steer their incompetents. These people may receive a plush office and a fancy title as long as they keep out of the way. In these departments nothing much is required and little damage can be done. But how many executives view this as a meaningful way of spending their lives? Naturally there may always be people who thrive in these situations, but most executives will feel very uncomfortable. A situation may be created for increased susceptibility to stress symptoms.

MANAGING AMBIGUITY

Executives who 'manage by ambiguity', particularly whose who experience a great need to be loved and, consequently, are reluctant or unable to make unpopular decisions, do not realize that they may be killing through kindness. In making their ambiguous statements and obscure organizational arrangements – thus avoiding a direct confrontation with the failure to produce – they contribute to an unpredictable, uncontrollable work environment. The subordinate exposed to this treatment becomes confused about standards of performance, about evaluation methods, and experiences a lack of authority and information to carry out his or her responsibilities. It is confusion of this kind which creates the conditions for the giving-up-given-up complex in organizations and contributes to the incidence of stress symptoms. The existence of this type of relationship between ambiguity and stress has been supported in various organizational studies.[8]

Ambiguity in organizations is related to the adequacy of information to do a job properly. This can be applied to both role definition and accuracy of feedback. When this information is missing ambiguity is experienced and so is helplessness. The greater the task uncertainty, the greater the amount of information that must be processed. Clarity in role definition is an important element in reducing ambiguity. Depending on the amount of accurate feedback available, ambiguity will intensify or decrease and so may stress symptoms. The validity of this latter relationship has found support in a number of physiological experiments done with animals.[9] These processes seem to be also applicable to human situations, as other experiments have indicated.[10] Relevant feedback and clarity in role definition make for a feeling of control, prevent the incidence of the giving-up-given-up complex, become a countervailing force against helplessness, and seem to have a stress-reducing impact.

In a study done in a large Canadian organization one of the conclusions was that the executive group (compared to the staff and lower level operations group) appeared to be less susceptible to stress symptoms.[11] Contrary to popular beliefs the executive group was the healthiest. To explain these differences a bureaucratic and a power effect was postulated, the first one referring to familiarity and identification with organizational processes, the second one pertaining to the possession of power and the ability to change organizational practices. The essence of this finding was that the possession of power, in particular, had a therapeutic effect, making for a perception of control over the environment, lessening the state of helplessness and thereby having a stress-reducing influence. It appeared that the upwardly mobile executive acquired reasonable clarity about role definition, was sufficiently exposed to information, and received adequate feedback. Consequently, there is an experience of having control over the immediate environment. As one top executive said: 'I don't have ulcers, I give ulcers'.

In organizations power is a scarce commodity. Each organizational participant is, in some way or another, engaged in a comparison process, assessing differences in relative power base. The rules governing this comparison process seem very much to be of a zero-sum-game nature: an increase in one executive's power base is usually perceived as a depletion of the power base of another. Thus, although power may be therapeutic and giving power to executives with a low power base may benefit their general state of health, very few executives will volunteer in this power sharing process. Altruism, particularly concerning the distribution of power, is not a common pattern of organizational life. Somehow the possession of power seems to be addictive.[12] The more you have the more you want. Not many individuals seem to be willing to give it up. The immediate holding on to power seems to be preferred to pushing power down to lower levels of the organization, in spite of its beneficial effects. In psychological processes short term needs tend to take priority over the long term.

Lower level executives, in particular, bear the brunt of the dilemma of wanting more power from people who are not in the least inclined to relinquish control over this scarce commodity.

Power seems to evoke very basic human emotions. The addictiveness of power makes power sharing a very reluctant process. Added to this human characteristic is the fact of organizational life that organizations are funnel shaped; higher-level management usually has more power than lower-level management and will be very possessive of that power base. And we have seen that ways of protecting this power base will include such actions as withholding of information, insufficient feedback, and unclear definition of roles and tasks.

This type of behaviour is exacerbated by other characteristics of human nature: for instance, the great need to be loved, which is closely tied into anxiety over the arousal of hostile reactions. Earlier we have argued that this human characteristic lies at the core of the reluctance of executives to tell their subordinates that they might have reached a plateau in their career path. Of course there are exceptions but the majority of executives will, at some point in time (assuming that the 'Protestant Ethic' is important), experience disappointment.

There is a deterministic quality to this conclusion; these basic dimensions of human nature imply that management by ambiguity is here to stay. Ambiguity seems to be an inevitable pattern of organizations; all we can do is to modify its potential for destructiveness. This conclusion points out the need for organizations and their executives to find a satisfying balance between management *of* ambiguity and management *by* ambiguity. But we have to recognize that the level of tolerable ambiguity will vary for each individual. Personality factors will have a buffering effect. Some executives will thrive in ambiguous environments while others, if placed in the same situation, would soon be hospitalized. They might feel more comfortable in organizations where rules and procedures are clearly spelled out and task uncertainty is less of a problem.

Although ambiguity can be found in any organization, some types of organizations are structured in more ambiguous ways than others. This seems to be the case particularly in organizations where boundary spanning activities are important. Since the threshold level for ambiguity will differ for each individual, the selection of the 'right' organization becomes important. Executives engaged in boundary spanning activities, having to deal with the interface of organization and environment or different organizational sub-units, are more likely to be subjected to highly ambiguous situations than executives who have very little or no contact with other organizational sub-units. We are here referring to such jobs as project manager, product manager, and systems analyst. Naturally, individual threshold level and the nature of the feedback mechanisms built into the organization will make a difference and will influence the manifestation of stress.

DISENTANGLING THE WEB

The therapeutic effects of power and the addictiveness to power in combination with the inclination to manage by ambiguity lead to a number of dilemmas. The task of the executive now becomes how to find a workable solution out of situations which, at first sight, appear as double binds. Management becomes the skill of balancing trade-offs.

The question becomes: what will be more stress-inducing? Is it telling a subordinate how the situation really is, or is it by disguising reality in ambiguity? Of course, as an added dimension, we cannot forget the organizational considerations. How effective are executives going to be if they really know where they stand in their career path, particularly if that position does not compare favourably with their own anticipated progress?

To reduce ambiguity and modify possible stress levels, the executive needs to embark on a continuous process of accurate self-observation and reality testing. This will necessitate a regular re-evaluation of life goals and achievements, and an examination of reactions to disappointment. In more severe cases therapeutic intervention might be needed.

If an attitude of honesty prevails, rationalizations and reconstructions of career events will be kept to a minimum. This re-examination process becomes really meaningful if frank feedback about performance and opportunities for advancement are given. Although most executives will support this philosophy in theory, in actual practice their attitudes may be quite different. The organizational fear of demotivating the individual and the more personal concern involving the need to be loved and the reluctance to invite aggression are deterring forces. Therefore, unfortunately, many executives, in dealing with their subordinates, eventually will take what seems to be the easier way out. Real feelings will be hidden, interactions will be of a ritualistic nature, platitudes will become the rule, and lack of disclosure will lead to ambiguity.

The choice between ambiguity and frankness is a difficult one to make. Ideally, the mere fact of knowing the implications of each alternative will make for wiser decisions. But whatever the choice, a certain amount of disappointment seems to be inevitable. The test of good leadership will be the way disappointment is handled, which, in the end, will influence the prevalence or absence of stress reactions.

Apart from the question of how to handle career-path decisions and the nature of superior–subordinate interactions, the issue of prevention can be mentioned. We are referring to selectivity in organizational entry to reduce or prevent the incidence of explosive, stress-inducing situations at a later date. Executives have to be selective in their choice of individuals entering the organization and the same statement applies to the individual selecting an organization. It becomes important to assess both the prevailing level of ambiguity in the organization and the threshold level of the individual to ambiguity. Although it will be difficult to make an exact 'fit' – ambiguity level measurement not being an exact science – consideration should be given to this criteria in selection and placement. Attention has always been paid to criteria such as salary level, nature of the industry, functional position, and the like. The time has come to consider type of organizational culture, prevailing ambiguity level, and prevailing stress level as selection criteria for entry. The use of these additional criteria will be particularly important for jobs of a boundary spanning nature where task uncertainty is high.

From an organizational design point of view, organizations need to set rules and procedures to define 'the rules of the organizational game' concerning roles and methods of feedback. Action of this kind can be viewed as a different effort to minimize ambiguity, prevent the abuse of power, and reduce stress reactions. Unfortunately, it is just not that simple. Anyone exposed to organizational life is aware of the negative side attached to these rules and regulations. What was once instigated to assure equity and fairness can easily transform into a representation of repressive action or abuse. I am referring to the fact that changes occur in goals and needs of organizations and their occupants necessitating different distributions of power. Then, rules and regulations may be used to prevent adaptation. What was originally set up to protect now becomes an instrument to block, leading to a sense of uncontrollability, unpredictability, and helplessness, which may foster stress reactions. The existence of this organizational pitfall points to the regular need for organizational renewal and the use of change agents, individuals whose main task will be to facilitate organizational change. Built-in adjustment mechanisms to deal with organizational change might also be needed. An organization learning atmosphere has to be created.

Executives have to come to grips with their own aggression and sense of guilt. They have to balance honest confrontation about performance, feedback, and the ability to motivate; they also have to make a choice between reality and rationalization. Executives have to realize the existence of the giving-up-given-up complex in organizations and find ways to reduce its destructive effects. They have to recognize that management by ambiguity, deriving from the need to be loved, is not necessarily an act of kindness. On the contrary, as a power-keeping strategy, this particular management practice is a contributory factor to the incidence of stress reactions, and thus, in many instances, can be viewed as an extremely hostile activity.

5

AN ALTERNATIVE VIEW OF POWER

Even in the most respectable of us there is a terribly bestial and immoral type of desire which manifests itself particularly in dreams. . .[1]

Plato

We have already noticed the enigmatic quality of power, a concept disconcerting to economists, sociologists, political scientists, psychologists, and anthropologists alike, each one of whom – depending on his particular orientation – is apparently engaged in the pursuit of a different animal. Even the philosophers have not been able to straighten out this state of confusion. Although Plato, Aristotle, Machiavelli, Hobbes, and Nietzsche have agonized about the nature of power they have also left us with a legacy of widely divergent opinions. Terms like power, control, influence, persuasion, coercion, manipulation and authority have been taken for granted, used indiscriminately and interchangeably, their meanings assumed to be common knowledge – a state of affairs which has contributed to the vagueness and lack of clarity of the concept. This situation of confusion in interpretations of power makes us wonder if it is even worthwhile to continue to pursue the topic. We might ask ourselves if power does not belong to that group of mythical creatures such as the unicorn whose existence really does not seem to matter. Maybe it would be better to drop the topic altogether and continue with the study of more worthwhile, less confused subject-matters.

Robert Dahl, a well-known student of power even stated that:

First (following the axiom that where there is smoke there is fire), if so many people at so many different times have felt the need to attach the label power, or something like it, to some Thing they believe they have observed, one is tempted to suppose that the Thing must exist: and not only exist, but exist in a form capable of being studied more or less systematically. The second and more cynical suspicion is that a Thing to which people attach many labels with subtly or grossly different meanings in many different cultures and times is probably not a Thing at all but many Things; there are students of the subject, although I do not recall any who have had the temerity to say so in print, who think that because of this the whole study of 'power' is a bottomless swamp. . .[2]

Dahl's comments about power are very timely and warrant serious consideration. He indicates that the concept of power may be the victim of a communication problem between groups of social scientists with different disciplinary backgrounds. An overview of social science research on power supports this contention. If we review the literature on power we can summarize these various orientations under the headings structural, interpersonal, and intra-personal theories of power.

Structuralists have been concerned with ways of classifying power. Their main emphasis has been on resources and means to exert power. For example, a fairly comprehensive and influential categorization of kinds of power has been prepared by French and Raven.[3] They distinguished between reward, coercive, legitimate, referent, and expert power. Reward power is based on B's belief that A can provide rewards. Coercive power rests on B's perception that A has the ability to provide punishment. Legitimate power derives from the internalization of common norms or values. Referent power is based on B's identification with A. Expert power comes from B's belief that A possesses some special knowledge or expertise. As an additional source of power we can also mention control over information.[4] Actually, in its most simplified form, we can summarize these bases of power as being control of physical resources (i. e. remunerations such as salaries, commodities, etc.), and symbolic resources (i. e. allocation of prestige and esteem, administration of ritual, etc.).[5]

Researchers interested in the interpersonal nature of power have suggested that power is a process whereby one party will try to influence the other through various means to bring about change in the original relationship.[6] Other writers with a similar orientation have looked at power as a social exchange activity, a dynamic process of opposing forces in search for mutual adjustment. Imbalance and equilibrium would follow each other in rapid succession contributing to a dialectical process of adaptation.[7] These interpersonal theories compare power to an asymmetrical influence relationship, a consequence of an extremely complex process of social exchange. The conditions under which these exchange processes occur will decide the attribution of power. The ability to engage in these exchange processes and to exert influence will be determined by the possession of, control of, or need for, valued resources. These resources become part of a bargaining procedure of stimulation or deprivation which is dependent upon the way in which the objectives of the other party can be hindered or facilitated.

Most students of power have concentrated on the structural and interpersonal dimensions of power. Instead, we would like to emphasize the intra-personal aspects of power; what power means to the individual in a psychological sense, and how we acquire a need for power. In presenting this relatively neglected point of view, we hope to arrive at a more balanced and eventually more integrated perspective on this subject-matter.[8]

INTRA-PERSONAL THEORIES OF POWER

The notion that power is an innate human drive can already be found in Plato's Republic. Other philosophers such as Hobbes and Nietzsche have supported these ideas. Nietzsche even went so far as to say 'that all driving force is will to power, that there is no other physical, dynamic or psychic force except this'.[9] Russell commented that 'of the infinite desires of man, the chief are the desires of power and glory'.[10] In his opinion the desire for power is an essential part of human nature.

Other writers have argued that a power motive is particularly peculiar to political people. For example Max Weber viewed the 'power instinct' as a normal quality of the politician, the striving for power being one of the basic driving forces of all politics.[11] This point of view was elaborated by the German psychologist Eduard Spranger who suggested that every personality is characterized by a number of cultural values.[12] One of these values, the pursuit of power and the need to dominate, is, according to him, the politician's only reason for existence.

One way of interpreting the previous statements is by looking at power as an autonomous motive, innate to human beings and actually beyond explanation. Power motivation then turns into a precursor of behaviour instead of a consequence of the intricate dynamics between individual and environment. Very few psychologists, however, will support this contention. What we can observe in most instances is that power as a motive is explained by theories based on compensatory motivation or by theories which look at power as an important outcome of developmental processes.

Power as a compensatory motive

The view of power as a compensatory motive is not new. Philosophers, political scientists, creative artists, and many journalists have been trying to explain political behaviour with the notion of compensatory motivation in mind. The main advocate of this point of view – drawing his ideas from a rather simplified version of psychoanalytic psychology – has been Alfred Adler.[13] He considered the striving for power as a compensation for organic or imagined defects. The smallness, helplessness and sense of imperfection of the infant in comparison with adults supposedly explained the development of feelings of inferiority, the latter being viewed by Adler as a universal problem of mankind. To overcome this 'inferiority complex' the mentally healthy person will try to master these feelings through accomplishment.

Karen Horney argues in a similar vein, except that she distinguishes between normal and neurotic strivings for power. While normal striving for power is based on a person's realization of 'his own superior strength, whether it be physical strength or ability, mental capacities, maturity or wisdom', the neurotic striving for power 'is born out of anxiety, hatred and feelings of inferiority'.[14] In her conceptualization, neurotic striving for power serves as a protection against anxiety, helplessness and the danger of feeling or being regarded as insignificant. Her notion about the intrapsychic aspects of power is similar to that of Adler but without the primacy which Adler gives to the inferiority complex. In her opinion Adler never recognized the central role of anxiety in bringing about such drives.

Harold Lasswell was strongly influenced by the ideas of Adler in his analysis of *homo politicus*. His 'key hypothesis about the power seeker is that he pursues power as a means of compensation against deprivation. Power is expected to overcome low estimates of the self.' Lasswell's main interest is the political person who, in his opinion, differs from the average individual because of the tendency to displace private motives on public objects and to rationalize these motives in terms of the public interest.[15] Although Lasswell modified this rather narrow view of the origin of the need for power slightly in his 'afterthoughts' to *Psychopathology and Politics*, written thirty years later, compensatory motivation remains at the core of his propositions, with its implicit emphasis on psychopathological processes.[16]

The psycho-biographical study of Woodrow Wilson by Alexander and Juliette George was guided by the notion of compensatory motivation.[17] In a later study Alexander George pointed out, however, that compensatory motivation is only applicable under special arousal conditions: '*Homo politicus* is likely to be a multivalued personality; his striving for power as compensation may be reinforced by, or conflict with, strong personal needs for other values that he may also pursue in the political arena'.[18] With this statement – although not explicitly – Alexander George points to the need to look at power in a developmental sense.

Power as a developmental process[19]

Freud, and later Erikson, in proposing a theory of infantile sexuality and development, viewed a person as passing through a number of stages, a process during which they learn to cope with sexual and aggressive drives.[20] These stages are connected with specific psychological developmental processes and social interactions. Child psychologists have indicated that the first three stages of the life cycle are of utmost importance in this process of human development and significantly determine later behaviour. These stages can be summarized respectively, to use Freud's and Erikson's terminology (whereby psychological development is closely tied in to physiological processes), as the oral stage (the stage where the polarity of trust and distrust stands central), the anal stage (the stage of autonomy versus shame and doubt), and the Oedipal stage (the stage of initiative and guilt). We can look at the acquisition of power in a similar manner. People's orientation to power, the intensity of this need, can be viewed as the outcome of a gradual developmental process, dependent on the individual's mastery of, and adaption to, the environment. We propose that during this process of mastery – analogous to the concept of the stages of human development – an individual also deals with three aspects of intra-personal power (each originating from one of the first three stages in the human life cycle) which we will call oceanic, controlling, and rivalrous manifestations of power.[21]

These three elements of power play a role in a person's personality make-up, but for each individual there will be a difference of degree and composition. The manner of coping and adaptation during the process of human development will determine the intensity with which a person experiences these intra-personal aspects of power, which will, in turn, influence how this power is used and the specific orientation and manifestation of leadership style. Depending on each person's unique life history, power needs will differ. Some will experience a strong need for power; for others it will be negligible.

Oceanic power originates in the oral stage of development and is based on the 'oceanic' feeling of unity, the experience of omnipotence and boundlessness. It is the period in time when an individual's narcissistic base is established. Not surprisingly, a close relationship exists between oceanic power and the notion of charismatic leadership. We will see later, in an elaboration of charismatic leadership, that the emotional ties between leader and those being led can partially be explained by a primitive process of wish fulfilment and attachment behaviour aroused in the followers which makes the leader's style so persuasive. Depression and mania are the most extreme personality characteristics which characteristically belong to this power orientation.

Controlling power is a legacy of a stage of development in which the child has learned the intricacies of control, of dominance, and deference. In contrast with oceanic power which is, by nature, somewhat vague, in the anal stage – after much trial and error – 'limits of power' are better delineated and circumscribed. In this mutual process of exertion and control, excessive rigidity in control can lead to conformity, excessive latitude to overconfidence. Stubbornness and compliance are common personality traits associated with this type of power.

Rivalrous power derives from a developmental period when competition and cooperation with parents and siblings are major issues. It is at this stage that the child experiences more fully the nature of prohibitions; a sense of retribution becomes established through the internalization of guilt feelings which centre around the dilemma between the wish to overthrow the rival and the fear of his retaliation. It determines the choice and balance between competitiveness and cooperativeness. The way an individual will deal with authority figures and peers later in life is influenced by the legacy of the rivalrous orientation to power.

ELEMENTS OF STYLE

The development of an intra-personal orientation to power is not an instantaneous process. Personality dynamics involve the gradual development of a sense of self, the components of which come from two different sources, i.e., the esteem in which we are held by other people and an individual's sense of competence and achievement in mastering their environment. Furthermore, this developmental process also implies a gradual set of actions leading to differentiation between these inner and outer sources of gratification. The degree of identification and differentiation during this process of development will determine the internalization of the intra-psychic aspects of power and the choice of a particular leadership style.

This developmental point of view can be applied to observable leadership behaviour. Each developmental intra-personal orientation to power will correspond to a specific power style (characterological power orientation) and specific power resources used. We do realize, however, that some individuals may experience such a low power need that no specific style is discernible. In contrast, the most dramatic examples of power orientation are usually to be found in the political sphere. Naturally the described power orientations are not mutually exclusive but can occur concurrently. We will present these 'ideal types' only for the purpose of clarification, to simplify an understanding of a complex world. In the reality of everyday life they are usually only found in combination.

The persuasive power style

We occasionally encounter rare people who not only act as if they need nobody else but, at the same time, evoke in other individuals dependency needs, the universal craving to be taken care of. The meeting of independent assertiveness and dependent nurturance is at the core of oceanic power and makes for this remarkable sense of unity between actor and audience. It also determines patterns of behaviour and the conditions and means by which power is exerted. These persons are quite narcissistic and impress us by their extreme self-confidence, self-centredness and assertiveness.

This pattern of behaviour which evokes such basic emotions does not develop overnight. This internalization of the intra-personal aspects of power is preceded by a process of trial and error during which a 'fit' is found between internal demands and external restraints. Compromise and disappointment here play an important role. It seems as if a purification ceremony is needed, a *rite de passage* out of which, on extremely rare occasions, individuals emerge who are characterized by behaviour of this seemingly independent, extremely persuasive nature. Max Weber's theoretically troublesome and confusing designation 'charismatic' has been the term often chosen to describe these people. These individuals convey the notion of extreme independence while, at the same time, catering to the dependency needs of others. Their great conviction in the visionary goals which they disseminate – frequently supported through the use of symbolic power resources – is extremely contagious. The persuasive style is at the core of the process of social change and transformation. Processes of this nature – the belief in an individual's invincibility – touch upon people's most inner feelings and become the catalyst for change. Due to the extreme confidence which these individuals radiate they are usually very effective in the use of power, given the right historical moment.

Mahatma Gandhi represents a good example of an individual who used this style predominantly. The *charkha* or spinning wheel, his advocacy for the return of handloom weaving, became to the Indians a symbol of a lost and regained identity. *Satyagraha*, or militant non-violence, was transformed in his hands into a pacific ritual which captured the masses. Fasting, an age-old ritual act, the Salt march and the Ahmedabad strike became symbols of self-chosen suffering and signs of martyrdom. Gandhi's inner experience of oceanic power as reflected in his private and public statements, his feelings of elation, his use of symbolic themes, made for an extremely effective persuasive style and contributed significantly to the process of bringing India to nationhood.[22]

The coercive style

We described previously how conflicts centring around control and submission are at the core of the controlling dimension of intra-personal power. Individuals who predominantly use the coercive power style seem to oscillate between aggressiveness and submissiveness, cruelty and gentleness, order and disorder. Such behaviour becomes particularly noticeable in an organizational setting. Complementary behaviour between individuals inclined toward the coercive style and their submissive counterparts in the interpersonal influence and social exchange process emerges as a key variable in the effective and efficient functioning of organizations. Rules, regulations, and procedures are the criteria which circumscribe superior–subordinate relationships and guide the control over resources which determine the nature of the social transactions leading to submission and control. We can also observe that the use of physical resources becomes an important pattern among individuals characterised by this leadership orientation. The power and politics of organizational life creates mutual reinforcement of behaviour on a spectrum whereby the dimensions 'control' and 'being controlled' turn into polarities. The management of uncertainty becomes very important in the coercive style. Control may lose the reference to its original objective in the social exchange and influence relationship and may degenerate into ritualistic behaviour. The mastery of the fear within oneself, of being subjected to a sudden unexpected controlling force lies at the heart of the coercive style.

The members of the Krupp dynasty can be taken as examples of individuals predominantly using this particular style. In this instance the coercive style probably reached its peak at the time of the rule of Alfred Krupp during the second world war. Apart from his own labourers, who were forced into complete submission under his totally paternalistic regime, 100,000 persons were working for him as slave labourers in Germany, the occupied territories, and concentration camps. 'Extermination through labour', accelerated by excessive working hours, hazardous working conditions, poor living quarters, and starvation became the fate of prisoners of war, concentration camp victims, and foreign civilians. Control was enforced by Krupp's own police force and SS guards.

A childhood under the complete control of his father, his role as the 'crown prince' with the constant example of his illustrious great grandfather held out before him, taught the young Krupp the meaning of the words *Verantwortlichkeit* and *Pflicht,* responsibility and duty. Krupp's later obsession with power of a controlling nature was reflected in his reliance on the *Generalregulativ,* a complex code of rules and regulations governing the conglomerate, and was illustrative of his excessive coercive style.[23]

The manipulative style

We have seen that emotions centred around conflicts about authority and feelings of rivalry make for the psychological basis of rivalrous power. The rivalrous dimension of power is a legacy of the Oedipal stage and in organizational life we can find the recurrence of these competitive and cooperative relationships. Coalitions and collusions can be viewed as manifestations of movements along horizontal and vertical axes in organizations and are ways through which cooperativeness and competitiveness become expressed. The wish for equality, simultaneously paired with the perception of inequality and the subsequent ambivalence about authority, determines a person's understanding of hierarchical relationships. The degree of acceptance of these perceived inequalities in interpersonal relationships, coupled with an individual's ability to tolerate frustration, makes for the sense of comfort or discomfort with which individuals function in an organizational setting.

Sensitivity to the trade-offs between competitiveness and cooperativeness in the social exchange and the influence process of interpersonal relations facilitates an understanding of the intricacies of bargaining in organizational life. Individuals predominantly guided by the manipulative style possess a great ability to assess the pluses and minuses of each social transaction. An overdose of competitiveness in controlling resources – particularly of a material nature – may be interpreted as rebelliousness and insubordination, may isolate the individual in the organization, and may eventually lead to the severance of the tie between individual and organization. Too much cooperation may be abused by others, leading to the loss of control over resources and resulting in career stagnation. Success in organizations is highly dependent upon the effects of the manipulative style. Thus, this style characterizes the highly mobile executive and the career politician. For example, the political career of Lyndon Johnson represents the style of the kind of individual who predominantly uses the manipulative style.

Johnson was an extremely skilful organizer and negotiator (with the possible exception of his period in the presidency during which time all the constraints placed upon him made him less effective). As the Democratic majority leader in the Senate he had a great reputation for compromise and effective action. His ability to manipulate people, his skill in taking advantage of opportunities offered and situations was legendary. His favourite Biblical quote was from Isaiah and it read: 'Come now, let us reason together'. He knew the value of information, which became in his hands a major bargaining tool. His emphasis on equality among his staff members underlined his special position and was a way of maintaining his place of power. He kept close contact with his constituency and associates, trading off rewards and favours to strengthen his power base.

Having been born to a large family he had experienced the pangs of rivalry early and knew the value of negotiation and bargaining. His manipulative style and his talent in using material resources as a way of exchange and influence process testify to that fact.[24]

A MODEL OF POWER

We have looked at intra-personal theories of power and suggested that the ability or need to exercise power is also a consequence of a very intricate developmental process. The proposition has been put forward that the orientation to power is made up of three dimensions which are not mutually exclusive but can occur concurrently with various degrees of intensity. These aspects are described as oceanic, controlling, and rivalrous manifestations of power.

From the point of view of characterology, considering observable behaviour, each developmental manifestation of power has a corresponding element of style, be it persuasive, coercive, or manipulative. Each style seems to have its preference of power resources attached, although the use of multiple resources will be more the rule than the exception. The person characterized by the persuasive style tends to give preference to the use of symbolic resources in the influence and social exchange relationship. Here the term 'charismatic leadership' is often applied. Individuals with a coercive power orientation often take recourse to physical resources while the manipulative style corresponds to a preference for material resources. Given the frequency with which the different power orientations occur, material and physical resources are probably the bases of power most often used. The combination of power orientation and the availability of resources will be a determining factor in the manifestation of leadership style and the means selected in the influence of the social exchange process.

Figure 5.1 suggests that effective use of leadership style will largely be determined by the 'goodness of fit' between the intra-personal power orientation and the availability and appropriateness of the power resources utilized. Naturally the other dimension will be the acceptance of the emerging style by the followers, which raises questions about the degree of favourableness of situation and the intra-personal needs of the followers. Whatever the nature of the situation or availability of power resources, the starting point remains the experienced need of the individual for power of whatever orientation and composition.

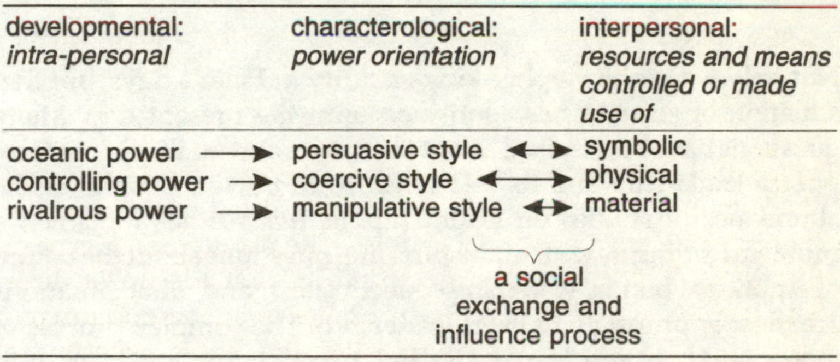

developmental: *intra-personal*	characterological: *power orientation*	interpersonal: *resources and means controlled or made use of*
oceanic power $\longrightarrow$	persuasive style $\longleftrightarrow$	symbolic
controlling power $\longrightarrow$	coercive style $\longleftrightarrow$	physical
rivalrous power $\longrightarrow$	manipulative style $\longleftrightarrow$	material

a social
exchange and
influence process

Figure 5.1 A model of power

6

LEADERSHIP AND PARANOIA

He who is the real tyrant, whatever men may think, is the real slave, and is obliged to practice the greatest adulation and servility, and to be the flatterer of the vilest of mankind. He has desires which he is utterly unable to satisfy, and has more wants than anyone, and is truly poor, if you know how to inspect the whole soul of him: all his life long he is beset with fear and is full of convulsions, and distractions. . .[1]

Plato

Not only were philosopher-kings a rarity in Plato's days, but that situation of scarcity has continued until the present day. Many questions have been raised about the nature and quality of contemporary leadership and its relationships to power. In spite of the abundance of studies on leadership, its essence has remained a problem leaving us with many puzzling questions about the nature of emotional bonds, leadership effectiveness, and what situations are most appropriate to exert leadership. The complex process of interaction between leader and led, necessitating congruence in values and objectives, and the conscious and unconscious imagery which accompanies these processes, has continued to mystify us. So have other aspects of leadership, particularly the destructive effects which the possession of leadership exerts on the leader as well as on the followers.

CHARISMATIC LEADERSHIP

I mentioned earlier that Max Weber introduced the concept of charisma as a way of explaining the mysterious influence which some leaders hold over their followers. To him, charisma consists of:

> a certain quality of an individual personality by virtue of which he is set apart from ordinary men and treated as endowed with supernatural, superhuman or at least specifically exceptional powers or qualities. These are such as are not accessible to the ordinary person, but are regarded as of divine origin or as exemplary, and on the basis of them the individual concerned is treated as a leader. . .[2]

Unfortunately, the indication of 'supernatural', 'superhuman' powers, and the mystification implicit in the assumption of the 'divine origin' of these, is not a satisfactory explanation; it is just descriptive and leaves out the psychodynamic forces at play which motivate individuals in a position of leadership. And most of the analyses of charismatic leadership remain at a purely descriptive level. Other statements continue in a similar vein and have a rather mystical overtone. A charismatic leader is 'called' and experiences the sense of having a 'vision'. What we can infer from such statements is that many of these individuals seem to belong to the realm of religious prophets. This type of assumption would partially explain Max Weber's indication of the 'divine origin' and the 'sense of a mission' among these leaders.

Most of the spectacular examples of charismatic leadership have been found in the political domain. Usually, these leaders emerge in a period of crisis which can be triggered off by various threats, frequently coming from an 'outside'. It is 'the others', those individuals not belonging to an 'inside' group, who become perceived as dangers. Wars between countries and civil discord are the most common examples of the consequence of these threats. But this phenomenon is not limited to the political sphere; it occurs in business organizations as well. The interactions of individuals who make up business organizations reflect, admittedly on a reduced scale, developments similar to those of a nation at large. In a business setting, it has usually been to that folk hero of business enterprise, the entrepreneur, that charismatic qualities have been attributed. And although the era of the great robber barons, as represented by the Krupps, the Rockefellers, and the Carnegies, has become part of history, the capacity of business leaders to influence the political sphere of a nation at large should not be underestimated.

A well-known example of the way in which a business leader can influence public opinion can be found in the first Henry Ford's Peace Ship adventure, his anti-Semitic campaign propagated through his newspaper, *The Dearborn Independent*, his fight against the unions, and his original unwillingness to aid the government in the production of war supplies during the First World War period.[3]

THE BOND BETWEEN LEADER AND LED

Charismatic individuals seem to distinguish themselves by their strong need to influence their followers and their ability to do so. Persons who possess this quality know how to use their power. The adopted power style is of a persuasive nature and, from a developmental point of view, contains oceanic elements. Charismatic individuals seem to hold onto infantile wishes of all-powerfulness. But in making this proposition we should keep in mind the possibility of two different life strategies. First, there is that person who has grown up in a relatively secure environment which spared him from any serious conflict with often painful reality. Continuous assurance made for a sense of confidence in dealing with power issues. In contrast, we can find individuals whose relationship to power is a reaction to early experiences of powerlessness. Power becomes an issue surrounded by conflict as the person attempts to combat early feelings of helplessness; this conflict continues to be a troublesome legacy of these earlier stages of human development. In this context I have made a distinction between constructive and reactive narcissistic development, the former the outcome of positive life experiences while the opposite is the case for the latter one.[4] What will become crucial to the later development of both types of individuals, regarding their competence in the exercise of leadership, depends on the level of unresolved intra-psychic conflict and the related competence in actual reality testing. Competence in leadership is largely dependent on the match between internal values and external reality; the greater the gap between the conscious and unconscious imagery surrounding power issues, and reality, the more problematic the need for, and exertion of, power becomes.

Given these two ways of looking at the development of persuasive power and the nature of charisma, the second group is particularly susceptible to a disturbance of a frequently delicate psychological equilibrium. We have seen that the balance between what is considered 'normality' and what belongs to pathology is an extremely fragile one. Excessive possession of resources through which power can be exerted – be it of a material, physical, or symbolic nature – can easily shift the balance in an otherwise 'normal' individual toward pathological behaviour patterns. We recognize that the management of power is not an easy task. The realization by the individual in a position of leadership of the 'boundlessness' of the stage on which he is acting – particularly when he becomes aware of his ability to transform his intra-psychic fantasies into reality for his followers – might be too much for him to handle. If the leader's sense of reality becomes impaired, or was unstable in the first place, one of the outcomes may be paranoid developments symptomized by delusionary ideas and megaloma-niacal fantasies. As we have indicated, the belief in one's own omnipotence has many attractions in situations of crisis. An atti-tude of this kind evokes what can be described as 'saviour imagery'. The leader becomes a symbol to his followers of the long-sought-after, and for common mortals never attainable, state of final independence. He appears to need nobody and thus seems the possessor of the envied ability to attain complete mastery and control over his environment. Followers will reactivate mankind's dormant tendency toward idealization, a characteristic essential in the early development of the self. What evolves out of this, is a transferential pull, a universal desire to ascribe to authority figures in the present the magical powers one once expected from the caretakers of the past.[5] Leaders and followers will have a regressive experience resembling a return to a state of childlike bliss in which fantasies of omnipotence and of being taken care of play a major role. The parallel with early childhood is striking. Power, appar-ently, not only 'corrupts' but may lead to a regression to attachment-type behaviour which is itself based on early interac-tion patterns between mother and child.[6] The state of dependency on the part of the followers is not only analogous to early childhood behaviour but reminds us of the belief in magic among primitive tribes. Attachment and omnipotence mutually reinforce each other. The belief on the part of the followers in the leader's omni-potence will reinforce the leader's illusions of grandeur and will strengthen his self-love, a process which will, in turn, strengthen the dependency needs of the followers. Omnipotence becomes a

71

'self-fulfilling prophecy' and during the operation of this process, nothing is off limits; everything is allowed.

The 'magic' influence of the leader over his followers becomes understandable if seen in the light of his ability to have the final word in decisions regarding life and death, advancement or stagnation. The threat of annihilation, the wish to survive, evokes one of the most basic, elementary emotions of man and may be viewed – besides regressive attachment behaviour – as a main explanation of the relationship of bondage between leader and followers. This explains why shared atrocities, no matter what kind, will even reinforce the tie between leader and led; it will lead to a communal atmosphere of guilt and anxiety.

In this psychological process a paradoxical development becomes more understandable. The leader may initially frighten his followers by indulging in atrocities. Hitler's purges inside the Nazi party, as well as the genocide of the Jews, are good examples in the political sphere, while in business situations this process may take the form of ruthless dismissal of subordinates, an occurrence which was extremely common in the Ford Motor Company, where the original five-dollar-a-day man, Henry Ford, became the tyrant of the 'Rouge', the Dearborn, Michigan plant. But surprisingly enough, the remaining followers will run for protection to the individual who started the process of terrorization in the first place. As has been indicated, the consequence of this process is a reinforcement of the group ties among the followers. Here again we can find the defensive reaction 'identification with the aggressor'. By imitating the aggressor, fears are alleviated and security enhanced.

Identification with the aggressor is one of the main processes in the development of group ties. The feelings of the followers will alternate between love, affection, and fear. Intra-psychically the leader transforms into a parental figure, with whom, analogous to the process which took place in the followers' early childhoods, it is easy to identify. The identification of the followers with the leader and, consequently, the identification with each other, will result in the establishment of group cohesion, since the leader supposedly disperses favours and imposes deprivations on an egalitarian basis.[7] The ideals, the goals, and the promises of the leader become common property; these goals will be taken up by the followers. It is the leader who offers protection against helplessness and enhances the followers' sense of self-esteem since, through identification, elements of perceived omnipotence are incorporated and the illusion is created that any threat can be warded off. Leaders of this type are experts in the creation of continuous tension among followers; this provides a background against which leaders can act out their fantasies of omnipotence.

Besides the manifestation of the illusion of grandeur in leaders, the ever-present potential for the development of delusions of persecution should be mentioned. Suspiciousness becomes a way of life. Preparedness for any form of emergency becomes a predominant pattern. Although preparations for emergencies may be viewed as positive developments, usually a gap will occur between perception and interpretation of events, and consequently distortion of reality becomes a common pattern. To describe the nature of these processes the psychoanalyst Fenichel once remarked: 'Just as the 'monsters' in a dream may represent 'amoeba' from daily life, so the monsters of paranoid delusion may be a misapprehended real microbe.'[8] Naturally he refers to the projective mode: an idea, no matter how trivial, which is perceived as internally threatening, is substituted for an external threat and exaggerated, a process which contributes to and reinforces the perception of persecution. Powerful political and business leaders are extremely susceptible to paranoid developments, particularly in crisis situations. They possess the power to externalize internal dangers and can turn the act of destroying the 'monsters' into a 'common good' for society.

THE VICISSITUDES OF LEADERSHIP

It is not an unusual phenomenon that once a person reaches a position at the top of a corporation or state they become surrounded by subordinates who, perceiving the leader's inability to accept critical remarks, begin to supply the leader with only positive feedback. The megalomaniacal heights to which continuous positive feedback may lead in pathological cases has been illustrated by Gustav Bychowski in his study, *Dictators and Disciples*, using Adolf Hitler as an example:

According to Gauleiter Wagner, he was the greatest artist of all time. His hypnotic fascination convinced the industrialist Wilhelm Keppler that 'The Führer has an antenna directly to God'. According to Ley: 'The Führer is always right. He is the only man in the world in the history of mankind who never makes mistakes'. And according to Goebbels, he was 'the greatest general of all time'.[9]

This, of course, is an extreme case, but even an American president such as Woodrow Wilson, a man usually considered a rational, well-adjusted individual, had a personality constellation which was extremely receptive to, and in desperate need of, positive feedback. This aspect of Wilson's character becomes clear if we analyze his relationship with his chief adviser, Colonel House. One of the factors which contributed to the deterioration of their relationship, eventually leading to a definite break, was Colonel House's occasional criticisms of the way in which Wilson handled the Senate with respect to the ratification of the Treaty of Versailles and the entry of the United States into the League of Nations. These disagreements were aggravated through the formalization of their relationship when House obtained a more official government position and thereby became gradually perceived as a possible threat.[10] In a business enterprise setting an example may be found in the case of the first Henry Ford. His assistants Liebold, Sorensen, and Bennett were his 'yes' men. Realizing the sacrosanctity of the Model T to Henry Ford, these men were ready to lay the blame for the Ford Company's reduction in market share on anything except the real cause: the Model T had simply become outdated.

The behaviour of the followers of the individual in a position of leadership is not difficult to understand. In the case of the leader who develops an unwillingness to confront reality issues, the followers soon realize that their position in the organization depends completely on a good relationship with the leader which is mainly determined by the supply of positive feedback. Those followers fail to realize, however, that they might be in pursuit of short-range goals. Their very position does not permit a very wide margin of error. Chronic suspicion as a mode of behaviour when leadership attains pathological dimensions leads therefore to continuous tension rather than stability. But this latter state contains exactly the type of conditions on which this type of leader flourishes.

In the case of the first Henry Ford, his main subordinates Liebold, Sorensen, and Bennett were not subjected to the ultimate fate of many henchmen of dictators – death – but were eventually dismissed from their initially secure positions. These followers refused to accept that one cannot live in a dream world forever and that when the awakening occurs, the shock will usually be destructive to both leader and led.

There are many other facets connected with the paranoid potential. The externalization of an intra-psychic threat into an objective danger by an individual whose paranoid potential gains pathological dimensions can result in a tragic 'search for an enemy'. We are referring to the need for scapegoats. These individuals are unable to merge 'good' and 'bad' images; their inability to establish relationships without polarization is frightening. In the case of dictators such as Hitler and Stalin, the 'need for an enemy' reached gigantic proportions. The existence of this particular displacement mechanism gives us a better understanding of the role which the Gestapo played in Germany during the Hitler period and that of the NKVD, the secret police force in Stalin's time. The role of Joe McCarthy in the House Un-American Activities Committee, Nixon and the Watergate scandal, and Reagan versus 'the Evil Empire', are other examples. A more positive side effect to scapegoating does also exist which is worth mentioning: initially it may foster a sense of group cohesion.

As an example of scapegoating in the business sphere we can again take the Ford Motor Company under the rule of the first Henry Ford. The casualties at the top of the organization were enormous. The role of Harry Bennett, an ex-boxer with strong ties to the Detroit underworld, is very similar to the previous illustrations. Bennett was put in charge of the Ford Service Department, the main task of which was apparently to engage in espionage and create terror in an effort to fight unionism. Scapegoats were easily found and fired. In the Montgomery Ward organization, under its late chairman and president, Sewell Lee Avery, casualties were also common, particularly in the period between 1939 and 1955 when some forty vice-presidents and four presidents left the organization.[11] In both cases the behaviour of the two business leaders, Henry Ford and Sewell Lee Avery, resulted in the near bankruptcy of their respective companies.

The delusions of persecution in the case of the individual in whom the balance of normality leans toward paranoia, and the frightening potential behind this paranoid development, is like an iceberg. The real danger lies below the observable surface. The delicate balance between paranoid and 'normal' behaviour often results in a belated recognition of the danger signals, as in the case of James Forrestal, the first US Secretary of Defense. Given his position, we can wonder about the role which reality played in respect to his fantasies. Were his obsessions about communism real, given the psychological climate created by the Cold War period? In his case the tragic circle of reality and fantasy ended with his suicide.[12]

The individual inclined to paranoid behaviour patterns, in his search for an enemy and in his need for scapegoats, usually follows the slogan that the best defence is a good offence and consequently projects or externalizes his delusions onto his direct environment. Followers and victims, who are often indistinguishable, may then 'identify with the aggressor'. In the case of Stalin, the scapegoats were the counter-revolutionaries; and in the case of a charismatic leader such as Sukarno, the scapegoats were the imperialists as personified by the Dutch; in the case of Hitler, the scapegoats were the Jews and the communists; in the case of the Bosnian conflict we can see rampant paranoia among the Serbian, Croatian and Bosnian leaders.

A similar need for scapegoats can be found in a business setting. Unions, Wall Street bankers, and Jews were the main targets for the first Henry Ford. Jews, blacks, Freemasons, and communists have been traditional scapegoats. Howard Hughes has been a very colourful example of an individual who viewed communism as a general personification of all that is evil in society. His ways of dealing with his subordinates, his numerous phobias, and the total secrecy of his movements indicate a variety of delusional processes. The case of the union leader, James Hoffa, has been another example. To him, Robert Kennedy and the FBI were the personifications of evil. In a much milder but similar vein we can cite Sewell Lee Avery's fight with the government and the unions. Every example, however, raises the question of how many of the acts of the previously mentioned individuals had a true basis in reality?

The individual who is inclined toward pathological paranoid behaviour patterns often continues his self-deception by shifting the burden of guilt onto others. In acting out this particular behaviour he will reassert his sense of righteousness and omnipotence. Unfortunately, suspicious thinking does not lead to a great sense of adaptability but usually results in behaviour patterns characterized by rigidity.

THE NEED FOR CRISIS

In the previous discussion, some of the dangers associated with the paranoid potential have been emphasized. But the paranoid potential can be the source of great strength as well. To use the words of Robert Waelder:

> It gives strength through the polarization of all tendencies in one direction and the complete intellectual conviction which eliminates doubts and ambiguities; here, clearly, the native hue of resolution is not sicklied over with the pale cast of thought.[13]

The polarization of the environment into 'good' or 'bad' imagery, the related 'search for an enemy', and the shared feelings of euphoria and triumph leading to group cohesion can thus also be the sources of great strength. For some people, having an enemy becomes their way of arriving at a sense of identity. The process of arriving at objectives shared by the leader and his associates may also be facilitated and aided by paranoid mechanisms. As has been well illustrated in the example of Henry Ford and his Model T, single-mindedness and hyper-alertness to the developments in the environment can initially pay off.

Analogous to the political leader who acquires the designation of being charismatic and emerges usually in a period of crisis, is the business executive who is brought into an enterprise by the board of directors with the specific objective of guiding the corporation through a critical period. The line drawn between the flamboyant, more charismatic entrepreneur and the more bureaucratically inclined business executive is a very thin one indeed. The organization man can also attain charismatic heights in certain situations. What these processes of the 'birth' of the leader have in common is the centrality of crisis situations.

Comparable to situations in the political sphere, the initially successful leader (for example an entrepreneur like Henry Ford) may create a crisis if paranoid tendencies in his personality gain the upper hand. One of the main stimuli for this development may be the activation of a delusional idea. Continuous positive feedback (a consequence of the idealizing transference) on the part of the entrepreneur's direct subordinates for even his most erratic actions may be responsible for a gradual deterioration of reality testing. In contrast, taking the case of an elected business leader, the crisis is usually responsible for the initial entrance of the individual with leadership capacities into the corporate domain.

Sewell Lee Avery is a good case in point. The management of crises was clearly his main strength. His skills as a cost-cutter and his ability to reverse declining profit positions were the reasons for his original election to presidency of US Gypsum and later, the department store chain, Montgomery Ward. Unfortunately, his need for crises never stopped. He adopted a policy of continuous preparedness which eventually became extremely detrimental to the growth of the company. The accumulation of reserves in the form of cash at the cost of capital expenditures became his 'blind spot'. His sense of reality testing became seriously impaired, indicated by his obsession with economic depressions and his suspiciousness about his subordinates' actions. Only a proxy fight and his resulting resignation reversed a development which was turning the company into a bank with a department store front.

Crises are conducive to regressive behaviour for leaders as well as followers. At these times susceptibility to change will be greater and the identification (and even idealization) of the employees with the new leader will be facilitated and may result in a rebirth of motivation among the employees and the general emergence of a long-sought-after group spirit in the organization. The attainment of shared objectives is then no longer an impossibility, facilitating speed of implementation of decisions. These shared objectives can take many forms, of which the introduction of new product lines, ambitious sales plans, cost reduction programmes, salary cuts and the willingness to work overtime are only a few examples. If the appointed business leader is successful in guiding the enterprise through its initial period of 'crisis', the foundation is laid for that leader's indispensability.

The difference between the appointed business leader and the entrepreneur is obvious. The entrepreneur, after initially going through a successful period, may acquire the characteristics associated with self-destructive behaviour. This process of self-destructiveness in the organization as well as within themself may occur if their sense of reality becomes clouded, a development usually brought about by the isolation which has a top management position will entail. If isolation results in pathological behaviour, with symptoms such as the leader distrusting subordinates and denying reality by accepting only positive feedback, there will be a good chance that the individual in a position of leadership will bring the company into a crisis situation because of their failure to make organizational, structural, and strategic adjustments. Contrary to the above situation where the entrepreneur brings a company into a crisis, the appointed business leader will be the one chosen to push the company through the very crisis itself.

After the appointed business leader has proven him- or herself by solving the crisis initially, both cases may become remarkably similar if the business leader is unable to deal with the source of power which the office holds. In pathological cases the likelihood always exists that business leaders, in a desperate effort to preserve their charismatic appeal, will pile crisis upon crisis to keep their subordinates in an extremely dependent position while, at the same time, taking care of their own need for omnipotence. Although the first crisis in the case of an appointed business leader may have served a useful purpose since it resulted in the establishment of social cohesion induced by the processes of identification, a continuous relationship of dependence may push the company down into a spiral of self-destructiveness. In general, however, crisis behaviour in the case of an entrepreneur is a far more common phenomenon.

Both the entrepreneur and the appointed business leader (who usually both have their share of fantasies centred around omnipotence) are frequently unable or unwilling to foresee the need for eventual succession. Continuation of crisis behaviour is not exactly the way to keep good management talent; it only leads to mediocrity in organizations. The process of the indicated corporate self-destruction, through the deterioration of the relationship with subordinates after the initial period of euphoria has been passed, the sacrosanctity of various objects (in Henry Ford's case portrayed by his unwillingness to change the Model T), the increasing rigidity in activities, and the inability to make strategic and structural adjustments, will push the company toward a crisis. Due to the crisis the entrepreneur and the appointed business executive with charisma may gain new strength.

We have now some notion about the strengths and weaknesses of the paranoid potential in organizations (see Figure 6.1). We notice that the original major strengths of leaders with a paranoid disposition can also become the source of their major weaknesses. No matter how successful their single-mindedness and their creation of high morale and group cohesion may be, self-destruction

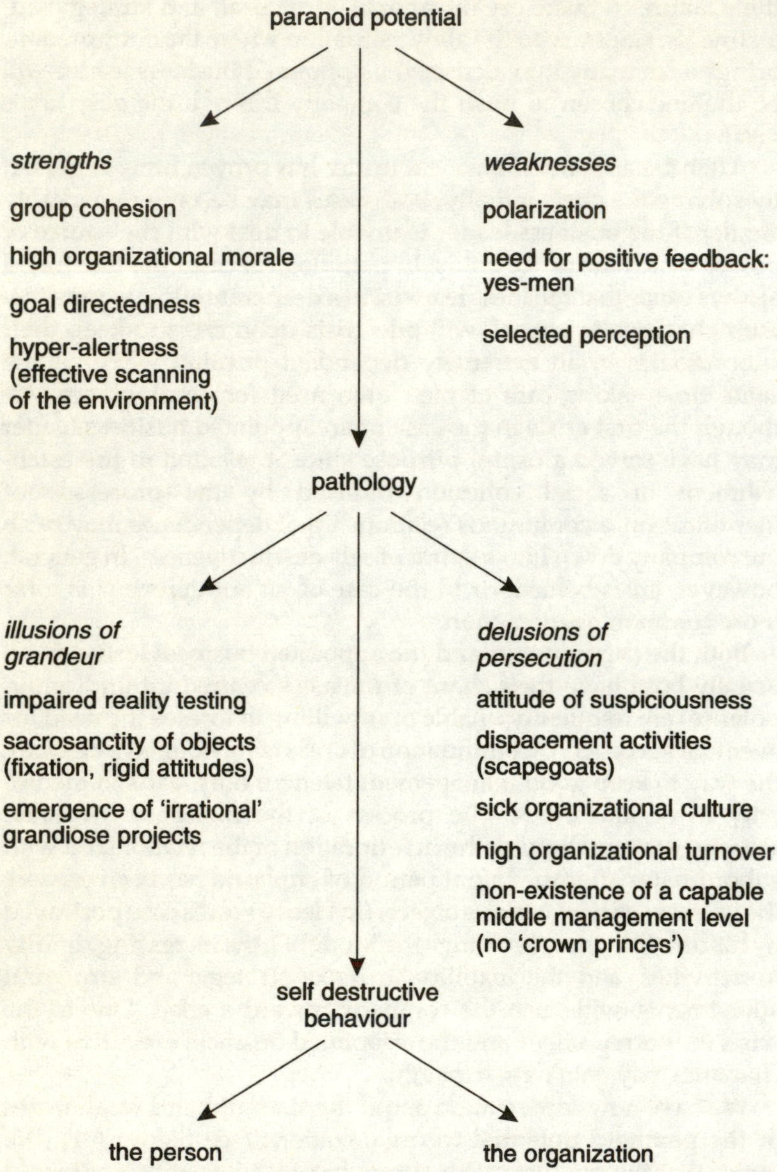

paranoid potential

strengths

group cohesion

high organizational morale

goal directedness

hyper-alertness
(effective scanning
of the environment)

weaknesses

polarization

need for positive feedback:
yes-men

selected perception

pathology

illusions of
grandeur

impaired reality testing

sacrosanctity of objects
(fixation, rigid attitudes)

emergence of 'irrational'
grandiose projects

delusions of
persecution

attitude of suspiciousness

dispacement activities
(scapegoats)

sick organizational culture

high organizational turnover

non-existence of a capable
middle management level
(no 'crown princes')

self destructive
behaviour

the person

the organization

Figure 6.1 Strengths and weaknesses of the paranoid potential

can emerge as a major problem as soon as reality testing becomes impaired.

REVERSING THE IRREVERSIBLE?

The undercurrent of the previous discussion of individuals in a leadership position has been a gloomy one indeed. The realization that a leader's paranoid potential can easily lead him or her into the realm of pathology is not a particularly pleasant one. Optimists might say that these developments are rare and throughout history leaders have emerged who are still remembered with warmth and affection: leaders such as Mahatma Gandhi, Truman and Winston Churchill. Naturally we might argue that perhaps only the positive sides of the potential for paranoia were observed in the cases of these leaders, but maybe there is more to it. Apparently some leaders manage to make their intra-psychic problems fit the societal needs at a given point in time in such a way that even behaviour that would otherwise be considered pathological becomes completely accepted. They might also possess the inner resources to circumvent the pitfalls of leadership. The potential for changing societal norms relating to pathological behaviour, however, is usually reserved for religious and political reformers. Even then, certain thresholds of pathology cannot be surpassed.

Returning to business leaders, we have indicated that the dividing line between pathological developments and corporate success is a rather thin one, which raises the question of whether there are any steps which can be taken to counter the forces leading to self-destruction and which can play the role of safeguards. In answer to this question I will mention a few safeguards which can be divided between internal and external controls.

Frequently we encounter within organizations a multitude of rules, regulations, and other impersonal arrangements which determine the relationships among the participants. These rules can be viewed as a way of depersonalizing relationships as a reaction to possible abuse of power. Public opinion, the government, unions, and the board of directors can be mobilized in case these rules are broken. It should be noted, however, that the presence of these rules and regulations is often a high price to pay if we consider the occurrence of associated 'bureaupathological' behaviour.

As a possible countervailing power, the government or the press are very important. Unions represent another important potential safeguard against the abuse of power by individuals in leadership positions. As the examples of Henry Ford and Sewell Lee Avery have illustrated, a struggle with government and unions is not an unlikely occurrence and, in fact, can become a major issue, particularly if the threshold of the potential for paranoia has been passed and the individual begins to be inclined toward pathology. In many countries, workers' councils operating within the organization also play a major role; however, the importance of these councils and their role as a countervailing force should not be overestimated. Very often we can observe ritualistic behaviour on the part of members of these councils so that, associated with that process, reality testing disappears. In many cases the balancing power of these councils is merely a fiction since actual decision making takes place outside them.

A failure in earnings, particularly in the case of a company directed by someone who does not possess a controlling equity position, might induce the board of directors, the stockholders, or banks to create pressures to balance the strength of the leader in power; in attempting to control the leader, these other power groups might even force his or her resignation. Unfortunately, in the case of stockholders, their role as a counteracting force is usually a fiction as well. In many instances they will remain unaware of the actual developments in the enterprise. In the case of business leaders with a controlling position in the company, the role of the board of directors and other stockholders becomes even less important. Henry Ford only relinquished control under severe family pressure at an age when he was nearly senile. In this case, the company was fortunate. His self-destructive behaviour resulted only in a reduction of its market share and not in bankruptcy. The effects of age played a similar role in the resignation of Sewell Lee Avery. As of late, it can be said, however, that institutional investors and supervisory boards (the latter group being encouraged to show greater vigilance because of the risk of legal liability) have become more active in taking on a monitoring role.

We can list as other countervailing forces consumer organizations, customers, and competition in general. Their influence in the enforcement of reality testing, however, is naturally very dependent on the degree of control of the business leader over the enterprise.

The pathological aspects of the paranoid potential remain an ever-existing threat even though the modern corporation provides more safeguards than has ever been the case. A periodic critical appraisal of one's values remains crucial. Unfortunately, as we have indicated, the atmosphere within the organization surrounding the individual exercising leadership is often not particularly conducive to a realistic re-evaluation. It is inevitable that the strengthening of a person's perception of reality and the ability to arrive at mature relationships with others should be emphasized. Outside help is frequently advisable to recognize possible 'blind spots' and emerging ritualistic behaviour patterns which surround this type of leader. But if paranoid processes have reached an advanced stage, if the individual in question is unwilling to be helped, and if he or she is in full control of the enterprise, there is often not much which can be done to steer the company away from its own self-destruction.

The realization, associated with the process of growing up, that one, after all, is not all-powerful, and the ability to test and re-evaluate reality remain the critical issues. If those processes are functioning we might be able to harness and transform the paranoid potential into a major force capable of strengthening any organization.

7

FOLIE À DEUX

> We shouldn't overlook the argument that folly finds favour
> in heaven because she alone is granted forgiveness of sins,
> whereas the wise man receives no pardon. So when men pray
> for forgiveness, though they may have sinned in full aware-
> ness, they make folly their excuse and defence. . .[1]
>
> Erasmus

Although the nature of interaction of leader with followers might
contain irrational elements and foster ambiguity, we have noted
that these behaviour patterns are usually not one-sided; more often
than not the other party is drawn into the process. We can take as
a good illustration the behaviour of Hitler. The Führer during the
last months of the war, isolated in his bunker in Berlin, increasingly
withdrew into his fantasies, then more than ever inhabited by
delusions. Encouraged by an intimate clique of old party members
(particularly Bormann, Goebbels, and Ley),[2] he increasingly de-
nied the reality of the approaching end.[3] Even one and a half
months before Germany's total unconditional surrender Speer tells
how he participated in an armaments conference during which
non-existent crude steel production, quotas for anti-tank guns, and
the employment of imaginary new super weapons were discussed.
At this conference the dismal record of the previous war years was
attributed to treason and sabotage by army officers. But since these
traitors had finally been exposed, the situation would be turned
around. Victory was near.

Speer recalls how in these twilight days of the Thousand Year
Reich innumerable fantasies blossomed among Hitler and his close
companions. Roosevelt's death was hailed as a sign of providence,
a turning point in the war which was compared to the way in which

history once had given victory to an apparently hopelessly beaten Frederick the Great at the last moment; another example was the delusionary idea that a new death ray was about to be invented, a weapon that would change the outcome of the war. All this occurred one month before the final assault on Berlin, a time when Germany was in a complete shambles.

The striking part of Speer's reminiscences is the delusional interplay of fantasies among Hitler and his inner circle. The reality of the approaching end was unacceptable to this group of people who, from the beginning of the Nazi movement, had always been disposed toward delusional ideas of a grandiose and persecutory nature. While most fantasies originated from Hitler, his close entourage not only participated in, but enhanced these irrational thoughts. In this small, increasingly isolated community the belief persisted that everything was not lost. Miraculous developments were just around the corner. Set-backs were only temporary. The only reason that the situation had deteriorated as far as it had was betrayal and sabotage by enemies. The spell was broken only by advancing Russian troops. Communal suicide and imprisonment followed.

We observe in this recollection the transferral of delusional ideas and unusual behaviour patterns from one person to one or more others who are in close association with the person primarily affected. The partners not only participate in the delusional ideas but frequently even elaborate them. This phenomenon has been known for some time in psychiatric literature as folie à deux.

Although the term folie à deux originally referred to the adoption of mental processes from one person to another and has been viewed as being limited to the behaviour of individuals within families, it can also be regarded as a collective phenomenon whereby entire groups of individuals become influenced by the delusional ideas of the affected person. The intensity and persistence of this influence process will differ. The influenced party may actually believe or pretend to believe the emerging irrational notions.

Given this more broadened point of view, organizations can be affected. I am referring particularly to the relationships between superiors and subordinates. I also believe that this disturbance has been given less notice than it probably deserves because of a tendency within relatively insulated organizational cultures to manifest a high degree of tolerance for unusual, or what is called 'eccentric', behaviour.

PSYCHODYNAMIC ASPECTS

At the end of the nineteenth century two French psychiatrists mentioned folie à deux for the first time.[4] From then on an extensive number of articles have been published to describe and analyze this phenomenon.[5] Other names for folie à deux have been double insanity, mental contagion, collective insanity, or psychosis of association. The reason for the latter term is that, in true folie à deux, the symptoms described are usually of a psychotic nature: e.g. illusions of grandeur and delusions of persecution. In a number of instances, religious, grandiose, and depressive delusions have been identified.[6] Whatever its specific content, folie à deux essentially involves the sharing of a delusional system by two or more individuals.

Etiology

For an explanation of these patterns, early childhood gives up some of the answers we need. It seems that the degree of success in developing basic trust reactions, particularly with the parents, largely determines susceptibility. Lack of basic trust and the arousal of anxiety because of frustrating, humiliating, and disappointing experiences can lead to unsatisfactory interpersonal relationships, a sense of betrayal, and a perception of the environment as hostile. The individual's personality will develop accordingly. Such a person, in dealings with the outside world, will be always on his or her guard and take precautions to be ready for any confirmation of expectations.[7]

Apart from an emerging paranoid disposition, lack of trust frequently will lead to an absence of closeness and thereby frustrated dependency needs. The world becomes a dangerous place where only a very few individuals are to be trusted. Contingent on the degree of deprivation, if an opportunity arises to satisfy dependency needs, attachment to the other person can become extremely intense, totally overpowering the individual's other behaviour patterns to the detriment of rational thought and reality testing.

The need for a high degree of similarity in general motif and delusional content of the partners' system of ideas is also mentioned in folie à deux. Individuals who engage in folie à deux accept, support, and share each other's delusional ideas. Folie à deux apparently creates a symbiotic type of relationship. This usually occurs under conditions of prolonged and close association.[8]

Not only dependency but also identification seem to be important aspects of folie à deux. Because of the extreme dependency of the participants on each other, total identification with the partner becomes a way of avoiding the intolerable thought of separation.[9] A feeling of closeness is preserved through identification which eventually necessitates acceptance of emerging delusional ideas of one party by the other. This appears to be a mutual, not a unilateral process. Both parties will depend upon and identify with each other. It is a process of identification and counter identification.

This identification process is of a special nature and seems to belong to the earlier described defence mechanism 'identification with the aggressor'. The dominant partner in folie à deux frequently acquires this symbolic role. Through 'identification with the aggressor', the more submissive partner defends himself against his own hostile and destructive wishes (a reaction to feelings of helplessness and dependency on the dominant party) and the fear of retaliation about these wishes. Strength will be gained through the alliance with the aggressor, rather than allowing oneself to be the victim.

If we now recapitulate the process of folie à deux, we note that the period preceding folie à deux is one where a participant is strongly dependent on the other and has few outside sources of gratification. The submissive partner's dependency needs are satisfied by the dominant partner. Eventually the dominant partner becomes preoccupied by the feeling (not necessarily consciously), that there is a danger somewhere out there. A stimulus for this perception may be the feeling that the less dominant partner is increasingly taking advantage of his or her (the dominant partner's) dependency needs. This may cause a certain amount of hostility on the part of the dominant partner. However, at the same time, he or she feels guilty about this rising hostility. Because he or she is afraid of giving up the relationship with the other party, a defence is formed against this hostility, usually of a projective nature. Hostility is externalized and attributed to others and, in most instances, takes the form of a paranoid delusion. The dominant partner needs the support of the more submissive individual and wants him or her to share the delusion. He or she is afraid to lose the close contact with the other party if the delusion is rejected and therefore has no choice but to induce this person to participate in the delusion.

If the more submissive partner resists, the dominant partner will become more overtly hostile towards him or her, instead of using the projective defence of blaming other people; he or she will, however, exclude the submissive partner from this accusation process. This will raise the level of anxiety and guilt for the submissive partner. The actions of the dominant individual will cause the more submissive one to be placed in a 'double-bind' situation. This person will be threatened with either the loss of gratification of his or her dependency relationship or the loss of reality. In some instances, he or she will see no alternative (not necessarily in a conscious sense) but to give in to this ultimatum, 'identify with the aggressor', satisfy dependency needs, and also deflect the hostility of the dominant party. The reason for this choice is probably that separation from the person who started this process is much more of a direct, conceivable loss than loss of reality.

Identification with the aggressor usually implies participating in the delusion of the existence of a common outside enemy. These persecutory fantasies also become the rationalization for the lack of fulfilment of the often elaborately constructed grandiose schemes of the dominant individual. Lack of success will be blamed on sabotage and opposition of this common enemy. The shared delusions are usually kept well within the limits of possibility and are based on actual past events or certain common expectations. Through participation in similar fantasies the source of gratification will be maintained, the level of anxiety and guilt will be lowered, and anger at the dominant party will be expressed in its projected form. The process resembles a mirror effect; the actions of the initiator become reflected in those of the more submissive partner and vice versa. Folie à deux becomes the means to save the alliance from breaking up.

CONTAGIOUS PARTICIPATION

Among the psychodynamic factors we observe in folie à deux are extreme dependency (which is mutual), separation anxiety (about the feared loss of the dominant partner, it being an attitude not without ambivalence), identification with the aggressor (the dominant partner), close association (frequently implying a condition of relative isolation), and deflection of hostility (usually through the mechanism of projection). The type of delusion is often of a persecutory nature. One explanation for the latter might be that paranoid reactions are among the most primitive and universal of all human reactions. Some support in reality for delusional ideas can always be found.

Examples from literature

The interplay of the variables creating folie à deux has been noted by playwrights and other creative artists. For example, Eugene O'Neill describes an incidence of folie à deux in his play *Where the Cross is Made*.[10] It tells the story of a retired sea captain who is waiting for his ship 'Mary Allen' which was sent out many years before on a treasure hunt. It is known, however, that it has been sunk for three years. This catastrophe, causing total financial disaster, becomes emotionally unacceptable to the captain who creates the delusion that the ship would return. His son, embittered because of increasing emotional and financial strain, is making preparations to have his father sent to a mental hospital. Not only is the mortgage on the house going to be foreclosed if his father continues to stay in the house, but the son is becoming more and more afraid of being drawn into his father's delusions. At the end of the play, when the moment of separation is coming near, the father declares that the ship has arrived, pointing at the blackness of the night, and then curses his son for turning traitor. The son cannot stand this pressure any longer, accepts the delusion and participates, agreeing that there is a ship out there. When the doctor comes to take the father away, the emotion causes the father's death by heart failure, but his son continues in the delusionary fantasy.

In Thomas Mann's story, 'The Blood of the Walsungs', a twin brother and sister named Sieglinde and Siegmund are acting out Wagner's opera *Die Walküre* in real life.[11] Brought up without economic worries in an emotionally impoverished environment, their contact with others becomes disturbing and is minimized. Eventually, the impending marriage of Sieglinde becomes the catalyst for total identification with their namesakes from the opera and leaves us at the end of the story with unanswered questions about incest and adultery.

In Bergman's film, *Hour of the Wolf*, we find another example of folie à deux. In this instance the film tells us the story of the painter Johan Borg who believes that he is tormented by demons during his stay with his wife on an isolated island. It is only at the end of the film that we discover that his wife, who originally appears to be a very earthy, sane, submissive individual, is a partner to his delusions.

From another perspective, the psychoanalyst Robert Lindner in one of his case histories, 'The Jet-Propelled Couch', tells how he gradually got drawn into the delusions of one of his patients, a scientist, who found escape from reality by constructing an extremely elaborate science fiction world.[12] Only with great effort was he able to wrest himself away from this world of the galaxies.

These four examples (and many others) indicate the similarities in folie à deux, e.g. the relative isolation of the characters, their closeness (family or otherwise), the existence of a dominant partner, and the emergence of a delusion. This process of change becomes analogous to that of brainwashing.

The analogy with other processes of behaviour change

In folie à deux, as in brainwashing, three phases can be distinguished: unfreezing, changing and refreezing.[13] We first discern a disorganizing or regressive phase during which the defensive structure of the submissive party is gradually broken down. A strong demand is made to fulfil heightened dependency needs. During this period motivation to change is induced. In brainwashing this process is usually facilitated through social isolation and sensory deprivation. Subsequently, change occurs through identification with the beliefs and attitudes of the aggressor. New responses are created based on new information. Finally, refreezing takes place, whereby the new responses are stabilized and integrated.

We can consider the process of change in belief systems of folie à deux from an experimental social psychological perspective. Such studies indicate the importance of 'group think' and social comparison on the behaviour of an individual subjected to this form of influence. Also it illustrates the role which sanctions play in the case of non-conformity.[14] The basic premise seems to be that individuals like to be correct in their perceptions and want to live up to others' expectations. This is particularly true for individuals with an insecure sense of self-esteem, often indicated by strong dependency needs. There are, however, differences in the degree of conformity. If private choices become similar to public ones then, because of these group pressures, the individual appears to be completely persuaded. If this is not the case, and the individual is only acting this way in public and is going against his own judgement to mollify the group, then his actions are more superficial and ritualistic.

The avoidance of punishment (such as rejection or ridicule by the others and fear of separation) and the obtaining of rewards (such as gratification of dependency needs) seem to be main motives in behaviour. The experiments of Milgram supported the notion that a large proportion of the population will cause pain to others in pandering to authority.[15] We seem to be dependent on others to validate our conceptions of reality. In cases of differences our sense of stability and security is quickly threatened and we try to conform.

Conformity can also result through others' behaviour being the only guide to appropriate action and determination of reality. Studies of cognitive dissonance point in that direction.[16] Individuals will go through great efforts to reduce the dissonance between two or more cognitions which are experienced as inconsistent with each other. When reality is unclear and uncertain other people become the source of information of how to behave. In this way social bonds are maintained.

A collective phenomenon

Folie à deux is contagious. Given our dependence on others for guidance, it illustrates why delusional ideas and actions can infect and spread eventually to involve an entire society. In this context the term 'folie à beaucoup' or 'folie collective' is occasionally used. Helene Deutsch noted the resemblance of group phenomena with folie à deux and once remarked:

> We also find the process as a mass phenomenon, where entire groups of healthy people are carried away by psychologically diseased members of the group: world reformers and paranoids, for example. Indeed, great national and religious movements of history and social revolutions have had, in addition to their reality motives, psychological determinants

91

which come very close to the psychological processes of folie
à deux.[17]

Prejudice, political attitudes and religious beliefs can be considered
as variations of folie à deux. These processes are facilitated in
situations of fear and terror during which individuals seem more
susceptible to 'mental contagion'. This is especially true during the
quieter periods of anticipation when the 'work of worrying' occurs
and the level of anxiety tends to rise.[18] In the same vein we can
mention ideas of religion and mysticism. These beliefs, frequently
promising alleviation of experienced suffering, become very com-
municable, particularly in periods of great upheaval and change.
The time of association will vary depending upon individual relationships, personalities, needs, and intensity of contacts.
Lycanthropy fears, witch mania, lynching and looting mobs, and
some religious cults such as the Sun Moon and Hare Krishna
movements, or the Branch Davidians of Waco, Texas are examples
of variations of folie à deux on a larger scale.[19] Senator Joe McCarthy's hearings and the Stalin purge trials are other illustrations.
Frequently, we find as a central image that of vast, mysterious, and
frightening conspiracy. This has been a common notion throughout history, be it represented by the Elders of Zion, the Jesuits, the
Freemasons, or the communists, and in the business sphere by
collusionary practices. It is a world in which absolute good is
fighting absolute evil, where there is a lack of compromise and,
consequently, unrealistic goal setting, which only heightens the
participants' sense of frustration.

REACTIONS TO FOLIE À DEUX

How permanent are the behaviour patterns and belief systems
instigated by folie à deux? Some guidance in this matter is offered
by Kelman, who suggests dividing the relative permanence of
conforming behaviour, or generally, responses to social influence,
into three kinds: compliance, identification and internalization.[20]

Compliance would be the mode of behaviour in response to the
desire to gain reward or to avoid punishment. This behaviour is
very short lived; it is a public shift in values and will last only as
long as the promised reward or threatened punishment.

Identification is a response to social influence based upon the
individual's desire to be like the influencer. The individual comes

to believe the values and opinions he or she adopts, but since the basis of the relationship is the attractiveness of the other person, this implies the maintenance of an active relationship between the two parties. The continuation of the relationship is satisfying since the other person becomes the model for self-definition. But the belief in the values and opinions of the other person is not necessarily very strong and will disappear in the absence of close interaction. We find here a parallel to charismatic authority.

Internalization becomes the most deeply rooted response to social influence using Kelman's classification. The beliefs or values are intrinsically rewarding and become part of the system of values. The basis of the influencer's power becomes expertise and credibility. These beliefs are independent of the other party's continued presence and therefore extremely resistant to change.

Since Kelman only identifies different forms of acceptance of social influence we can add to this list the group of people who resist influence in any form. The name non-conformers seems most appropriate for these individuals.

Except for the group of the active non-conformers it is often difficult from the observer's point of view to distinguish between compliance, identification and internalization. A subordinate may seem to be engaged in a folie à deux but the intensity and seriousness of the reactions will remain open to question. Only an understanding of the subordinate's private motivations and the nature of his behaviour after the two parties have been separated will yield insight into the type of social influence process. Only in the case of identification and internalization can we speak of true folie à deux and allow that the previous description of the psychodynamic processes is applicable.

Naturally, the 'influencer' does not necessarily have to be a superior; peers, subordinates, and even complete outsiders can set this process in motion. But given the effect of authority in behaviour and the usual prevalence of a relationship of dominance-submission in folie à deux, this disorder will be most common in superior-subordinate relationships.

If we now take responses to social influence as one of the dimensions with which subordinates can react to the behaviour patterns of their superiors, and take as another dimension the level of activity or dynamism with which a manager reacts to his environment, we arrive at a matrix which conceptualizes the various ways in which we can observe folie à deux in organizations (see Table 7.1). We realize that this classification presents merely ideal types. Obviously there will be areas of overlap.

Table 7.1 Subordinate behaviour patterns in folie à deux

responses to influence	level of activity	passive	active
non-conformance and oportunism	non-conformers	withdrawal into routine low key activities participation in delusions avoided retreatistic behaviour	leaves organization (resignation or dismissal) occasionally playing the role of change agent
	compliers	participation in delusions without private conviction ritualistic behaviour	participation and enhancement of delusions without private conviction
folie à deux	identifiers	participation in delusions with private conviction relationship relatively unstable	participation and enhancement of delusions with private conviction relationship relatively unstable
	internalizers	participation in delusions with private conviction stable relationship	participation and enhancement of delusions with private conviction stable relationship

Non-conformers

Both active and passive non-conformers refuse to participate in the irrational behaviour patterns of their superiors. The group which has a more passive orientation usually withdraws into routine, non-essential activities. Immersion in the technological aspects of the job (as long as these are not an emotionally important part of the delusionary frame of reference of the superior) will be their solution for avoiding participation in the behaviour patterns of the superior. The basic strategy is to avoid activities considered essential to organizational leadership. Because of this low profile (given the pressures inside the organization for conformity and participation) there are usually no rewards for this behaviour regardless of its importance to the organization. Career stagnation or demotion are often the logical consequence. In contrast, the more active non-conformers will refuse to participate in the delusions or other irrational behaviour patterns of their senior executives. By taking a more active stance the wrath of these individuals may be provoked. Eventually, the non-conformers' choices will be limited; they either leave the organization voluntarily or the organization forces their resignation.

In some instances active non-conformers will play the role of change agent. Because of their active stand the delusionary spell may be broken and the organizational participants brought back to reality. This is, however, a relatively rare occurrence. The power and authority of active non-conformers are usually limited – therefore so is their effectiveness in instigating change.

Compliers

Active and passive compliers will participate, if irrational behaviour patterns emerge in the organization, but without private conviction. The only reason for participation is a sense of opportunism because the reward system of the organization encourages conformity to the wishes of the superior. While the behaviour of the passive complier is of a more ritualistic nature, characterized by an 'I am not sticking my neck out', or 'I am playing it safe' attitude, the active complier not only participates but will enhance any emerging delusion of the executive in charge.

Identifiers

Identifiers participate in delusions and other irrational behaviour patterns with private conviction. The only difference between the active and passive group is that the active group will elaborate upon the delusions. Executives who use the response of the active

95

identifiers probably belong to the most true and common variety of folie à deux. Continuous association between the parties is needed for the delusions to hold. The alliance remains relatively unstable since the subordinate usually stops behaving according to the delusionary frame of reference of his superior when the relationship breaks up.

Internalizers

The final group, the internalizers, will not only participate in the delusions and other irrational behaviour patterns with private conviction, but continue in these beliefs even after the relationship is broken. Change is more complete and definitive. This can be considered the most deeply rooted variety of folie à deux. The difference between active and passive identifiers depends again on the willingness to elaborate on these delusions. But, according to clinical evidence, this variety is relatively rare.[21]

In presenting this conceptual scheme we realize that each category of response can evolve into another. This implies a progression of intensity and degree of participation with the activities of the senior executive. Mere compliance in situations of prolonged exposure may eventually transform into internalization, making for a sense of commitment and performance.

AN ORGANIZATIONAL THEATRE OF THE ABSURD

We can assume that as a rule folie à deux in organizations is not diagnosed as such. These contagious behaviour patterns are simply accepted and often rationalized as one of the consequences of an eccentric leadership style. The non-clinical manifestation of folie à deux might be more common than expected, particularly among relatively isolated groups, frequently in situations of inadequate leadership.

In reviewing the literature we can find only one incidence of folie à deux diagnosed under this particular name.[22] It concerns a partnership of two barbers. One of the partners suddenly became preoccupied with the idea of starting a barber college. The financing would come from a number of mysterious millionaire friends and, according to his description, the proceeds from this college would be phenomenal. This rather unrealistic, grandiose plan resulted soon in business losses which were blamed on a group of people (unknown) operating against both of them. The more submissive partner believed completely in these grandiose plans and delusions. The delusions eventually become so serious that both partners had to be hospitalized.

This case is an exception. In most instances the occurrence of folie à deux in organizations is probably not diagnosed as such. Usually the explanation is given that the organization was run under poor leadership. Although this might be true, it is not merely that simple. As we have indicated, other dynamics can play a role. Frequently and without great effort executives are drawn into situations which resemble folie à deux. Power, attractiveness or expertise of an individual in a position of authority easily leads to conformity, identification or internalization of behaviour patterns by executives in subordinate positions. Not all executives have a sense of personal identity strong enough to withstand the pressures placed upon them. Giving in, be it only compliance, is usually a much simpler process.

The need for a mirror image

In spite of the emphasis given to independent-mindedness of subordinates, when it comes down to actual practice many senior executives find this attitude hard to deal with. They frequently possess relatively closed belief systems. They like to see their subordinates' belief systems congruent with their own. In their way of thinking, independent-mindedness creates only non-obedience to authority, confrontation and other disturbing forms of behaviour leading to anger, anxiety and guilt. Therefore, they prefer – though they may not necessarily state as much – their subordinates to be mirror images of themselves, compliant to their wishes.

This tendency has serious consequences in so far as it concerns entry and career advancement in organizations. Individuals with these attitudes will select subordinates who have compatible behaviour patterns and belief systems. Many executives who might have reacted in an active non-conforming manner, unwilling to participate in possible irrational behaviour patterns, are automatically excluded. Others are dismissed or resign soon after joining the organization. The process of organizational socialization becomes the phase where compatibility with existing organizational norms and values are tested. Difficulty in adjustment to the organizational culture will make for exclusion.

The same can be said about career advancement. Reward systems will be based on participation in similar behaviour. To the subordinate, the alternative to compliance, identification, or internalization of the norms and values predominating in the organization is far from attractive since it frequently implies dismissal, demotion, or other forms of career stagnation. Because of this selection and reward system (which does not necessarily exist in a formal sense) existing delusional patterns in the organization will be enhanced, creating a fertile territory for folie à deux. Subordinates and superior may find themselves trapped in unrealistic fantasies whereby the original objectives of the organization lose out and solidarity leads to distorted external reality.

The search for the enemy

Occasionally we can observe dysfunctional elements of clique formation in organizations which can be considered a side effect of folie à deux. Within these groups organizational myths and fantasies (frequently completely unrelated to reality) flourish and are enforced. The sight of the organization's overall goals will be ignored; reality testing is often absent. Actions will not necessarily be in accordance with the information and data available.

The members of these groups live in a polarized world where only two views are acknowledged. It is a world of inclusion and exclusion which does not accept any nuances; only 'good' and 'bad' are recognized. Executives unwilling to participate in the prevailing myths and fantasies are ostracized and are viewed as outsiders. They are the scapegoats and will be blamed as incompetent, ineffective or out of touch, or will be considered as candidates for transfers or early retirement.

Because of reasons of organizational structure, sub-groups tend to overlap with departments or other organizational units. Areas of responsibility will be jealously guarded. Boundaries between units can lead to conflict. Seeking or accepting help from other groups will be viewed as a weakness or betrayal.

This excessive sense of rivalry leads to a narrowness of perspective, defensiveness, and over-control. It makes for organizational differentiation without integration, to the detriment of communication, morale and performance. Instead, the organizational participants will take refuge in policies and procedures, politics and other forms of organizational gamesmanship. Cooperation will be rare, priorities nonexistent.

This organizational behaviour pattern induced by folie à deux makes for a situation where conflict becomes stifling, where creativity is discouraged and distrust prevails. Emergencies will be met by withdrawal reactions or the blaming of others. Fear will be the undercurrent of the organizational climate. Means and ends are confused. We are dealing with organizations which seem to drift along without well-defined goals and strategies.

The susceptibility of family firms

Family firms, given the intensity and closeness of relationships, are particularly prone to folie à deux. The founder of the firm, the entrepreneur, is frequently an individual who masters feelings of dependency, helplessness, and rejection by using a proactive style characterized by a strong need for control and an exaggerated concern for autonomy. The relationship of the entrepreneur and the enterprise is usually extremely intense and conflict-ridden, due to the symbolic emotional significance of the firm to this individual. In view of their personal history, the behaviour of entrepreneurs in the firm can be extremely erratic. Hoarding of information, playing off favourites, inconsistent handling of company policies, and the creation of other ambiguous situations, are not uncommon. That is why a considerable number of entrepreneurial firms have no strong layer of capable middle-management. The non-conformers leave; the yes-men remain. The latter will spend a great part of their efforts in political in-fighting, enhancing the irrational behaviour patterns and beliefs of the entrepreneur.

If more than one member of the family works in the firm, the family relationship not only makes for close association but can often lead to far more open and intense psychodynamic processes than is the case in public organizations. Conflict arises because of non-conforming behaviour. Frequently, however, the ideas of one family member, even if irrational, prevail and the others participate.

Organizational dramas

This is not to say that folie à deux does not occur in publicly owned organizations or government institutions. In both privately owned and public organizations we can see how, on many occasions, subordinates begin to share the fantasies and delusions of the chief executive officer. The common threat or 'enemy' often becomes symbolized by the government, competitors, labour unions or consumer organizations.

Only since J. Edgar Hoover's death has the world became aware of the bizarre ways in which he ran the directorship of the FBI.[23] Hoover, as an administrator, was an erratic, autocratic individual banishing agents to Siberian posts for the most whimsical reasons, terrorizing them with so many rules and regulations that adherence to all of them was an impossibility. His directorship was infallible, dissent equalled disloyalty, toleration of disloyalty was punishable, adulation the only way to rise in the organization. No whim of the director was considered insignificant enough to be ignored. For example, non-obedience to an anti-obesity programme was likely to incur the wrath of the director; the appearance of his agents might provoke his irritation (required were white shirts, subdued ties, jackets worn in the office, and short hair); chauffeurs had to avoid making left turns while driving him (he once got struck by a car making a left turn). What to other people might appear as trivial and unimportant was transformed in meaning if the order originated from Hoover. Then a directive would become transformed out of proportion, and warranted serious attention and some form of calculated action, even if the meaning was unclear. Trouble would follow if an agent did not take his directions seriously. These directions often assumed a life of their own, perpetuated and nurtured by the organizational participants. Their value to original organizational objectives would no longer matter. Discussions of real problems in the field could be fatal to the career of the special agents in charge. Only slavish obedience to the rules and statistical accomplishments counted. These statistics summarized such activities as monetary value of fines, number of convictions, and apprehended fugitives. Trouble would follow if these figures were not increased each year. Naturally, those agents who embraced the concept of the director's omnipotence were more likely to succeed. To ensure compliance inspectors would be sent out into the field in search of substantial violations in the field offices (the breaking of some obscure rule or instruction). If a 'contract was out' on the special agent in charge, cause for punishment would inevitably be found. The inspector's own future was at stake if no violations were found because, in turn, a contract might be issued for him. An atmosphere of anxiety and fear pervaded the halls and offices of the FBI. Participation in many of these absurdities was unavoidable for survival; nobody was excluded.

Some of the behaviour patterns found in ITT under Harold Geneen can also be viewed as a non-clinical variety of folie à deux.[24] The rigorous system of financial controls, the special meetings with Harold Geneen playing the role of the grand inquisitor, the preoccupation with espionage in the company, its intelligence system and use of spies, all carried elements of folie à deux. Checking and cross-checking described the predominant leadership style of Harold Geneen; nobody could really be trusted with the exception, possibly, of a small inner circle at head office. The prevention of leaks within the company has always been a constant obsession at ITT. Subsidiary controllers reported directly to head office and were only in an advisory role vis-à-vis their own chief executive. Product line managers, divided along product planning and marketing lines, officially operating only in an advisory capacity, were the feared extensions of head office. They played a dreaded role during the monthly meeting at headquarters. Geneen's reactions during these meetings determined the actions of these product line managers. If Geneen zeroed in on a division manager, the staff group immediately followed and provided evidence leading to complete humiliation. If Geneen smiled and reminisced about old times, total restraint was in order, no matter how much evidence of incompetence was uncovered.

The way the late Robert Maxwell dealt with his subordinates can be seen again as another example of folie à deux. The only way to survive in his organization was to play the role of sycophant. He intimidated everyone around him. His management style was unequivocal; he was the master and his employees were to follow him in lock step. Even small disagreements would be interpreted as major threats, and Maxwell would react with violent explosions of anger.[25]

These examples of well-known executives illustrate the contagiousness of folie à deux in organizations and the infectiousness of the behaviour of the executive in charge. In the cases of J. Edgar Hoover and Robert Maxwell we observe how originally functional behaviour became increasingly dysfunctional to the organization. The behaviour of their subordinates only encouraged them in their views. Very few were willing to stand up to them. Opposition was crushed; non-conforming behaviour ended in dismissal.

This does not mean that folie à deux is always dysfunctional from an organizational point of view. Initially, it can be a source of great strength because it can make for group cohesiveness and goal directedness. Unfortunately, in the long run, the tendency to organizational pathology will be substantial.

ITT under Harold Geneen can be viewed as a much milder variety of folie à deux and indicates how difficult it often is to draw a line between functional and dysfunctional organizational behaviour. In spite of set-backs such as the scandal about ITT's involvement in the overthrow of the Allende government in Chile, the company continued to be profitable during his tenure. However, the kind of organizational culture he had created – as distrust prevailed – lacked the essential elements of a learning organization. Not surprisingly, soon after his retirement, the company found itself in serious difficulties.

In each of these three examples it is difficult to determine how much of the behaviour of the subordinates involved can truly be called folie à deux and how much more was compliance to an eccentric leadership style of the senior executive. But as we have mentioned previously, mere compliance if performed long enough can easily evolve into identification or even internalization.

DEALING WITH FOLIE À DEUX

Given the susceptibility of executives to folie à deux and its contagiousness in organizations it becomes important to recognize the danger signs. Awareness of the symptoms can make for prevention and limitation of its dysfunctional effects. Recognition of the danger signs is necessary for initiating coping behaviour.

Watching the danger signs

An executive who is predisposed to folie à deux, and consequently possesses paranoid characteristics, can be recognized by a number of behaviour patterns. In describing these behaviour patterns I am referring particularly to the primarily affected person, the superior, the instigator of the process of folie à deux. When the 'mental infection' spreads the newly affected persons will show similar behaviour traits although (in most instances) not of such a deeply

102

rooted nature. Initially, however, the main noticeable characteristic of the executive subjected to 'infection' by a superior susceptible to folie à deux is that of excessive dependency. These executives often stand out because of their extreme subservience. In contrast, the reactions toward their own subordinates are frequently exactly the opposite.

Executives predisposed to folie à deux are usually characterized by attitudes of conceit, arrogance and righteousness. We can look at these attitudes as compensations for underlying feelings of inadequacy, inferiority and low self-esteem. Their rigid concepts and ideas are extremely difficult to alter by any appeal to logic or reality because of their uncompromising, hostile and aggressive stand. These executives possess a façade of bravado, self-sufficiency and unrealistic pride. Feelings of sexual inadequacy and incompetency are common.

The predisposed executives will stand out because of their need to dominate and control the persons around them; any form of use of authority toward themselves, however, is strongly resented. These executives will be in a continuous state of defensiveness against the threat of a superior force. Hyper-alertness, hypersensitivity, suspiciousness, guardedness, and a critical attitude toward others become ways of life. There is a preoccupation with hidden motives, a search for confirmation of suspicions. Details are amplified and elaborated.

These executives feel easily slighted, wronged, or ignored. Lack of trust and confidence in others make them extremely self-conscious, seclusive, reserved and moody. They tend to be inconsiderate, querulous and insensitive to others. Mood swings are common. If there is an attitude of friendliness and companionship, this façade is quickly shattered by the slightest provocation, after which the full force of hate, mistrust and rage will break loose. Playfulness and a sense of humour are usually absent.

Besides the characteristics of the executive, the danger signals of folie à deux can also be detected in the peculiarities of the organizational culture. Unusual selection procedures, excessive risk aversion, strange decision-making patterns, uncommon information systems, excessive control and extreme secrecy often can be taken as danger signs. The excessive manifestation of stress symptoms (such as gastro-intestinal and cardio-vascular disorders, alcoholism and drug addiction), a high turnover of executives, absenteeism, frequent changes in organizational goals and the existence of grandiose, unrealistic plans can be viewed as other indications requiring closer investigation.

COPING

We have seen, from our three case examples, that even awareness is not much of a help when the phenomenon involves a very powerful executive. This is particularly true in corporations when this person is also the main shareholder, and the options open to the subordinate are usually either participation, dismissal, or resignation. Early diagnosis, however, will improve a subordinate's chance of preventing involvement, or even slow down or stop the process before he or she becomes one of the players, and, increasingly cut off from reality, joins the roller coaster ride to destruction. Recourse can be had through support of a countervailing power such as the government, the unions or the press who, by taking preventive measures, may be able to steer the organization away from a path determined by folie à deux. This will often imply the removal of the original instigator of this process from the organization. Also, contemporary pressures toward flatter organizations and empowered executives can be viewed as another way of preventing, or at least limiting, the emergence or proliferation of folie à deux.

For the person who started the process of folie à deux in the first place the route to reality is not that easy. A paranoid disposition is a difficult burden to overcome. Confidence and trust have to be obtained to enable a manager to begin to doubt the original validity of assumptions made about the world. Realistic self-appraisal can begin only then. But substituting reality for fantasy is a very slow process of adjustment which usually needs professional help.

The outlook of the affected subordinates is more positive and less time consuming (with the possible exception of those subordinates who have internalized the beliefs of the primarily affected person). Removal of the affected senior executive is usually sufficient to break the spell. But because it was the susceptibility of these subordinates to influence (originating from an insecure sense of self-esteem) which made folie à deux possible, strong reality-orientated leadership is needed in the period of transition to provide for their dependency needs. A strong leader will be accepted as a substitute for the disturbed leadership style of the initially affected person and make for the organization's revitalization.

The freedom to choose in organizations, to solve problems in a realistic manner and limit susceptibility to influence, implies a secure sense of identity. Only executives with the willingness for self-examination have the ability to establish mature working relationships to create a healthy organizational culture. When this willingness is absent, susceptibility to folie à deux increases, and a crisis in leadership may follow.

8

THE ENTREPRENEURIAL PERSONALITY

Sometimes I have visions of myself driving through hell, selling sulphur and brimstone, or through heaven peddling refreshments to the roaming souls...[1]

Brecht

Entrepreneurs seem to be particularly susceptible to the vicissitudes of leadership. Their ups and downs in fortune may be one of the reasons for our continuous fascination with their ventures. The theme of individual success and failure represented by entrepreneurship has always been a highly popular topic awakening the rebellious spirit present in each of us. Prometheus and Odysseus seem to have been replaced by these folk heroes of the industrial world, entrepreneurs. They resemble the last lone rangers, bold individualists fighting the odds of the environment. They are the people who, after enduring and overcoming many hardships, trials and business adventures, finally seem to have 'made it'. But frequently there is an epilogue to these fairy-tale endings. The 'and they lived happily ever after' theme is missing. Analogous to Greek myths, success may lead to *hubris* and a tragic fall. As the histories of many entrepreneurs illustrate, success is a very fragile state indeed, easily followed by failure.

Take for example the story of Bernard Cornfeld and Investment Overseas Services.[2] This tale tells us of a displaced person born in Istanbul of Jewish parents. His family emigrated to America. The father, an unsuccessful actor, died when Bernard Cornfeld was very young, leaving the mother to take care of the family, having to work extremely long hours. The story continues by describing how Bernard Cornfeld, after many difficulties, became an investment professional (thereby ending his career as a social worker)

106

and began to sell mutual funds overseas (not necessarily to the benefit of the investors), being extremely successful at this activity. But his funds became like a chain letter game, financial controls were lacking, and chaos prevailed in the company. Eventually Cornfeld was deposed, leaving the remains of the company wide open to plunder by a mercenary financier, Robert Vesco.

Another entrepreneurial saga tells the tale of the rise and decline of An Wang, the founder and presiding genius of Wang Laboratories. This brilliant Chinese immigrant built an empire from scratch and became one of the leading players in the computer revolution that transformed the way we work. In its prime, Wang Laboratories was one of the premier companies in the world, employing more than 32,000 people, generating 30 straight years of increased profits. The meteoric rise of his company created an aura of mysticism and invincibility around Wang. But this incredible story is one of *hubris* as well as success. Ambition and glory were followed by an equally spectacular collapse, due to a series of miscalculations and fatal errors. An Wang's obsessive desire for control, his increasing remoteness, his unwillingness to listen to the advice of his key executives and his customers, combined with his insistence on passing the leadership of his empire to his inexperienced eldest son, contributed to the company's downfall. Wang Laboratories is now listed at the top of *Fortune*'s annual hit parade of the 10 *least* admired companies in America.

An Wang's family history is another tale of extreme hardship and deprivation. It is the story of a young boy growing up in China during a period of terrible upheaval. Both the Nationalist Guomindang led by Chiang Kai-shek, and the Chinese communists led by Mao Tse-tung, were battling for control of China. As if this was not enough, the Japanese invaded China during this time. The Chinese have given this period the very appropriate title of the Age of Confusion. As Wang would write later in his autobiography, the incessant fighting disrupted every aspect of his childhood.

During An Wang's early years, his father lived with the family only at weekends. Wang himself left home at the age of thirteen after having been admitted, because of his talent in maths and science, to a prestigious high school in Shanghai. He would never again live with his family, other than for brief visits. While he was living in Shanghai, the Japanese assaulted the city and massacred hundreds of thousands of Chinese. Wang was spared, as he lived in the nine-square-mile French concession, where he would spend his remaining years at college. Although he was relatively safe, the terrible circumstances in the rest of China must have caused an enormous amount of anxiety about his family, from whom he was separated. Unfortunately, his fears were justified. During his freshman year in college, he received word that his mother had died. A few years later he was informed that his father had been killed, and shortly after, his older sister. He would not see any of his remaining siblings for forty years. He later described his life under the Japanese occupation as extremely hard. Finally he was able to emigrate to the United States where he founded his company. Wang Laboratories was extraordinarily successful initially, but in the end, the company failed dramatically.[3]

These two stories are spectacular but not uncommon examples of the rise and fall of entrepreneurs. While other stories might be less dramatic and often limited to the successful part of the entrepreneur's endeavour, closer analysis of these various stories reveals that most of these tales of hardship and success contain a number of common, rather familiar, themes. We are usually introduced to a person with an unhappy family background, an individual who feels displaced and seems a misfit in their particular environment. We are also dealing with a loner, isolated and rather remote from even their closest relatives, a person who gives the impression of a 'reject', a deviant, a perception certainly not lessened by the frequently conflict-ridden relationships with family members. The environment is perceived as hostile and turbulent, populated by individuals who like to control and structure their activities. We observe an individual who utilizes innovative rebelliousness as an adaptive mode (with occasional lapses toward delinquency) and as a way of demonstrating an ability to break away, to show independence. But these reactive ways of dealing with feelings of anger, fear and anxiety do not relieve tension altogether, since 'punishment', in the form of failure, may follow suit. Failure is expected and success is often only perceived as a prelude to failure. Interrelated with this strange pattern of elation and despair, of successes and failures, we also observe a type of person who demonstrates a remarkable resilience in the face of set-backs. Entrepreneurs possess a great ability to start all over again when disappointments and hardships come their way.

The person we are describing, the entrepreneur, or the 'creative destructor' to use a term from Schumpeter,[4] is a highly complex individual, and is certainly not the simpleton or automaton which many economists would like us to believe. The entrepreneur is obviously not that 'lightning calculator of pleasures and pains', as Veblen once cynically described them[5] and bears no resemblance to that mythical mechanical creature of economic theory, the economic man. On the contrary, we are dealing with a very active individual, often inconsistent and confused about motives, desires and wishes, a person under a lot of stress, who often upsets us by seemingly 'irrational', impulsive activities.[6]

ENTREPRENEURIAL ROLES

Economists have always looked at entrepreneurs with a great deal of ambivalence. The often unpredictable, irrational actions of entrepreneurs have not fitted the economists' rational, logical schemes; they tended to disturb the implicit harmony of the economists' models. Generally speaking, the attitude of economists toward entrepreneurship has been one of 'benign neglect'. Baumol's exasperated statement that 'the theoretical firm is entrepreneurless – the Prince of Denmark has been expunged from the discussion of Hamlet'[7] is not far from the truth.

The term entrepreneur, derived from the French word *entreprendre*, to undertake, has been defined and redefined by historians, economists, and sociologists.[8] Forgetting conceptual niceties, students of entrepreneurship usually describe the entrepreneur as that individual instrumental in the conception of the idea of an enterprise and the implementation of this idea. In this process the entrepreneur fulfils a number of functions which can be summarized as the innovation, the management-coordinating, and the risk-taking functions.

The *innovation function*, particularly, has been emphasized by Schumpeter who stated that 'entrepreneurship.... essentially consists in doing things that are not generally done in the ordinary course of business routine'.[9] Schumpeter's entrepreneur is an idea person and a person of action who possesses the ability to inspire others, and who does not accept the boundaries of structured situations. These people are catalysts of change, able 'to carry out new combinations', instrumental in discovering new opportunities which make for the uniqueness of the entrepreneurial function.

Less spectacular but essential is *managing-coordinating* which is often regarded as a second function of entrepreneurship. Here the distinction between an entrepreneur and a business executive becomes blurred.[10] Some may even argue that the terms 'manager' and 'entrepreneur' are actually mutually exclusive. It raises the question of at what stage of an organization's development the more 'bureaucratically inclined' manager is likely to take over.

As a third function of entrepreneurship *risk-taking* is worth mentioning. This notion has particularly been promoted and developed by Knight who views the entrepreneur as the taker of non-quantifiable uncertainties.[11] But with the division of ownership and management, the use of resources other than the entrepreneur's personal capital, the entrepreneur can be considered more a creator of risk than a taker of it. Although the entrepreneur does not necessarily bear the financial risk of an operation, he or she is, however, exposed to a considerable degree of socio-psychological risk. More often than not a great decline in prestige and status income is a common phenomenon in the initial phase of entrepreneurship. The 'purgatory of entrepreneurship', i.e. the period preceding public recognition of one's entrepreneurship abilities, can be a time of extreme hardship during which considerable socio-psychological sacrifices have to be made. Naturally, a certain tolerance for economic risk is necessary but a tolerance for socio-psychological risks might be more important.

IDENTIFYING ENTREPRENEURSHIP

Testing entrepreneurial behaviour patterns

Empirical studies of the entrepreneurial personality have not brought us much further in understanding the particular behaviour patterns common to this individual. Most of these studies have not excelled in conceptual clarity. Not only is there a recurring confusion in definition of differences between entrepreneurs and executives but, in addition, many of these studies have focused exclusively on specific entrepreneurial sub-groups such as the high technology entrepreneur, or have concentrated on specific personality characteristics which might contribute to successfulness in company performance. Furthermore, the great diversity in test instruments has prevented or at least hampered the possibility of making more general comparisons. The psychological picture which has emerged in using a variety of personality tests on entrepreneurs has remained unclear. Some elements, however, have stood out. For example, it appears from these studies that particularly high achievement motivation is an important aspect in the entrepreneurial personality. In addition, autonomy, independence and moderate risk taking are contributing factors. The entrepreneur also emerges as an anxious individual, a non-conformist poorly organized and not a stranger to self-destructive behaviour. Although power motivation is important, the degree of power motivation varies and has an influence on effective leadership style. Entrepreneurs seem to be 'inner directed', are 'internals' on locus of control, present themselves as self-reliant, and tend to de-emphasize or neglect interpersonal relations. And finally, entrepreneurs possess a higher than average aesthetic sense which may contribute to their ability to set up 'new combinations'.[12]

Entrepreneurial types

It is very possible that entrepreneurs do not make up a homogeneous group. This notion has been emphasized by a number of researchers. For example, one researcher has suggested two different types of entrepreneur: the craftsman-entrepreneur and the opportunistic-entrepreneur.[13] The craftsman-entrepreneur is described as the individual narrow in education and training, low in social awareness and involvement, possessing a lack of competence in dealing with the social environment, and a limited or circumscribed time orientation. In contrast, the opportunistic-entrepreneur exhibits breadth in education and training, a high social awareness and involvement, a high confidence in dealing with the social environment, and an awareness and orientation toward the future. These two 'ideal' constructed types have been related to type of firm (defined as rigid versus adaptive). The craftsman-entrepreneur is supposed to build a more rigid firm while the opportunistic entrepreneur would create a more adaptive firm (rigidity and adaptability being dependent on customer and product mix, production methods, dispersement of markets and production facilities, and plans for change). A main discriminating factor between these two types seems to be education. Unfortunately, this typology seems overly simplistic. We have to get beyond this simple demographic differential. A more in-depth analysis of personal history and non-work environment is necessary to see if there are distinctly different personality patterns. Only then are we on more solid ground to explore the possibility of two different types.

Most of the efforts in distinguishing entrepreneurial types, however, have been directed at the spin-off, high technology, research and development (R&D), or technical entrepreneur.[14] The common background of this 'type' of entrepreneur is usually previous work experience in high technology organizations or universities. What characterizes entrepreneurship of this nature most of all is the higher tolerance for formal education (average education of Master of Science degree). In addition, we notice the regular incidence of entrepreneurial teams (a possible indication that interpersonal relations and need for control might be less problematic) for this suggested sub-group.

Although it is very possible that the R&D entrepreneur is distinctly different in personality make-up, insufficient evidence exists at this point and more research is needed. The relationship between the opportunistic and R&D entrepreneur is not yet very clear. The type construction can be questioned. Overlap in types is very likely and the question of other types can be raised.

Naturally, there is the possibility that a new type of entrepreneur is emerging: an individual who is better educated, not as impulsive, less concerned about control and independence and more adaptive to the environment. If this is a trend in entrepreneurship, its impact on existing large companies (as far as internal entrepreneurship is concerned, i. e. creation of new product ventures and new technology divisions in existing companies) could be enormous. Intrapreneurship, 'internal' entrepreneurship in large bureaucratic organizations, may be the inevitable response to organizational decay and inertia.

Socio-cultural elements

The hypothesis is also put forth that the possession of, and belief in, different value systems from that of the mainstream of society will contribute to the development of unconventional patterns of behaviour – entrepreneurship being one of them. Hagen, a student of social change, postulates a cycle of events which culminates in the emergence of the entrepreneurial personality.[15] In a society characterized by traditional values (as reflected in child-rearing practices) status deterioration of a particular segment of the population may cause a psycho-social disequilibrium leading to a situation of withdrawal of status respect and of self-esteem. Anger, anxiety and suppression of traditional values follow eventually, contributing to a state of retreatism for this particular group as reflected in the phenomena of normlessness, shiftlessness and anomie. This is an unstable state, however, and it may trigger off certain personality transformations. The existence of individuals who have gone through this process may be one of the contributing factors to the emergence of creative, innovative, entrepreneurial activity. These changes in personality can be explained by the fact that the old patterns of behaviour of social group and family are not respected and acceptable any longer; therefore new innovative modes have to be found to integrate the individual with society. According to Hagen four types of events can produce this process of status withdrawal:

1 displacement by force (i. e. by political upheavals and wars);
2 denigration of valued symbols (i. e. religion);
3 inconsistency of status symbols with changes of the distribution of economic power;
4 non-acceptance of expected status of immigrant groups.

We can observe repeatedly how members of minority groups are exposed to some form of discriminatory treatment which prevents them from obtaining one of the more established, usually higher status-bearing roles in society. As a consequence there is often no other choice open to these groups than doing something new, something which has not been done before.[16] New roles are created out of necessity since many existing occupations are closed or barred to these individuals. Immigrants and political refugees who also have to deal with changes in original status position obviously fall into this category. There are other types of minority groups suffering from displacement.

Besides the fact that entrepreneurs frequently come from ethnic, religious or some other form of minority group, there is another pattern which stands out. Many entrepreneurs come from families where the father or other significant caretaker has been self-employed in one form or another.[17] The vicissitudes of self-employment, its ups and downs, its turmoil and other psycho-social uncertainties can have a profound effect on the family situation and may influence career orientation at a later stage. The saying 'better the devil you know than the devil you don't' seems appropriate. It appears that in spite of the hardships so often experienced by significant care takers, children frequently follow their footsteps because, paradoxically enough, familiarity with the fact that obstacles, in some way, have to be overcome has an assuring quality. Moreover, frequent early exposure to risk may increase one's tolerance to it.

But these conditions do not necessarily make for entrepreneurship. We can only postulate that – given these special background factors – individuals originating from selected segments of society might have a greater disposition to developing entrepreneurial characteristics. We are not describing a causal relationship but probably only a part of a more complex phenomenon which contributes to the emergence of entrepreneurship. Changes in institutional patterns such as the legal and tax systems, infrastructure, technology, the political situation, resource availability and the existence of 'incubator organizations' such as found in Silicon Valley in California, route 128 in Boston, or Sophia Antipolis in the South of France, will be other important dimensions.

ENTREPRENEURIAL FAMILY DYNAMICS

In view of these frequently encountered general background factors of entrepreneurs and the importance of turbulence in the environment, it follows that the childhood of many of them is portrayed as a very disturbing experience. Discussions with male entrepreneurs are more often than not filled with images of endured hardships.[18] Desertion, death, neglect and poverty are themes which continue to be brought up in their conversations. And in these conversations facts and fantasies about hardship intertwine and become indistinguishable. This pattern seems to belong to entrepreneurial mythology and the entrepreneurs usually oblige. It is worth realizing that, as far as personality dynamics are concerned, the difference between perceived and real hardship is rather slim. For the impact on personality development it is perception that counts, even if distorted. Narrative truth not historical truth is what creates a psychological impact.

In these 'memories of things past' the father appears to be the main villain in the life history of male entrepreneurs. He is frequently blamed for deserting, manipulating, or neglecting the family. And death may be interpreted by a child as the ultimate form of desertion or rejection. What these conversations and study of life histories of entrepreneurs indicate is that a remote or absent

114

father makes for a poor role model for the child. The lack of familiarity and unpredictability of a remote father image leaves its scars in the developmental process. It may leave the child and later the adult troubled by a burdensome psychological inheritance centred around problems of self-esteem, insecurity, and lack of confidence. Repressed aggressive wishes toward persons in control are common and the resulting sense of impotency and helplessness contributes to these feelings of rage, insecurity and low self-esteem.

Given the nature of family dynamics, the absence or remoteness of the father image in the family is often complemented by the activities of the mother who assumes part of the father's role. In conversations with entrepreneurs their mothers usually come across as strong, decisive, controlling women who give the family at least some sense of direction and cohesiveness.

A CONCEPTUAL APPROACH

One way of looking at the family dynamics of entrepreneurs and their role in emerging career orientations is by using a simplified conceptualization of basic personality dimensions. Here, I am referring to the selection of the polarities high control–low control and acceptance–rejection attitudes expressed by parents toward their children.[19] The way parents relate to these dimensions becomes extremely important for later personality development. The eventual personality make-up of the adult will depend heavily upon the way in which these parental attitudes are emphasized and expressed by the parents and eventually assimilated and internalized by the developing child. Combinations of these personality dimensions lead to four possible configurations applicable to each parent. (Respectively: acceptance and high control; acceptance and low control; rejection and high control; rejection and low control.) Naturally, constitutional disposition, the existence of siblings, the nature and intensity of inter-sibling rivalry, the competition for parental affection, and the latters' reactions, add to the complexity of the dynamics of family life.

Consistency in childrearing assumes that parents will take a similar stand toward these personality dimensions. But, given each person's unique psychological make-up, this situation will be rare, in spite of the fact that generally accepted child-rearing practices encourage parents to make a concerted effort to appear as a 'closed front' to their children. But it is obvious from our previous discussion that the parents of entrepreneurs usually do not fall into that group which practices consistency in childrearing. At the risk of over-simplification, a possible configuration in the family of the potential entrepreneur (postulating a father who is remote or absent and a mother who is dominant but supportive) gives the impression of the father as low on control and basically rejective (in the child's fantasy world remoteness easily becomes synonymous with rejection) while the mother will be perceived as high on control and accepting. Naturally, the child's perception of the intensity of each dimension in respect of each parent will vary. And we can observe how, in spite of the limited integration of these perceptions by the child (the great dissonance between parental attitudes makes integration of the child's perceptions very difficult), some integration of these images will occur and be assimilated and internalized by the child. We hypothesize that, in the case of the potential male entrepreneur, a perception of high control and rejection usually becomes the predominant influence.

The lack of integration of these parental configurations, in addition to each parent's stand on these two personality dimensions, leaves the child with a feeling of inconsistency, confusion and frustration. On one hand, the child may submit to the control of the mother mainly with fear, anxiety and a sense of helplessness, while, on the other hand, the perceived rejection by the father is also resented and leads to aggressive retaliatory fantasies. A state of anger may be the legacy of this particular type of family dynamics, anger which may be directed toward the self or projected onto others, contributing to a sense of guilt and undermining self-confidence. In a later stage of personality development this tendency toward hostility and anger may injure relationships with peers.

What may also lead to retaliatory fantasies is a somewhat different scenario. In his rivalry with his father, the male child has obtained an 'Oedipal victory' having become the favourite of the mother and taken the place of the remote father. Being in this position, however, comes with a price attached in the form of an imagined fear of retaliation by the father for being displaced. Again this fear of retaliation may be transformed in ambivalence toward authority figures and paranoid tendencies.

In the instance that the predominant attitudes of parents are rejection and high control, the psychologist White (a researcher of longitudinal life histories) comments that:

When combined with rejection, high control still exerts a pressure for docile compliance but there is now a problem connected with hostility. Rejecting parents offer the child a meagre ration of love in return for his sacrifices of freedom. He submits mainly out of fear, and with resentment. A variety of consequences follow, which are easily understood as different dispositions of the hostility. This may be directed at the self, creating a sense of guilt that eats away at self-confidence and that sometimes plays a part in the development of neurosis. It may injure the relation to other children, promoting either a quarrelsome tendency or, to avoid this, a withdrawal from contact. It may produce half-hearted compliance with authority in which socialized behaviour is performed with sour resignation. It may be displaced to more remote objects such as outgroups seen as enemies of sound values. It may finally come into focus on the parents or on authority in general, producing a belated and often difficult rebellion.[20]

The combination of a dominant, controlling, somewhat nurturing mother and a remote father perceived as rejecting and somewhat threatening, can lead to problems in identity formation, and career orientation, a process accentuated by the general inadequacy or unacceptability of the prevailing role models. A person with this type of family background may experience difficulties as an adolescent in deciding upon an occupational identity. Consequently, rebellious activities will be quite common as a turnabout from originally half-hearted compliance toward authority figures. Confusion about career choice may not be temporary but may persist throughout life.

THE REACTIVE MODE

Before society at large recognizes his capabilities, the potential male entrepreneur enters a period of disorientation, without apparent goals, but also during which he is testing his abilities and ascertaining his strengths. The future entrepreneur drifts from job to job, encounters difficulties in the acceptance of his ideas, in conceptualizing and structuring possible 'new combinations'. He is perceived by other people as a 'deviant', a person out of place, frequently provocative and irritating because of his seemingly irrational, non-conformistic actions and provocative ideas.

117

Researchers of entrepreneurship such as Collins, Moore and Unwalla point out this non-conformist stand:

> The way of the entrepreneur is a long, lonely and difficult road. The men who follow it are by necessity a special breed. They are a breed who cannot do well in the established and clearly defined routes available to the rest of us. The road they can follow is one that is lined with difficulties, which most of us could not even begin to overcome. As a group they do not have the qualities of patience, understanding and charity many of us may admire and wish for in our fellows. This is understandable. In the long and trying way of the entrepreneur such qualities may come to be so much excess baggage. What is necessary to the man who travels this way is great imagination, fortitude, and hardness of purpose. The men who travel the entrepreneurial way are, taken on balance, not remarkably likeable people. This too is understandable. As any one of them might say in the vernacular of the world of the entrepreneur, 'Nice guys don't win'.[21]

Non-conformist rebelliousness becomes the entrepreneur's mode of behaviour, his way of exerting power and control over an environment perceived as dangerous and uncontrollable. The entrepreneur's actions do not derive from inner strength and self-assurance which a secure, consistent family upbringing would have provided. On the contrary, the confusing and disturbing family interactions frequently force the entrepreneur to react to situations out of inner insecurity. Optimism and resilience are the manifestations of a defensive reaction originating from a basic narcissistic conflict and become a form of characterological adjustment. Driving ambition may be viewed as a need to contradict strong feelings of inferiority and helplessness. Tangible achievements become the entrepreneur's way of telling the world that it should pay attention. Hyperactivity becomes a way of covering up passive longings. Passivity changes into activity as a reaction against anxiety.

The future entrepreneur *reacts* against the early demands imposed upon him by his family and immediate environment. If he originally perceives himself as being rejected, he will now counteract his helplessness, seize control, and do the rejecting himself. But it is behaviour not based on a secure sense of self-esteem and identity. No matter how strong his actions, doubt remains. Feelings of rejection, helplessness, and low self-esteem remain haunting issues.

The 'reactive mode' makes for a sense of impulsiveness whereby speediness, abruptness, and a lack of planning on a long-term basis determine the entrepreneur's actions. It is short-term, operational planning for the purpose of instant gratification which predominates and makes for success in actions. These people seem to possess a low tolerance for frustration and tension and a low attention span, seemingly in pursuit of immediate gains and satisfactions. For the entrepreneur the initial impression, 'the hunch', often becomes the final conclusion without a further serious search and deliberation process. There seems to be an absence of concentration, of logical objectivity, judgement, and reflectiveness as if the process of cognition is impaired and does not fulfil its integrative function. A lack of analytical thinking, an absence of active search procedures and self-critical reflections, becomes a predominant mode.

THE PARADOX OF SUCCESS

Thus, due to the frustrations and perceived deprivations experienced in the early stages of life, a prominent pattern among entrepreneurs appears to be a sense of impulsiveness, persistent feelings of dissatisfaction, rejection, and powerlessness, forces which contribute to an impairment and depreciation of their sense of self-esteem and affect cognitive processes. Many entrepreneurs are people under a great deal of stress, continuously badgered by their past, a past which is experienced and re-experienced in fantasies, daydreams, and dreams. These dreams and fantasies may have a threatening content due to the recurrence of feelings of anxiety and guilt which mainly revolve around hostile wishes against parental figures or, more generally, all individuals in a position of authority. Distrust and suspicion of everyone in a position of authority force the entrepreneur to search for non-structured situations where control and independence can be asserted. The entrepreneur is also an individual who tends to deny hostile wishes and projects these onto the outside world. Entrepreneurs are very quick in seeing others as enemies. And given their particular outlook, it is extremely hard, if not impossible, for individuals with an entrepreneurial disposition to integrate personal needs with those of organizations. To design their own organizations, to create and structure organizations centred around themselves, often becomes the only alternative.

The 'reactive mode' which characterizes entrepreneurial behaviour makes for a very unstable personality make-up. Since prestige, power, and self-confidence are used as reassuring weapons to deal with low self-esteem, inferiority, and related feelings of anxiety, any perceived depletion of these outward symbols may cause a psychological disequilibrium and trigger off impulsive reactions. If self-confidence is weak and inner hostility provokes guilt feelings, punishment is unconsciously expected. Any sign of failure means that expected punishment is at hand, any sign of success may be interpreted as an achievement not really deserved which again indicates that punishment is not far off. Although the entrepreneur fears failure, for some, the 'irrational', unconscious notion prevails that punishment is deserved, be it only for hostile wishes against authority figures. Using the same kind of logic, success only means that punishment will follow immediately and thus causes anxiety about future failures and punishments. Given the existence, at an unconscious level, of fear of success and fear of failure, combined with impulsivity of action and the absence of thorough deliberation and adjustment, it is not surprising that the careers of many entrepreneurs appear to be a remarkable succession of business successes and failures. Actually, because of this psychological process some entrepreneurs may feel at their best when they have reached 'rock bottom'. Their feelings of guilt being 'paid off', they are 'free', unburdened, able to start all over again.

We notice how many entrepreneurs emerge as psychological gamblers subjected to a high degree of psycho-social risks. Due to intra-psychic transformations, original feelings of helplessness, dependency and rejection are replaced by a proactive style in which power, control and autonomy become predominant issues. What used to be an inclination toward submission and passivity changes into an active impulsive mode of behaviour. The role of the passive, helpless victim is replaced by acting the role of the one in control.

We have indicated before that the often self-employed father was frequently an undependable and anxiety-provoking influence upon the young entrepreneur. Now the roles have changed; after having been continuously manipulated at an early age, the entrepreneur will do the manipulation him or herself and thus identify with the original aggressor. The entrepreneur will be reliving these actions as a form of mastery of these early frustrations and as a kind of 'protective reaction' against, first, his or her father and, later, authority figures in general. The inability to function in structured situations makes it necessary for the entrepreneur to design an organization where he or she is in control and at the centre of action. It becomes a way of obtaining narcissistic gratification. His achievements in setting up enterprises become important tangible symbols of prestige and power and a way of bolstering an easily depleted, unstable sense of self-esteem. But these achievements are not sufficient to ward off a persisting sense of anxiety and other stress indicators. Rejection, dissatisfaction, and a sense of failure follow the entrepreneur like an inseparable shadow. (A summary

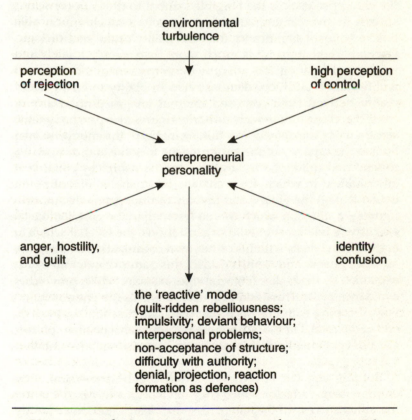

Figure 8.1 Psychodynamic forces influencing the entrepreneurial personality

of the various psychological forces working upon the potential entrepreneur is given in *Figure 8.1.)*

THE ENTREPRENEURIAL WORK ENVIRONMENT

We have indicated that the preparation period for many entrepreneurs is accompanied by authority conflicts, failures in organizational socialization, difficulties in adapting to organizational structure, and predictable job-hopping behaviour which sets the stage for the very unique relationship of the entrepreneur with his or her enterprise. Expectedly, the enterprise becomes the new setting where the entrepreneur's problems in adaptation and conforming to structure are accentuated and dramatized. Naturally, the enterprise itself is the tangible symbol to the entrepreneur of success in 'overcoming odds' and assumes a much greater symbolic emotional significance than the reality of the situation may warrant. The enterprise is much more than merely a vehicle for profit maximization; it is not only the entrepreneur's contact with reality but, in addition, demonstrates an ability to create a new reality derived from confused internal images centred around conflict and frustration with authority figures. In a psychodynamic sense – using the defence reaction formation – the enterprise symbolizes the capacity of the entrepreneur to solve and compensate for endured childhood frustrations and hardships by creating an environment in which, for a change, he or she is in control, not dependent on the whims and favours of undependable authority figures – a situation which was so resented in the past. Unlike the executive's relationship with organizations, the level at which an entrepreneur deals with his or her own organization is, therefore, far more intense and conflict ridden; this pattern cannot merely be explained by the higher financial risks at stake. While, previously, avoidance of structure and organizations was the entrepreneur's way of coping with life, his or her own organization becomes the end of the road. For the entrepreneur there seems no other place to go, a development which contributes a narcissistic investment in the enterprise.

But this very fact of complete psychological immersion of the entrepreneur – a factor which may have been a key ingredient in the initial success of the enterprise – can lead to serious dysfunctional developments in the future if the enterprise continues to grow. What we sometimes encounter in an entrepreneurial

122

organization is an organizational structure and work environment completely dependent on and dominated by the entrepreneur. In such a situation, the enterprise is run in a very autocratic, directive way whereby all the decision-making processes centre around the entrepreneur. We are faced with an individual who refuses to delegate, is impulsive, lacks any interest in conscious, analytical forms of planning, and engages regularly in bold, proactive moves. These impulsive actions were responsible for the initial successes and may have contributed to the continued success of the enterprise, but due to the absence of a conscious planning effort also carry a high risk component. The entrepreneur refuses to distinguish between operating, day-to-day decision making, and more long-term strategic moves. Furthermore, the impulsivity of this style, the lack of deliberation and judgement, and the importance of 'hunches' make for a rather limited time horizon. The entrepreneur has no sense of priorities and may spend as much time on the greatest trivia as on major strategic decisions.

Within such organizations, power depends on the proximity to the entrepreneur, who is constantly changing, and creates a highly uncertain organizational environment. This state of affairs contributes to a highly politically charged atmosphere where changing coalitions and collusions are the order of the day. As we have seen, folie à deux and paranoia are not uncommon in these organizations.

The suprastructure is poorly defined, a formal organization chart is outdated by the time it is drawn, or non-existent. The organization basically resembles a 'spider web' with the entrepreneur in the centre, constantly changing loyalties and keeping subordinates in a state of confusion and dependence. The organization usually has a poorly defined or poorly used control and information system (no sharing of information); there is an absence of standard procedures and rules and a lack of formalization. Instead, we notice the use of subjective, personal criteria for the purpose of measurement and control. Job descriptions and job responsibilities are inadequately defined or non-existent. This contributes to highly ambiguous situations which in turn contribute to stress reactions. Withdrawal or avoidance behaviour and a reduction in communication among employees also become symptomatic. Information hoarding turns into a common practice and contributes to the general state of disorganization. In addition, given the 'spider web' structure, the number of people reporting

Table 8.1 Entrepreneurial work environment

leadership style	autocratic directive
decision making	centralized lack of delegation impulsivity lack of conscious planning bold, proactive moves mixture of operating and strategic decision making
time horizon	short
power	proximity to entrepreneur
organizational environment	high uncertainty lack of sharing information prevalence of yes-men
suprastructure	poorly defined absence of formal organization chart 'spider web' structure
infrastructure	frequently poorly defined or poorly utilized control and information system absence of standard procedures and rules no formalized systems (use of subjective, personal criteria) poor integration of activities poorly defined job descriptions and job responsibilities (high degree of ambiguity) large horizontal span of control

to the entrepreneur will be large, adding to a general state of confusion. (See Table 8.1 for a summary of the dimensions of the entrepreneurial work environment.)

Although such entrepreneurs in the initial stage of development of the enterprise may have had the ability to inspire their subordinates, the mere fact of growth has complicated this process. Their aversion to structure, their preference for personalized relationships, and their reluctance to accept constructive criticism make growth, with its implicit need for a more sophisticated infra- and suprastructure and greater decentralization, increasingly difficult to handle. Hoarding of information, inconsistencies in day-to-day interpretation of company policies, playing of favourites, and refusal or reluctance to let people really know where they stand does not contribute to an efficient and effective organization. If this pattern becomes predominant and prevails, few capable subordinates will remain in the organization; the ones left will usually be of a mediocre calibre, spending a great part of their effort on political in-fighting. It is the absence of actual responsibility with authority which causes capable people to leave while the yes-men – individuals who do not really challenge the entrepreneur's authority – will stay on.

What we are describing is the potential danger of the entrepreneurial mode; that given the nature of the entrepreneur's conflicts and his peculiar leadership style – useful as these qualities might have been initially – growth may lead to the eventual destruction of the enterprise if the entrepreneur remains rigid in his attitudes and refuses to formalize the organization and change decision-making patterns. In case of continued growth of the enterprise, the effectiveness of the organization structure and the way of decision making become increasingly insufficient in coping with the complexities of the external environment.

For example, we can see how, in an organization such as Apple Computers, the reign of Steven Jobs became increasingly destabilizing, creating eventually a palace revolution leading to his exit.

The degree of environmental dynamism (change in technology, market behaviour, and competitors' reactions), heterogeneity (differences in needs and behaviour of organizational constituents), and hostility (cut-throat competition, resource shortages, etc.) determine how long the entrepreneur will be successful in pursuing the old style. Obviously, in a very static industry segment the strain on the organization is not so quickly noticeable. And while the time period may vary before the organizational strains become intolerable, utter disorganization, the increasing necessity of coping with the environment, and eventual financial losses frequently become the inevitable outcomes of the entrepreneur's leadership style. It is this obsession with control, the unwillingness or inability to 'let go', which eventually leaves a rather unpleasant inheritance behind with the word bankruptcy written all over it. But, as we have mentioned before, failure does not come as a surprise; somehow it has been expected by the entrepreneur.

SUCCESSION

Given the rigidity in attitudes and the inability to modify behaviour, abdication and succession is often the only alternative if the continued growth of the enterprise is a major goal, given the self-limiting nature of the entrepreneur's leadership style. But management succession is easier talked about than implemented if we take the emotional investment and symbolic meaning of the enterprise into consideration. Although, from a rational point of view, it may be better for both enterprise and entrepreneur if the entrepreneur distances himself and starts something new, from an emotional point of view this is not such an easy transition. Many rationalizations to prevent this type of transition are used by the entrepreneur. Usually, we will hear the argument that there is no one good enough to take over, a statement with the implicit message that there is no alternative for him but to stay on. The paradox of the situation is that the entrepreneur has created a work environment of high dependency. He has always looked at any potential infringement upon his position of power and control with suspicion, and therefore it is naturally highly unlikely that a capable administrator could have risen through the ranks, making his statements about the impossibility of stepping down a self-fulfilling prophecy.

Family members are certainly not excluded but are as suspect, or more so. They are easily labelled as possible intruders threatening the entrepreneur's position of control. The presence of family members seems only to intensify the eruption of conflicts over succession. The pre-eminence of folie à deux in family firms is indicative.

We can observe a confusion of roles between the social system of the family and that of the enterprise. At the base of these conflicts are feelings of rivalry, whereby the conflict-ridden attitude which the male entrepreneur possessed toward his parents is transferred toward his son. Daughters of entrepreneurs seem to have an easier time. In the case of sons, however, frequently a re-enactment of the old 'family romance' occurs, meaning that the son of the entrepreneur is exposed to the same treatment the entrepreneur feels he once endured. But now it is the entrepreneur who is in the position of authority and control and his son who is dependent on his whims, vulnerable to his erratic and unpredictable behaviour, and kept in an infantile position. That the idea of abdication, of stepping down, is resented by the entrepreneur has become obvious, but that succession by his son is even more resented and traumatic has now become less mysterious in view of the reliving of these old feelings of rivalry with their connotations of frustration and despair.

For example, Edsel Ford's relationship to his father, the first Henry Ford, is a good illustration of the abrasive dimensions these conflicts can reach and the destructiveness of this type of rivalry to the enterprise. Henry Ford's refusal to change strategy, to make alterations to the Model T, and his unwillingness to encourage Edsel Ford in his efforts to build a solid organizational infra- and suprastructure, brought the company to the edge of bankruptcy.[22]

Successful entrepreneurs who manage to guide the enterprise through the formative period of development into a stage of growth and maturity tend to follow a path which eventually may lead to their own functional self-elimination. They are people at the crossroads, enigmas, on one hand highly creative and imaginative, but, on the other hand, highly rigid, unwilling to change, incapable of confronting the issue of succession.

Succession becomes identified with loss and losing out and thus takes on the meaning of a taboo. But the issue of succession is inevitable, not only for reasons of age but also because of increasing maturation and growth of the company. The entrepreneur is no longer alone; other interest groups such as employees, family members, bankers, customers, suppliers, and the government are getting involved. The strength of the entrepreneur's position of power determines his influence on the policies of the enterprise. But change by this type of pressure is usually only of a modest character. A more drastic type of change is needed for continued growth and success of the enterprise apart from changes caused by old age or death. We imply here the attainment of a sense of psychological maturity on the part of the entrepreneur. This means a willingness to assess one's personal strengths and weaknesses, to master conflict-ridden behaviour and transcend the problems of the past. But adaptation to present-day reality and foregoing the legacies of personal history require considerable doses of self-awareness and insight. Important as this psychological state might be for the continued survival of the enterprise, for overcoming rigid behaviour, and for greater flexibility in operating modes, adaptation of this kind is rare and hard to attain. More often than not, involuntary separation from the enterprise by the entrepreneur in one form or another turns out to be the only alternative for the purpose of survival. This development highlights the depressive facet of the entrepreneurial dimension. While the entrepreneurial spirit is one of the strong countervailing forces preventing decay and decline of the economy as a whole, in the final deliberation the entrepreneur pays an extremely high price in an emotional sense in this process of economic growth.

9

THE MID-CAREER CRISIS: A RENEWED SEARCH FOR IDENTITY

Midway in our life's journey, I went astray from the straight road and woke to find myself alone in a dark wood. How shall I say what wood that was! I never saw so drear, so rank, so arduous a wilderness! Its very memory gives a shape to fear.[1]

Dante Alighieri

The crises of leadership become increasingly noticeable from mid-life onward. It is a period in time which introduces many frustrations and much discontent. The opening stanzas of the *Divina Comedia* exemplify the nature of the emotional experience of one man, in this instance portraying the poet Dante's sense of bewilderment about his life achievements and the feeling of loss, failure and disappointment about his past political career after his banishment from Florence. The poem presents a person in the pangs of a mid-life crisis, troubled with identity and career. The quotation illustrates the impact and significance of the mid-life transition and its vicissitudes.

At the age of 35 Dante reached the zenith of his political career. He was elected one of the six supreme magistrates of the city of Florence. Barely two years later, in 1302, his fortunes had turned. He was banished from his beloved native city and spent his remaining nineteen years largely with a series of patrons, roaming the various courts of Italy.

In *The Inferno*, his drama of a journey through hell, Dante tries to cope with this critical mid-point of his life and work through his distress and grief. The poem turns into a mystical journey of personal insights wherein the choices of life are evaluated. It becomes an effort to integrate past with present, to master feelings of anguish and disappointment about his political career and the hardships of life as an exile.

More than two hundred years after Dante's forced departure from Florence, a monk and young professor at the University of Wittenberg nailed to a church door ninety-five theses attacking the system of indulgences (an ingenious procedure suggesting the possibility of the accrual of credit in heaven) propagated by the Catholic Church. Through this symbolic act, Luther announced his break with Roman Catholicism and the beginning of his new career as church reformer and leader. A sense of moral indignation experienced as intolerable at mid-life drove him to the act which symbolizes the beginning of the Reformation.

Although Dante's and Luther's trials and tribulations are unique, as are the external events which expedited their sense of bewilderment, the experience of a mid-life and mid-career transition is not. It seems to be a universal experience varying only in intensity. Sceptics question its ubiquity and caution about the danger of a self-fulfilling prophecy: when you expect it, you may create it. Social indicators, such as health and marriage statistics, however, prove differently.

The study of mid-life and the coinciding mid-career passage indicates that it is a time of re-assessment when the executive must come to terms with past and future. The executive is beginning to become aware of boundaries set by retirement and death and starts to assess the realism of original dreams and achievements. As Jung commented:

Middle life is the moment of greatest unfolding, when a man still gives himself to his work with his whole strength and his whole will. But in this very moment evening is born, and the second half of life begins. Passion now changes her face and is called duty; 'I want' becomes the inexorable 'I must', and the turnings of the pathway that once brought surprise and discovery become dulled by custom. The wine has fermented and begins to settle and clear. Conservative tendencies develop if all goes well; instead of looking forward one looks backward, most of the time involuntarily, and one begins to take stock, to see how one's life has developed up to this point. The real motivations are sought and real discoveries are made. The critical survey of himself and his fate enables a man to recognize his peculiarities. But these insights do not

130

come to him easily; they are gained only through the severest shocks.[2]

This turning point usually starts around the mid-thirties and continues for a number of years; the exact length of time varies with the individual. The experience of a mid-life transition is very much tied into career. The notion of a mid-life career crisis is a closely related phenomenon, the point in life when the executive evaluates original career aspirations and choices and the degree to which these have been fulfilled. Mid-life passage here refers to a transitional period within a broader context, i.e. considering factors beyond the work environment. Mid-career transition is used more in the context of job and work.

A striking example of mid-life and mid-career crises is portrayed in Joseph Heller's book *Something Happened*.[3] This novel deals with the life of Bob Slocum, a middle manager in a large corporation. In a dispassionate way the principal character of the story describes his sense of failure, fatigue and boredom with his job, his inability to rebel, and his state of anxiety and fear about his career, the latter not only experienced by him but by most of his colleagues.

Bob Slocum is a man plagued by insomnia, headaches, nervousness and depression. On some occasions he even fears that he is losing his mind. Career problems are not his only worries; his marriage has reached rock bottom. His wife is unhappy and is becoming an alcoholic. He turns to extra-marital affairs, but these do not give him any real sense of satisfaction. Even his children are unhappy. His daughter is troubled by low self-esteem and suffers from depression while his little boy is having difficulties at school.

The story confronts us with the frightening portrait of an individual who is desperately unhappy about missed chances and opportunities. Slocum is an executive undergoing a period of stress. He is stuck in his job and frightened by the prospect of gradually turning into a 'living machine'. He is worried that he is changing into a robot, unable to feel real emotions, nor show any real involvement with family and work environment.

Slocum's story is an illustration of a maladjusted way of coping with mid-life and mid-career transition. It indicates how stressful the onset of the 'prime of life' can be. This situation is aggravated by it being the period of heaviest responsibilities. Men, as well as women, pass through a time of turmoil and unsettlement. For men, the term 'male climacteric' is occasionally used, for women this period is often considered to be tied in with the approaching menopause. Psycho-neurotic and psychosomatic tendencies become more noticeable. Divorce, health problems and incidence of death show a sudden peak. It is a time when careers are viewed in a different light. Goals and aspirations may turn into resignation or belated attempts at achievement.

Naturally, it is possible that the mid-career crisis is specially applicable to our achievement-orientated society, an unfortunate by-product of the 'Protestant Ethic'. Given limited room at the top, many executives have to be disappointed. Mid-career thus becomes the period where many a dream will be shattered. Although adaptation problems become more pronounced, there are, however, many executives who show very few signs of stress and adjust well to the pressures of this critical period in their career.

THE MID-STAGE OF LIFE

We can look at a person's life as a series of stages with critical turning points when decisions have to be made about developmental tasks, life goals, values and career orientation. In using the concept of stages of human development we make the assumption of progressive, sequential changes of patterns of behaviour and functions during the life cycle. For that reason, stage theory becomes probably most applicable to childhood. It is during that period that there exists a close relationship between physical and mental developmental processes. It is also a period during which the basic criteria of stage theory, the need for sequence, universality and purpose are more easily met. In adulthood, these relationships become more tenuous because of the increasing complexity and influence of the external psycho-social environment. In spite of its limitations, however, stage theory does give us some insight into the dynamics of adult development and the problems associated with mid-life and the mid-career crisis.

Bühler was an early investigator of the life cycle concept.[4] She views the human life cycle as a curve of expansion and contraction analogous to biological patterns of increase and decrease of functions, represented by a progressive growth phase, a period of stability, and a phase of decline. She suggests that in the first part of their lives, people are concerned with the enlargement of opportunity; then a plateau will be reached and, eventually, a period of restriction will set in.

After reviewing about three hundred biographies, she discerns five stages in the life course. The mid-career period is the stage during which individuals examine their careers to determine to what extent they have achieved their life goals. Frenkel-Brunswik, building on Bühler's work, mentions the culmination period of life succeeding the period of definite choice of vocation and establishment of a home.[5] It is at this point that an executive enters the most fruitful and productive period of life. She mentions that the transition from the culmination period to the next stage is usually accompanied by psychological crises, symptomized by a renewal of unrest such as wanderlust and frequent change of residence. In addition, she indicates a transitory inclination toward daydreaming and loneliness.

One of the best known researchers of the human life cycle probably has been Erikson.[6] In his models of eight life stages, the last three stages comprise adulthood. The stage of generativity placed in contrast to stagnation has the closest association with the critical period of mid-life and mid-career. This stage turns into a crisis about the meaningfulness of life. Generativity becomes 'the concern in establishing and guiding the next generation' and will include 'such popular synonyms as productivity and creativity, which, however, cannot replace it'.[7]

The sense of generativity is critical for organization and society. There comes a time when it is necessary to devote resources and energy to the development of the younger executive to assume continuity of organizational processes. When generativity fails, psychological and organizational stagnation follow. Executives heavily involved in the pursuit of personal satisfactions and glory have no time to care for others and fail in their interpersonal relationships.

Levinson and his associates have focused on the adult stages of man and refer to the mid-life transition, the bridge between early adulthood and middle adulthood.[8] Levinson views this stage (which he positions between the ages of 40 and 45) as the turning point in a person's life since it delineates the period during which the individual moves from the apprentice role to the role of the expert. Three major tasks are worked on during that period: a reappraisal of the past, a modification of life structure, and the process of individuation (more definite establishment of boundaries between self and world). A sense of independence is acquired from other significant adults such as father, superior, or mentor. Mentors are likely to have particular influence over executives when they are in their twenties and thirties. During this period, mentors are guides and advisers in the world of work – then the time comes for independence. For Levinson, the mid-career transition is a

> matter of goodness of fit between the life structure and the self. . . He [the person] is having a crisis to the extent that he questions his life structure and feels the stirring of powerful forces within himself that lead him to modify or drastically to change the structure.[9]

After the mid-life transition, a period of stabilization sets in.

When we move to the realm of vocational studies we can also find the concept of developmental stages, but here more focused upon career paths. For example, Super has distinguished five stages whereby he takes career as the central concern, it being a symbolization of self-concept and the realities of the work environment.[10] In his conceptual scheme, the period of establishment becomes crucial. During this time the executive is modifying or implementing his self-concept depending upon how he deals with the opportunities and requirements offered in his work environment. From there, the executive will move on to a maintenance stage. Other researchers such as Schein also recognize a maintenance stage attained after the trials and hardships of mid-career when the executive makes a final attempt to test his or her field of work.[11]

All these theories have the common view that mid-life and mid-career is a period of turmoil and disruption, preceding the stabilization of middle age. They also point at possible dilemmas in the transition process. Finally, they present the notion of sequence, progression, and, possibly, fixation and regression.

THE COMING OF MIDDLE AGE

When individuals reach the mid-point of their lives a number of changes occur.[12] Although the environment still seems full of opportunities, the preoccupation with inner life becomes more important. There is a greater sense of introspection, self-evaluation and reflection. We notice an existential questioning of self, values and life. There is a sudden awareness that we are growing older, that more than half of our lives has already been lived. For some, this leads to a sense of depression, for others it will heighten the commitment to make life more meaningful.

Physical changes that may be uncomfortable are occurring. We notice the concern with 'body monitoring', the urge to keep the middle-aged body at given levels of performance. For women, the menopause becomes an approaching reality; men experience a reduction in the sexual drive.

Taking stock has come and with that a restructuring of time. The future is no longer of unlimited duration. Life is viewed in terms of time-left-to-live instead of time-since-birth. The decline of the body and death of friends of the same age group are contributing factors. Little time seems left to shape the behaviour of the children. A sense of urgency arises to impart values to them with which we can feel comfortable. There exists a general perception of losing control and the realization that the mistakes in child-rearing are taking a more definite form and becoming irreversible.

In a larger social context, the realization dawns upon us that we are fulfilling the role of 'bridge' between the older and the younger generation. The young become distant and the old close. Executives at mid-life are suddenly realizing that they are being responded to as full-fledged adults, as grown-ups or authorities by the younger management generation. We notice that the reference group is becoming the peer group. A movement from 'player' to 'coach' is noted by the deference accorded in work and social interactions. Parents will be perceived in a different light. It is as if a role reversal takes place as they become more dependent on their children. Many executives at mid-life perceive the changes happening to their parents as a harbinger of what will happen to themselves. All these transformations can be very anxiety provoking, creating fantasies of being unprotected, of feeling left alone and becoming a target. We are referring to the work disorder success or promotion depression.

Life line and career line are closely compared, which makes for a sense of being 'early' or 'late' on the 'career clock'. There seems to exist a prescriptive timetable for the ordering of major events such as marriage, children and, particularly, career. Some executives begin to realize that a plateau has been reached in their careers.

The coming of middle age can be a period of optimum capacity in handling a highly complex environment, a consequence of a previous build-up of learning capacity which has given the executive a better grasp of the realities of life and increased control over impulse.

A critical element of the onset of middle age becomes the need to come to terms with accomplishments and, at the same time, to accept the responsibilities which accompany achievements. For many, this is the time which brings a greater readiness and willingness to take responsibility for actions and decisions. For some, there is a fear of aging and an over-responsiveness to social norms. This can lead to a conflict between perceived freedom, limiting social constraints and personal potential, the latter acquired over time. For a number of people this will cause a profound and disturbing crisis. As Jung once said, 'the wine of youth does not always clear with advancing years, sometimes it grows turbid.'[13]

THE MID-LIFE CRISIS

The term mid-life crisis was probably coined by the British psychoanalyst and organizational sociologist Elliott Jaques.[14] It is the crisis which predates the coming of middle age. Jaques found, in studying the histories of creative artists, that the age of 35 figured prominently in the lives of these individuals. He discovered a sudden jump in the death rate between the ages of 35 and 39, a rate which returned again to a lower level in the late forties. Jaques attributed this anomaly in death rates to the sudden realization of the inevitability of one's own personal death which many experience as a period of psychological disturbance causing a depressive breakdown.

In addition, Jaques felt that there was a significant difference in the creative work of the artists studied, depending on the time period during which their work was produced. He distinguished between the 'hot-from-the-fire', more intense, spontaneous form of creativity of the twenties and early thirties, versus the more mature, 'sculpted' creativity of the later stages of life when breadth of experience begins to count.

The notion that creativity is not only an early life phenomenon, but continues to appear later in life has been supported by various studies.[15] For all groups studied (and that included the social and the natural sciences and the arts) the most productive decade was the age of 40 to 49; if not, the record was only a little below that of the peak decade. Creative people in the arts and literature tended to be more productive in their twenties and thirties compared to social and natural scientists.

Mid-life crisis and the problems associated with mid-career are phenomena not limited to creative artists, scholars and scientists. For most people the transition to the maintenance stage of their career means exposure to a multitude of forces and pressures which makes this period such a trying one.

A survey conducted by the California Institute of Technology of over a thousand middle-aged men in professional and managerial positions revealed that five out of six managers or professionals had gone through a period of intense crisis which started as early as their late thirties. Moreover, one man in six never fully recovered from this crisis.[16]

This sense of crisis can be brought about by a number of incidents: a physical event such as change in appearance (baldness, wrinkles, paunches etc.), or menopause in women, or sexual problems, or a breakdown in health. It can also be caused by psycho-social transformations such as marital strife, disappointments with children, or the after effects of the children leaving the home; it can be career trouble such as disappointment with advancement, awareness of having made the wrong career choice, attainment of a career plateau, demotion, or termination of the job.

How these events are experienced depends upon the individual. We usually observe that crisis at mid-career is the recognition of the limitations of life in general, of one's own life and abilities, and of one's physical and psychological potential. A sense of regret is experienced about what has not been done rather than what has been done. But whatever psychological processes take place, at the core seems to be the realization of mortality (the eventual coming of one's own death), in combination with the awareness of the loss of capacity to reproduce.

Three major categories of problems occur at this critical point in life: difficulties with marriage, career and health. These problems can be looked at as social indicators pointing out a person's strength in adaptation.

MARRIAGE PROBLEMS

Marianne, one of the marriage partners in Ingmar Bergman's film *Scenes from a Marriage* asks her ex-husband Johan:

Why did things turn out like this? What went wrong? When did the children get bored with you? When did you get bored with them? What became of all the love and solicitude? And all the joy?[17]

Johan's reply is:

We are emotional illiterates. And not only you and I – practically everybody – that is the depressing thing. . . We're abysmally ignorant, about both ourselves and others. . . it doesn't dawn on anyone that we must first learn something about ourselves and our own feelings. Our own fear and loneliness and anger. We're left without a chance, ignorant and remorseful among the ruins of our ambitions.[18]

At mid-life Johan and Marianne experience a sense of flatness, a lack of joy, a feeling that their lives are 'mapped out into little squares', confined. Johan sees himself as a failure in his career and his marriage. His extra-marital affair becomes his last fling, his attempt to escape and break the monotony and flatness of his life. Unfortunately he fails. In spite of his divorce and remarriage, the sense of meaninglessness hangs on.

Problems centred around marriage are myriad at mid-life. We can give as one explanation that individuals develop, grow and change at a different pace. At mid-life they start to become aware of these differences. Marital breakdown and social isolation is a common occurrence at this time. Mid-life seems to be a period when marriages start to go flat and fall apart. For example, in a study of American middle-class families, it was found that there were very few good man-woman relationships at mid-life. The predominant type of family was devitalized, numb, apathetic, or just getting along adequately.[19] We may hypothesize that the fit which made for the original marital choice seems to deteriorate over time because of the psychosocial and physical changes to which the marital partners are subjected. This creates a situation of increased dissatisfaction and disenchantment in the later years of marriage.

Marital dissatisfaction seems to be most severely felt by middle-aged women [20] (though we should keep in mind that many of the studies that come to this conclusion refer to women in traditional households, rather than to women who have followed a career). That this is the case is not surprising given the changes to which the middle-aged woman is subjected. The social norms stressing beauty and youthful appearance, a husband who is becoming less attentive, combined with the loss or upcoming loss of reproductive capacity, all put a lot of pressure on these women. The 'empty nest syndrome' will be another factor of influence in overall mental health. When the children start their own independent lives the parents feel less needed and experience a deeper sense of aging.

It is also a period when marital fidelity becomes a problem; adulterous activities are common. It can be seen as an often desperate attempt at some form of revitalization. For men, the new, 'trophy wife', may come onto the scene. In many cases, declining sexual interest in the marriage partner is a contributing factor.

In the traditional family marriage usually implies to women a belated resolution of the crisis of identity (symbolized by a change in name). It indicates the establishment of a sense of intimacy with the marriage partner, particularly since, in traditional households, occupational choice has been highly tentative until that time, dependent as it has been on courtship, marriage and family life. It is only at the verge of middle-age that employment and career become concerns. In these instances, for men, the situation is quite different because of the usually greater vocational commitment. Marriage is important, but does not have that exclusive connotation.

'Rehearsal for widowhood' and increased concern over the health of the husband is not unusual after the launching of the children. And there is an element of reality to these concerns. One British study indicated that at the ages of 40 to 44 married women with husbands outnumber the widowed and divorced by nineteen to one. At the age of 55 this ratio falls to less than five to one.[21]

After the children leave home or reach school age there will be a surge of married women going back to work. Many of them do so with much more energy and enthusiasm than can be said for their husbands who may be suffering from occupational burn-out. The launching of children can also make for a new sense of relaxation. It may enable the couple to spend more time together. This can be either a burden or a new opportunity for increased closeness and marital satisfaction. Actually most studies indicate that marital happiness and contentment increase with age; it seems that the marriage partner, after a mid-life low period, becomes more valued at a later stage in life.[22]

Frequently, the cessation of the parenting function seems to leave a vacuum and demands a major reorientation of purpose and goals. The behaviour of the adolescent child may have made a critical impact on marital relations. In many cases, it evokes memories of one's own adolescent turmoil and conflicts over life's purpose and goals.

A number of delayed divorces may occur, delayed because the couple may have decided earlier in life to wait until the children were grown before dissolving a basically unsatisfactory relationship. We can also observe how after the launching of the children a renewed interest in friends and social activities may occur. During mid-life the level of extra-familial relationships has usually been rather limited.

Renegotiation may be needed in the husband–wife role at the mid-life point. This may be provoked by an often vague feeling by both marriage partners at this time that something is missing in their lives. As we have indicated before, because of a combination of pressures, at this point in time women more than men have the tendency to look at the future as something bleak, empty, out of their control. Feelings of unhappiness, psychosomatic complaints and thoughts of suicide are frequent. This, however, as we have stated, is usually a temporary state and after the mid-life transition has been worked through, marital satisfaction usually improves for both marriage partners.

There is an element of irony in the fact that after the mid-life crisis has passed satisfaction with life for most women is on the upswing. While satisfaction with life for women was at its all-time low during this period, men reach this point in their sixties and seventies when retirement comes accompanied by a great sense of meaninglessness and futility. For women, from the mid-life transition onward, a sense of renewed usefulness comes with involvement in a new career, pursuance of a discontinued career, or through the pleasures of the grandmother role.[23]

Belated self-actualization can come through the reversal of traditional sex roles. The partners may feel less constricted by the prescribed social roles which were originally needed to fulfil a particular task requirement. Men may become more supportive, more 'feminine', possessing a greater willingness to express feelings and emotions, while women may become more aggressive, less sentimental and more 'masculine', feeling less guilty about egocentric inclinations.[24] Perhaps acceptance and security of competency in one role will lead to experimentation and trial of new ones; the outcome may be a moderate degree of role reversal. But even these reorientations are not without conflict because they imply a tendency toward more symmetrical arrangements, often necessitating reluctant compromise and change.

CAREER PROBLEMS

As executives get more settled in their careers, a timetable of expectations evolves, tracking progress in working life. On this 'career clock', we find critical points such as possible dates of advancement, peak productivity periods, highest earning-power, and retirement. By positioning themselves on the career clock, executives are constantly assessing their progress over the career life cycle and evaluating if they are ahead or behind schedule.

Careers can be a major source of stability but, as we have seen, also a major source of frustration. Career plateaux are the natural consequence of the organizational funnel, particularly in periods of limited growth. The inevitable consequence is that most executives will come to some form of a halt in their career. From mid-career onward management by ambiguity becomes more prominent.

For some executives, mid-career brings the feelings of being burned out, of boredom with the job, and a sense of being trapped, the latter mainly for financial reasons. Financial burdens are usually greatest in middle age. The price for maintaining social obligations and personal possessions is the feeling of being locked in. It is the period when not only the younger and older family members have to be taken care of, but, in addition, provisions have to be made for one's own retirement and old age. Rigid responsibilities, obligations and duties make for a perception of lack of options and a sense of frustration.

Sofer found in his study of men at mid-career that the middle group of his sample (ages 35 to 44) was the least satisfied with their work of all age groups studied.[25] What this group of executives frequently did was to resort to some form of rationalization to accept a situation which was perceived as unsatisfactory. Some individuals tended to blame others for their situation or would adopt a defeatist attitude to be prepared for 'the worst'. A few would leave the organization.

Mid-career often brings professional obsolescence. If people experience a sense of achievement in the attainment of their career

141

aspirations, they make a strong effort to stay abreast of current developments. If that sense of achievement is absent, and instead a sense of personal frustration and failure prevails, rapid obsolescence is often the consequence. It seems that, from a relative state of obsolescence at the entry point of career, executives become progressively more up-to-date until the mid-thirties when this trend starts to reverse. Naturally, apart from direct obsolescence effects, behaviour of frustrated, dissatisfied executives can cause deterioration of organizational morale and productivity.

In a positive vein, modern Western societies yield power and leadership to the middle-aged. They represent norms and make decisions, sources of gratification and fulfilment. Many of the more successful executives will look forward to this time. For many women, seeking replacement activities after having been preoccupied with children, the opportunity to begin or continue a career comes as a revelation.

HEALTH PROBLEMS

Many physical abilities decline by the time an individual reaches his or her forties, e.g. lung capacity, eyesight, hearing, strength of grip, and particularly for men, sexual ability. This seems like a grim picture. The total outlook, however, is not completely a pessimistic one, since an important matter such as mental ability will hold up and can actually improve with time.[26]

Mental dullness often seems to be caused by lack of stimuli, not the decline of mental ability. This observation points to the need to prevent 'rut formation', a behaviour pattern which may cause dogmatism and rigidity. Mental flexibility particularly becomes an issue at mid-career since the individuals now have reached, or are getting close to, attaining the peak in their career. For some people success may result in having a fixed opinion about most matters. This tendency may be accompanied by an unwillingness to consider different patterns of thought and action. For others, failure may cause a similar reaction. We notice the relationship with career obsolescence.

Career path is very closely linked to stressful experiences and satisfaction with life. In one study, almost 50 per cent of the men questioned reported that changes in life satisfaction were attributable to work in contrast to women where children appeared to be the principal focus of stress.[27] For men, excessive goal-striving behaviour and frustration because of failure to reach set goals seemed to contribute to the etiology of stress symptoms.

Women reported many symptoms associated with attitudes and changes related to the menopause. For men, there exists no evidence for a comparable physical change. The term 'male climacteric' is really a misnomer. For women this physical change is a reality. Menopause often plays a 'catch-all' role comprising a large number of physical and emotional disturbances. Many of the problems associated with the menopause seem to have a psychosomatic or psycho-neurotic origin.

We have to realize that the menopause is a significant symbolic event for women at the later part of the mid-life period. For some, it comes with a sense of personal achievement and satisfaction with child-rearing and other activities. The menopause is viewed by these women with a sense of anticipation and as an indication of the end of the child-rearing years. They now look forward to a new period when energy can be redirected.

Some women fail to acquire this sense of generativity. For them menopause means growing old. Some seek to grasp missed opportunities vicariously through their children. Others experience bitterness and a sense of stagnation which may be accompanied by psycho-neurotic and psychosomatic symptoms.

Sexuality can, particularly for men, become a major concern at mid-life. Impotence is not uncommon. In most instances of chronic impotence psychological, rather than organic causes, have been found. Excessive alcohol intake, drugs, fatigue, anxiety and overwork seem to be major contributing factors.

Common psycho-neurotic or psychosomatic patterns of illness at mid-life are heart neurosis, headache, backache, feelings of tiredness and obesity. Research by the cardiologists Friedman and Rosenman indicates that mid-life is the time when heart troubles begin, particularly for the hard-driving, ambitious, frequently overworked executive.[28] Increased tension of the job is reflected in a rising number of executives with high blood pressure.

In conjunction with 'body monitoring' and the awareness of physical changes, hypochondriasis may emerge. There exists a tendency to fall back on ill health as a way to avoid serious problems in career and family life. Apparently, failure in career due to ill health is more palatable than failure caused by an inability to perform. For men, hypochondriacal concerns tend to peak around thirty years of age, for women around forty. The upsurge of hypochondriasis for women at this age is probably due to associ-ations with the menopause. In the case of phobic reactions and hypochondriasis, the most important at mid-life is cancer (which has some base in reality, given its increasing frequency). In this context, we can postulate that concern about death and about the ability to sustain social and sexual roles aggravated by the first deaths among the peer group provoke fear of disease.

Insomnia is another serious problem of the middle years. The impairment of the ability to sleep, accompanied by a preoccupation with anxiety and guilt, may be considered signs of a mid-life depression. Insomnia and depression are particularly prevalent among the hard-striving, frustrated executives, the ones most af-fected by a mid-career crisis. The realization by the executive that the original enthusiasm about his or her life's work has been unwarranted plays a role in the etiology of these stress symptoms. Other indicators of depression are thoughts of self-denigration, pessimism, loss of interest, lack of motivation and a decrease in efficiency and concentration. Concurrently, we may observe a neglect of personal appearance, mood swings (agitation), loss of appetite and weight, and suicidal thoughts. Manic depression is not uncommon.[29]

It is also worth mentioning that figures from the US National Center for Health Statistics indicate that accident proneness seems to be highest among the 35–44-year-old group.[30]

There exists a steady climb in mental hospital admissions with advancing age. Sexual insecurity, frustration, realization of lack of occupational success, and fear of death seem to be contributing factors to these cases of mental illness. We observe a comparatively high incidence of mental breakdown of supposedly 'normal' people at middle age when on vacation or away from home, or immediately after return, raising questions about the traditional advice to go on vacation as a way of coping with depressive anxiety.

WAYS OF DEALING WITH THE MID-LIFE CRISIS

At mid-career, executives are likely to have their first 'face-to-face', their first confrontation with themselves. They will not only take account of what they have done, but what they have not done. Personality factors in combination with external circumstances will determine their style of coping with this mid-life review, in particular their way of dealing with career and marriage. Some executives will adjust badly. Types of stress symptoms manifested will be a function of coping style, e.g. both depressive reactions or over-activity contributing to the incidence of heart attack can be responses to the feeling of being trapped due to obligation and failed aspirations.

For the purpose of further clarification of ways of coping with the mid-life and mid-career passage, we will isolate two dimensions (in the form of polarities) representing the executive's orientation to the external world. The first polarity is the activity–passivity dimension indicating the pattern of activity and sense of dynamism with which the executive relates to the outside world. The second dimension represents the degree of reality with which the individual interprets and perceives his or her environment. Some executives accept reality – as disturbing as it might be – and deal with substantive issues. Others have not attained this more mature psychological state and may resort to regressive, ritualistic, or distorted activities as a way of avoiding painful experiences. We call this polarity 'the reality' versus 'the distorted' orientation.

By combining these two dimensions we arrive at four major

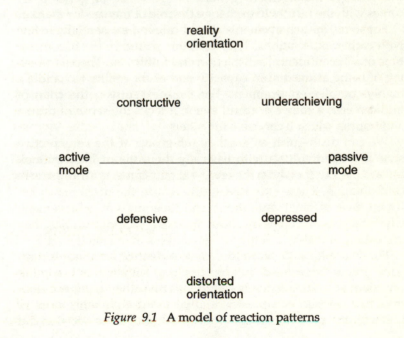

Figure 9.1 A model of reaction patterns

145

styles with which these executives interact with their environment (see *Figure 9.1*).

These styles are respectively

1 the constructive
2 the underachieveing
3 the defensive
4 the depressed.

We should keep in mind that these conceptualizations present 'ideal types'. Our objective is clarification. In real life, the simultaneous manifestation of more than one style by one individual is not uncommon.

Constructive style

Some executives are willing to engage in realistic stock taking and have the ability to restructure their experiences with new information and learning. These executives possess a sense of heightened reflection which comes with increased insight. They are able to share resources, skills and creativity to aid in the development of the younger management generation. A sense of generativity comes with the faculty to exchange the role of mentee for mentor.

For some, the achievements at mid-career are essentially in line with earlier expectations. Therefore this period in life becomes a time of self-confidence, satisfaction and fulfilment. There is a feeling of being at maximum capacity and of the ability to handle a highly complex environment. For these executives, the crisis of mid-career is a rather peaceful event; it lacks the sense of drama and trauma which it can have for others.

We can distinguish as another sub-group of the constructive style those individuals with basically the same realistic outlook toward life, but for whom the review at mid-career is a more severe confrontation. These executives now realize the discrepancy between their original aspirations and their present achievement. Given their sense of realism about abilities and opportunities, they are willing and able to settle for less success than anticipated.

For example, a 45-year-old vice-president of an apparel company gradually realized that her life-long ambition of becoming president was unrealistic. Over the years two other younger executives had reached vice-presidential positions with skills more in line with the present company needs. Although the decision did not come as a surprise to her, she was still disappointed when the president told her that she would appoint one of these two as her successor. But she understood the rationale of the decision and was able to deal with it emotionally. Soon after the new president was appointed, she could be seen devoting most of her energy to assisting the new woman in overhauling the overall company strategy. In addition, she began to fulfil a senior statesperson role at the meetings of the executive committee where her advice was eagerly sought, thus increasing her effectiveness and benefiting the organization.

This example illustrates that individuals belonging to this group might have the ability to face reality, even in the face of setbacks. Moreover, individuals who adopt this style possess the psychological strength and maturity to work through their feelings of disappointment with a minimum of bitterness while modifying their original aspirations. A sense of generativity and of concern for the next generation are integral parts of the behaviour of this group.

In addition to the two sub-groups mentioned previously, we can discern two other forms. Again, the term 'constructive style' is applicable, although the way of dealing with mid-life and mid-career crisis is more dramatic for these groups. Here we find executives who may decide on a career change.

The first group can be described as relatively successful in their careers but without the expected sense of satisfaction. The mid-life review comes with an emotional letdown described so well by Nietzsche as 'the melancholia of everything completed'. The opening lines of Goethe's *Faust* express these feelings perfectly:

Philosophy have I digested,
The whole of Law and Medicine,
From each its secrets have I wrested,
Theology, alas, thrown in
Poor fool, with all this sweated lore,
I stand no wiser than I was before.[31]

In spite of his success as a scholar and scientist, Faust dealt with his restlessness, his sense of meaninglessness and distress at mid-career by closing a pact with the messenger from hell, Mephistopheles. In this way he hoped to attain a greater knowledge of the meaning of things and break the stalemate in career experiences.

As another example of career change, we can name the group of executives who begin to realize that they have been building castles in the air, that they will never meet their original aspirations in their present careers. They ask themselves if their original career choice was a wise one. If they conclude that their choice was wrong, this group is willing to take the consequences.

For example, at the age of 35, Gauguin decided to end his career as a stockbroker's clerk and devote his life to painting. The decision did not imply a complete change since he already had previous experience as an amateur painter. With this break (he was soon unable to support wife and children) his life as a wanderer began, leading to his eventual fame as a painter of Tahitian people and landscapes. In 1890, one year before his first departure to Tahiti, he wrote to his wife: 'May the day come, perhaps very soon, when I'll bury myself in the woods of an ocean island to live on ecstasy, calmness and art. With a new family, and far from that European struggle for money.'[32]

Gauguin made a complete break and moved from one career to another in a fundamentally different field. This is, however, rather an unusual phenomenon. Transfers to different departments within one organization or transfers to another organization (in the same area or a related area) are far more common. In most cases (and Gauguin is no exception), if a total career change takes place, the individual has already tested the requirements for success in the new field thoroughly and possesses the necessary skills and experiences. Executives who belong to one of these four sub-groups making up the constructive style show the highest degree of adjustment in coping with the mid-career transition and the least amount of stress symptoms. They possess a sense of generativity, a genuine concern for the next management generation. And they will be the executives who become the backbone of organizations, assuring continuity and growth.

Underachieving style

Some executives look at the environment in basically a realistic way but possess a more passive mode in relating to the outside world. These can be called the underachievers. These persons have no high aspirations and are easily satisfied. Their lives seem to be without turmoil; they do not 'rock the boat'. In these cases it may be an exaggeration to talk about a mid-career crisis. Most of their interests seem to be directed toward activities outside their work environment. Mid-career passes without drama. We can assume that these individuals comprise a large group in organizations.

The hero of Hašek's famous novel *The Good Soldier Svejk* is a person belonging to this category.[33] He is Mr Everyman who is continuously caught up in the wheels of bureaucracy, keeping a low profile, reacting to situations, making the best of things. He has simple desires and is basically very satisfied with life. His underachiever's style makes for his great resilience.

Hašek often resorts to caricature in describing the adventures of Svejk, as, for example, in describing Svejk's responses to an interrogation. When asked what he is thinking about, he says:

> Humbly report, I don't think because that's forbidden to soldiers on duty. When I was in the 91st regiment some years ago our captain always used to say, 'A soldier mustn't think for himself. His superiors do it for him. As soon as a soldier begins to think he's no longer a soldier but a dirty, lousy civilian. Thinking doesn't get you anywhere'.[34]

Not only does this particular response serve a comical purpose, but it also points at some salient features of the underachieving style. These individuals may be passive and unambitious, but they possess a great sense of realism and personal insight into their own strengths and weaknesses. But we will certainly not find any *conquistadores* or robber barons among them. Their low profile, their lack of organizational participation, and the absence of achievement make for a high incidence of obsolescence. Many executives among this group would be considered 'plateauees', 'shelf sitters', or 'retirees on the job'. In spite of career stagnation and lack of career progression, these executives seem reasonably satisfied, accept their present status, and usually show few stress symptoms. Only a dramatic event, such as dismissal, will interrupt this tranquil state. In the present climate of downsizing, however, this group of people may have had a rude awakening, being the first to find themselves without a job.

Defensive style

The combination of the active mode and a distorted, unrealistic world orientation makes for the defensive style. This group of executives is more likely to suffer from stress symptoms. Life is endured and often experienced as somewhat tedious. Here, we find executives prone to a sense of panic when realizing that their lives may have been directed toward the wrong ends. The incidence of job obsolescence is fairly common among executives belonging to this group. Dismissal or demotion is not unusual. There exists a great resistance to changes in work behaviour and little attempt to improve managerial and technological skills. This pattern is accompanied by a reluctance and unwillingness to help develop the younger management generation, an indication of failure to attain generativity as a life stage. The younger management generation is often viewed with bitterness, jealousy and envy.

To illustrate, a 42-year-old director of finance of a medium size electronics firm began to complain about insomnia and stomach problems. His career until five years previously had been a successful one, marked by regular raises and steady promotions. Then, suddenly, this tranquillity was shattered due to the arrival of a new, younger man in the organization. This new man was given the coveted vice-presidency of finance, a position desired and expected by the director. It was some time later that he began to suffer from the symptoms mentioned earlier. Additionally, some changes in his behaviour became noticeable. He started to dress differently; he began to wear tailored stylish clothes aimed at younger age groups. At the same time his colleagues started to complain about his moodiness and unpredictability. His easy irritability was symptomized by the rapid succession of younger executives reporting to him. None of these younger executives seemed to be able to live up to his standards. Although he spent more time than ever at the office his effectiveness seemed to decrease. Deadlines were frequently not met and the quality of his work declined.

Closer investigation revealed also that his personal life was suffering. His relationship with his wife had deteriorated substantially over the past few years. After work he spent more and more time at nightclubs, often until early morning. Eventually his engagement in extra-marital affairs caused a divorce. Moreover, a drinking problem became more noticeable, and led to his dismissal from the company.

This example symptomizes a number of prominent modes that can be discerned in the defensive style. These modes represent various defence mechanisms which usually occur in combination and only occasionally in isolation. The most common defensive modes found within the defensive style are scapegoating, denying, and the 'manic' defense.

When executives begin to realize that it will be impossible to achieve their original career objectives but are unwilling to make any drastic changes, adaptations or modifications, and lean toward self-justification – placing the blame on others or circumstances – we are dealing with the *scapegoating* mode. We can find here those executives who are unwilling or unable to accept that their unrealistic ambitions are not going to be achieved. They will be angry at their present situation and blame others for their misfortunes. A sense of rigidity may be an accompanying feature. Unable to reconcile themselves to their lack of appreciable gains, they may fall back into paranoiac hostility or adult delinquency, or take flight in illness.

Executives who resort to this mode may experience a great sense of rivalry toward the younger management generation, a pattern sometimes called in this context the 'Reverse Oedipus Complex', because in the Greek myth King Laïos tried to kill his son Oedipus. Executives belonging to this group are easily threatened by younger people who represent new skills and management techniques. This mixture of envy, rivalry and anger can bring these executives to an abuse of their power. Under various disguises they may set up the younger executive as a target.

For example, the disguise of 'developing younger executives' may be used. In using this form of deception they give these younger executives responsibilities beyond their present capacity with failure as a predictable outcome. A high turnover of basically talented junior executives working under specific senior executives can frequently be explained, after closer investigation, as a result of this mode. Not only are these senior executives able to destroy career paths of others working under them, but their actions will have a negative effect on organizational morale.

The *deniers* refuse to admit their inability to actualize their unrealistic goals at mid-career. They may escape into alcoholism, sexual promiscuity and psychosomatic illness. In the case of men, affairs with younger women and hypochondriacal concerns over health and physical appearance become their ways of denying the aging process. These are the 'Peter Pans' engaging in a belated second adolescence. They often cling to their physical powers as the most important part of their self-concept. But physical powers inevitably decline and their resistance and manic activity make them increasingly ineffective in work and social roles. These executives often deny or ignore the fact that they have reached plateaux in their careers or have been demoted. A sense of being unreal emerges, of participation without real involvement. Pretending becomes a way of life. Organizational life turns into one of role playing and acting and often combines denial with elements of the 'manic' mode.

Johan, one of the marriage partners in Bergman's film *Scenes from a Marriage*, is one of these individuals, but in this instance, one possessing an unusual level of insight. In despair about his failures, and with the bitter taste which a period of 'Peter Panism' has left him, he says:

> viewed objectively I'm already a corpse. For the next twenty years I'll go around embittering my own life and other people's merely by existing. I am regarded as an expensive, unproductive unit which by rights should be got rid of by rationalization. And this is supposed to be the prime of life, when you could really make yourself useful. . . I'm so goddamn tired. . . If I had the guts I'd make a clean break and move to the country or ask for a job as a teacher in a small town.[35]

As we can read from this speech, Johan's defensive structure is badly shaken because of the stress of the mid-life transition. He may be in for a serious depression.

A very similar behaviour pattern characterizes executives who resort predominantly to the 'manic' mode. We can find here a close relationship with the frantic activities of the deniers. We are reminded of the myth of Sisyphus. These executives come across as living machines, hyperactive, ever unable to reach their desired goals. They are the classic examples of the coronary-prone individuals. Stimulated by what is sometimes called by the Germans, *Torschlusspanik*, the panic over the 'closing of the gates', they engage in frantic work activity as a last effort 'to make it big', and attain their originally set goals. For some, compulsive work activity becomes an escape from unsatisfying family interaction. These people tend to deny the reality of the situation, making for a close tie with the previous mode. For others, frantic activity is only career related. Naturally, we can view the sexual promiscuity of the Peter Pans also as a reaction to this sense of *Torschlusspanik*.

Even if these executives are successful in their careers it will not bring relief from their hyperactive, overcompensatory behaviour. Actually their sense of weariness and joylessness may increase. Success can make them anxious. Not only has Nemesis to be paid, but they will pursue other, even more unrealistic goals. The future may shrink into a monotonous demoralizing present that holds little hope for change. This pattern of behaviour can be viewed as the sign of a threatening depression and mental breakdown. Bob Slocum, the hero of Heller's novel *Something Happened*, is an individual who belongs to this group. His description of the company and his job reveals an organization man no longer able to separate his own identity from that of the company. He goes through ritualistic, compulsive activities to delay an upcoming depression and deal with his various stress symptoms.

Depressive style

We can look at the depressive style as an outflow of the defensive style. We are referring to a combination of the passive mode and a distorted orientation of life. Many of the frantic activities of the executives resorting to the defensive style, which combines the scapegoating, denial, and compulsive mode, mask the emergence of a mental breakdown. Self-denigration, a sense of failure and pessimism characterize these executives. They feel that they have not met their original aspirations. The life course has been pursued in vain, and a reason for continued existence is absent. They lack confidence for new departures or in their ability to continue learning and developing. A strong sense of doubt exists about ever being appreciated. For them, the mid-career point brings a sense of always being too late. It gives a feeling of finality and doom, of opportunities forever lost. They start to dwell more in the past; the present only evokes painful memories. Previously sustained ambition, optimism, satisfaction and good health are now exchanged for a sense of isolation, for purposelessness and for psychosomatic disorders. This sense of devitalization and withdrawal may lead to inactivity, work impairment and dismissal. In some cases it may end in suicide.

In Bergman's movie, *Face to Face*, the main character, a psychiatrist, is faced with a serious mid-career crisis. In a move of desperation she decides to end her life. She dictates a last letter on a tape to her husband and says:

I've been living in an isolation that has got worse and worse – the dividing line between my outer behaviour and my inner impoverishment has become more distance. . . Our sex life – I felt nothing, nothing at all. I pretended. I did, so that you wouldn't be anxious or start asking questions. But I think the worst of all was that I lost touch with our little girl. A prison grew up all around me, with no doors or windows. With walls so thick that no sound got through, walls that it was useless to attack, since they were built from materials I supplied myself. . . We live, and while we live we're gradually suffocated without knowing what is happening. At last there's only a puppet left reacting more or less to external demands and stimuli. Inside there is nothing but a great horror.[36]

Her attempt at suicide fails.

A NEED FOR CHANGE

In the future, increasing life expectancies will lengthen the potential working life of men and women even more. This trend, in conjunction with zero-population growth, makes for an ever larger proportion of executives in the middle and older age groups. Given greater concern about the quality of working life, a need to view career paths and length of productive life with less rigidity emerges. Commitment to one organization and to one career is becoming a less common phenomenon. We see a trend in the future toward more flexible and varied careers. We can look at this changing perception of career as a way to improve our use of the wealth of talent and skills which the middle-aged have to offer in work, family and community, a wealth that is now often wasted. The mid-career transition could become an opportunity for reassessment, re-evaluation and positive action. Several steps can be taken to facilitate this process.

The need for counselling

In view of the many problems executives encounter at mid-life and mid-career, great need for counselling seems to exist to help break unsatisfactory established behaviour patterns. Counselling refers to career counselling undertaken by organizations and more personal forms of counselling such as marriage counselling by psychotherapists, or counselling done by independent non-company career advisers. The problems of career, health and marriage are closely intertwined.

In advocating a greater use of counselling, we are not only thinking of intervention in instances of severe crisis, but also of a more preventive form of counselling at a time when 'repair' is less difficult. We observe that usually counselling is sought for cases of breakdown while no steps are taken to help the much larger number of demoralized. Identification of periods of high risk for marriage and career might facilitate the counselling process. In this context, counselling does not only mean inventory taking and redirection, but also dealing with the mastery of disappointment, grief and restitution.

An important function of counselling will be to teach executives the importance of attaining a sense of generativity by helping the younger management generation to progress and develop in the organization. For the executive at mid-career, generativity will be a counter-balancing force, helpful in breaking the spell of encroaching rigidity and resistance to change, and of feeling comfortable with past behaviour.

Career and management development can play a major role in facilitating learning in organizational settings. It becomes important to help executives to learn how to learn, to assist them in acquiring the ability to engage in a continuous process of problem solving, and also to help them develop an openness to new challenges. Therefore, the notion of compartmentalization of education, and limiting it as we do now to the first twenty years of life, is under question. Access to adult learning, a right atmosphere of support and confidence, and openness to change at home and in the organization, might prevent 'rut' formation and redundancy. In this era of change the challenge becomes to create the kind of learning organizations that prepare their executives for the year 2000.

Career monitoring could become much more of a company policy. Most executives are becoming aware that the critical points of the career cycle are entry, mid-career and pre-retirement. Currently, the major emphasis and the bulk of resources have been directed to the entry point of career. Only very recently has the idea of pre-retirement counselling taken hold. Mid-career counselling remains neglected.

The notion of a mid-career clinic and career redirection workshops is worth consideration. They will provide individuals with a chance to assess abilities, interests and opportunities. The workshops might become outlets for information exchange which will help executives in their decision-making processes. Here, the goals of working life can be re-examined and the appropriate and desired modifications in career direction can be made.

The creation of the awareness that there are special problems associated with mid-career is important. Not only will awareness make for a sense of preparedness, but it will also become a source of support. The mere expression of feelings about mid-life experiences might have a real relieving function.

A greater preparedness might be needed to handle multiple careers. This will not only necessitate vision, but also a search for alternatives going beyond individual company boundaries. As we have indicated before, we will observe not only more dramatic career changes taken by executives who are stuck in their jobs and are becoming redundant, but also by relatively successful executives who seek new avenues for growth. Organizations have to become more aware of these phenomena and be prepared to deal with these changes.

In this context the notion of the 'Protean career' has been suggested by Hall, implying a career more shaped by the needs of the individual than by the organization, and subject to regular redirection, depending upon the life changes experienced by the executive.[37] Through work-related flexibility and individual self-confrontation, the transition at mid-career will be facilitated and its dysfunctional effects reduced.

Turning to the family environment, we see that marriage counsellors usually deal with acute cases. Like vocational counsellors, they do very little preventative work. An expansion of marriage counselling services may be advisable to stir the flatness of many marriages experienced at mid-life. Help might be needed for couples at this stage to redefine their problems and break out of routine, demoralizing relationships. This may imply participation in community and cultural affairs, a reassessment of jobs, and frequently for women, a return to work, if they have not been working all along. The danger of dual-career families, however, is that both husband and wife become unhealthily involved in their careers to such an extent that they may suddenly find themselves with very little in common and without a reason for a continuation of their relationship.

Marriage counselling can also lead to an accelerated dislocation of those marriages which exist without any basis for mutual satisfaction. With the help of a psychotherapist, the partners may discover that, although their marriage may have been appropriate earlier, they have grown apart and would both be happier going their separate ways.

Prevention of obsolescence

Executive obsolescence is fostered by the rapid increase in knowledge and information, and changes in technology, managerial practices and occupations. We have observed that there exists a great need for training from mid-career onward when the danger of obsolescence begins to increase progressively. For some executives, obsolescence and 'levelling off' can be prevented through the upgrading of skills or retraining for new careers in related, and occasionally even unrelated, fields. Some organizations make extensive use of job rotation, a moderately successful way of preventing obsolescence at mid-career and subsequently. A few ease the mid-career passage through grants and sabbaticals, while some organizations prevent obsolescence through extensive in-house training efforts.

Naturally, the executives themselves have a strong responsibility to deal constructively with the mid-career transition and prevent their own obsolescence and redundancy. This will mean a continuing realistic assessment and evaluation of goals and opportunities. As they say at Apple Computers, 'We will provide you with opportunities, you have to manage your career.'

Executives at mid-career should be very alert to signs of personal obsolescence and indications of possible redundancy due to changes in the company and its environment. Only through this type of involvement will they be able to appraise the future outlook of their present situation and take appropriate action. For example, they should assess very carefully the impact of reduced profits, top executive changes, mergers, technological transformations and changes in market needs. Only through a high level of organizational participation and an attitude of achievement orientation will satisfactory personal growth and sensitivity to environmental change be maintained. Moreover, the prevalence of stress symptoms may suggest that something is wrong and maybe a change is needed with respect to family or work environment.

Sir William Osler once stated that one of the surest ways to assure a long life was to have a mild heart attack at life's mid-point. The shock would make the individual more receptive to a change in the life course. We hope, however, that continuous personal assessment and frank self-evaluation will invalidate this draconic recommendation. Nevertheless, stress symptoms remain as important indicators that all is not well with career or family life.

Every individual has the responsibility to reassess the satisfaction and pleasures derived from career and personal life. This suggestion implies a reduction of self-indulgence, the opportunity to express feelings about personal life and career, the willingness to engage in mutual problem solving, and a sense of generativity toward the younger management generation. These matters become important for both individual and organization, and will enable the executive to traverse the quicksand which can be mid-career, and make it a station on the route to personal growth and generativity, instead of the marking point of decline.

10

IS THERE LIFE AT RETIREMENT?

> Do not go gentle into that good night,
> Old age should burn and rave at close of day;
> Rage, rage against the dying of the light.[1]
>
> Dylan Thomas

Once upon a time there was a very old man who was no longer able to earn his daily bread and who lived with his son and daughter-in-law. His eyes had grown dim, his hearing was not what it used to be, and his hands were no longer steady. At mealtimes he had difficulties in holding his spoon and would spill food on the table cloth. This was a source of great irritation to his son and daughter-in-law who finally placed him out of sight, in a corner, behind the stove. The little food he received was put in an earthenware bowl. At mealtimes the old man would look sadly at the table with tears in his eyes thinking of happier times. One day, he could not hold his earthenware bowl, dropped it out of his trembling hands and it broke into pieces. His daughter-in-law replaced it with a wooden bowl from which he ate from then on.

During one meal his little grandson was sitting on the floor fitting pieces of wood together when the father asked the child what he was doing. The son replied: 'I am making a trough for you and mother to eat out of when I'm grown up'. Hearing this, his father and mother wept and brought the old grandfather back to the table. There he ate until the end of his days and nothing was said even when he spilled some food.

If they lived 'happily ever after' is not told in this old German folktale, but whatever the outcome, the story leaves us with a bitter aftertaste. Not only does this story illustrate man's denial of aging, but also man's contempt for old age. In addition, this folktale

159

contains a moral centring around the fear of role reversal: what I do to you, you might do to me. It portrays how in the first stages of life the children are the ones who are dependent, then the roles are reversed and with that grows the uncertainty of what treatment to expect. It is one of the reasons for our somewhat ambivalent attitude toward the elderly; on the one hand we express love and affection, on the other hand we show hostility and resentment, remnants of the power that older people had once wielded.

This tale has a moral for our own youth-orientated culture where responsibility for retired persons is often accepted very unwillingly. Gerontocracies such as the one once existing in old China have become rare. Reverence for the elderly is a low priority item. And paradoxically enough, politicians – a group among which septuagenarians and octogenarians are not strange – have shown until recently a remarkable callousness toward the interest of their own age group, which has become a neglected part of their constituency. Tax and civil laws have made disinheritance – a powerful tool to the elderly in previous centuries – less of a threat.

We do not kill our kings or high priests any longer when their power is waning, but this does not necessarily mean that there are no substitutes for these killings, and that we have put aside our bias against the elderly. Retired executives belong to this group of second-class citizens. Their low social status reflects their loss of power and responsibilities. It is therefore not surprising that retirement has become one of the most stressful points in the career life cycle. At an economic level it usually implies a reduction in the standard of living. At a psychosocial level it is perceived as a judgement of the inability of a once able executive to perform in a coveted role. This can lead to a sense of anxiety and fear and a feeling of being discarded like an old rag.

Shakespeare's drama *King Lear* illustrates this fear vividly. Lear's decision to retire, to leave the management of his affairs to younger strengths and invest his three daughters with the power of office, led to his betrayal by his daughters. Only his youngest daughter, Cordelia, who really loved him, was sincere and therefore unwilling to participate in the foolish 'trial of love', a verbal competition to assess which daughter loved Lear best. Cordelia refused to engage in empty flattery and thereby forfeited her share of the kingdom, which was then divided between the elder two. The story tells how, soon after, the older daughters abuse their father and even begrudge him the small remnant of royalty, his

160

retinue of a hundred knights. We observe the tragic Lear, unable to bear this ingratitude and stay at their castle any longer, riding out in the fury of a storm; he ends up wandering the land in madness and beggary.

Although such phrases as 'golden age' and 'senior citizenship' are being used, these words seem to be euphemisms, thinly disguised covers for age discrimination. Retirement is looked at with a large degree of ambivalence. The cynical statement by the British statesman Disraeli that 'youth is a blunder, manhood a struggle, and old age a regret' hits a sensitive chord. But are these bitter words really necessary? Does retirement have to be such a traumatic episode?

These questions and others are particularly important if we look at the rise in the number of retired executives in society, a consequence of increased life expectancy and even earlier retirement ages. While at the turn of the century two-thirds of the older men were still working, this percentage has now been reduced to one quarter. The United States Census Bureau estimates that 64 million people will be in the age group of 65 years and older by the year 2030.[2] While in the past retirement was only justified when an individual was unable to continue work because of physical or mental impairments, at the present it is explained as a reward for a lifetime of work, inevitable whether or not the person has psychological or physical defects. Retirement has become one of the luxuries of Western societies to which we are gradually getting accustomed. Given the magnitude of this new social phenomenon, the process of retirement is becoming an increasingly important issue for individual, organization and society alike.

RITES OF EXIT

Retirement can be viewed as a more dramatic, highly visible transition point than mid-career, a 'rite of passage' guiding the individual from one social position to the next. It becomes a symbol of old age. This psychosocial transition point can be celebrated with a banquet, a commemorative gift, or special treatment during the last day or days on the job. The purpose of these 'rites of exit' is to help the executive define and accept his or her new role as retiree and announce this change in position to the outside world through differential treatment. This usually takes the form of a celebration of past accomplishments accompanied by declarations of gratitude about services rendered. The emphasis will be on the past; very little will be said about future challenges and opportunities.

But all these congratulations and pleasantries cannot hide the fact that the executive is being divorced from his job, his world of work, and ending his career. Feelings of separation and loss are the emotions aroused during these rites of exit. Retirement is thus often experienced as a period of mourning and exile; feelings well hidden under the thin veneer of smiles, handshakes and tokens of appreciation. The event re-awakens the pain and sadness of separation, feelings of abandonment, loneliness and uselessness. The expression 'retirement rot' is indicative of this emotional state.

Churchill reacted with great bitterness and sorrow after being ousted from power as a result of the devastating defeat of the Conservative Party immediately following the Second World War. He would write later:

> On the night of the tenth of May (1940), at the outset of this mighty battle, I acquired the chief power in the state, which henceforth I wielded in ever growing measure for five years and three months of world war, at the end of which time all our enemies having surrendered unconditionally or being about to do so, I was immediately dismissed by the British electorate from all further conduct of their affairs. . .[3]

Churchill tried to ward off the feeling of what he called 'unemployment' and an emerging depression by engaging in therapeutically helpful activities, in his case painting and the writing of his memoirs.

When Verdi's statue was unveiled with great pomp and circumstance at the Scala in Milan the famous composer reacted with the following grievous words: 'It means that I am old (which is true, alas!), that I am an old soldier fit for honourable retirement... I did deplore this ceremony and I do deplore it now.'[4] Verdi was 68 at the time. He set about recasting *Don Carlos* and conducted the rehearsals himself. He did not retire then as his later operas *Othello* and *Falstaff* testify.

We can make the distinction between the active statement, 'I am retiring', versus the more passive comment, 'I am being retired'. In fact most people do not have much of a choice, the decision is made for them, and they are retired. Thus to many, retirement becomes synonymous with banishment from active life. Retirement takes on the meaning of a symbolic rejection; it signifies an expression of regret in the loss of a role and serves as an indication to society that the executive is no longer useful or able to perform his work activity.

There is a strong emphasis in Western societies on being involved in something utilitarian, a moral orientation which conflicts with the enjoyment of leisure time. In view of the 'Protestant Ethic', inactivity and leisure are not seen as legitimate sources of self respect. The biblical statement 'Man should live by the sweat of his brow', is still perceived as a social truth. Retirement violates the doctrine of the work ethic and is therefore approached in an ambivalent manner. Although it can be perceived as an extended holiday, it is frequently experienced as being thrown out on the scrapheap. But, however it is viewed, people prophesying that we will not be able to cope with the demands of increased leisure time are hard to silence and continue to create feelings of uneasiness in dealing with this newly acquired richness in the form of leisure time. Given the importance of work for social and personal well-being and the continuing ambivalence toward leisure, retirement can become an extremely traumatic event. The institutionalization of idleness and the acceptance of leisure time have quite some way to go before this situation changes.

A NEW IDENTITY CRISIS

Retirement can be viewed as a developmental milestone, a major event on the 'career clock' of the executive. It intensifies awareness of a process which reverses many of the developments which took place in childhood, adolescence and young adulthood. But contrary to the physiological transformations of adolescence, which with all its *Sturm und Drang* (storm and stress) overtones is far more dramatic and tormenting, aging is much more of a gradual process and does not show this sudden change. The realization of change occurs in a different manner. What actually happens is that many aged executives often come to feel old through the labelling of others, and therefore adopt 'age appropriate' behaviour. For example, we are expected to behave in prescribed ways when we have grandchildren or when we are retired. Some individuals may even be regarded with ridicule, as is sometimes the case with aged movie actresses who act and dress in 'age-disappropriate' ways.

It is not so much the 'milestone' of reaching retirement that creates problems of adjustment, but the transition and the

163

age-grading associated with retirement and old age. Just as the age of 21 has traditionally been the milestone of adulthood, the arbitrarily fixed age of 65 or 70 has become the mark of retirement and the onset of old age.

Changes

Retirement presents both men and women with serious problems of adjustment. It will usually imply alterations in the daily schedule of activities, a reduction in the standard of living, changes in social roles and status, a decrease in responsibility, changes in social and family relationships, and, often, declining physical health and vigour.

The spouse can become a source of stress. In the case of traditional role patterns whereby the woman manages the household, the wife may be unaccustomed to suddenly having a 'stranger in the house' disrupting her activities. The husband often leaves the world of work to enter an environment which customarily has been his wife's realm and where he feels lost and out of place. This change may be hard to take. In a case where the wife is working, a shift in family roles may have to be made. Apart from these adjustments, the retirement of an executive frequently necessitates the need to redefine and find common concerns and interests with the marriage partner. For years, both parties might have been living beside each other while effectively leading separate lives.

Just before retirement there tends to be an increase in humanitarian and moral concerns. Male executives are particularly preoccupied with leaving a legacy behind, making a tangible contribution to society, while religious life may take on a new meaning for women.[5]

The retired executive may experience not only loneliness but also self-denigration. The loss of work and social relationships leads the executive to question the very meaning of his or her existence. This journey of personal self-discovery can cause a sense of discontinuity and stagnation due to a disruption of daily life patterns and the new experience of operating in normless, unstructured situations.

The life review

Already, much earlier in life, executives have become aware of a

decline in their physical capacities which brings about a disquiet-
ing sense of insecurity. The preoccupation with the body starting
at mid-life is continuing. 'Body monitoring' is becoming a way of
life. Intra-psychic processes also continue to be more important and
make for an increased inner-worldly orientation. We often observe
greater conservatism as well as psychic rigidity, attitudes which
can be viewed as a defence against anxiety about problems of
adaptation to an ever-changing world. Greater rigidity can also be
a result of some diminished capacity for new learning due to
physiological deterioration but is more often a consequence of a
lack of new stimuli and the resulting 'rut' formation formed
through habits. With the life review comes also the awareness that
adjustments are needed to arrive at a realistic balance between
active management and contemplation.

Although the mid-career transition has set the stage the realization is now more final that life is a one-time matter without the
chance for repeats. Erikson calls this transition of the 'social clock'
the crisis of *integrity* versus *despair*, the last stage of the human life
cycle.[6] The theme becomes that of increased introspection whereby
the need for a life review becomes central.

In this context the psychologist Jung once said:

> Ageing people should know that their lives are not mounting
> and expanding, but that an inexorable inner process enforces
> the contraction of life. For a young person it is almost a sin,
> or at least a danger, to be too preoccupied with himself; but
> for the ageing person it is a duty and a necessity to devote
> serious attention to himself. After having lavished its light
> upon the world, the sun withdraws its rays in order to illumi-
> nate itself. . .[7]

When the future holds little and thinking about it arouses thoughts
of death, interests will turn regressively to the past. The life review
becomes a progressive return to consciousness of past experiences
causing the re-emergence of unresolved conflicts. The process is
one of a reassessment of life whereby the executive tries to integrate
and resolve the 'unfinished business' of the past. Politicians demonstrate the process of life review when they engage in memoir
writing.

Tolstoy describes the life review process masterfully in his story
'The Death of Ivan Illyich'. It tells of one man's struggle with dying
and the desperate search for the meaning of life. After an initial

period of pain and suffering, of despair about loneliness and meaninglessness, Illyich begins to recollect memories and assess his life. Eventually, finding value in past experiences and in himself, he arrives at a new sense of identity and with that an acceptance of death.

The life review makes for an increasing awareness about the finality of life and the proximity of death. The accomplishments during the earlier stages of life are important for acquiring a sense of the meaning of things, that one's 'one and only' life has not been wasted or should have been lived differently. If a feeling of waste prevails, a sense of despair and disgust may be all that remains. Integrity implies the personal experience of approving of one's own past achievements without the influence or the judgement of others. Life becomes now a period of consolidation, a triumph of reason over unbridled emotion as well as a period of resubjectification, meaning an increasing preoccupation with the self.

Loss of loved ones

The process of retirement is one form of loss which makes it necessary for the executive to make certain marital adjustments to arrive at a mutually satisfactory family life. Other losses which need some form of adjustment may occur concurrently. While the young adult is in the process of sharing his or her life intimately with another person, old age sooner or later will be accompanied by the loss of the person with whom one has shared one's life. The period of retirement is the time when the older executive will lose friends and spouse.

The most difficult adjustment to a new role occurs when a person loses a spouse. For many people this loss causes a severe disruption of life patterns and is accompanied by serious grief and depression. Losing spouse, friends, or relatives means a loss of daily companionship, a shared world of memories and recollections, and a source of support for common values and social norms. These losses cause a disruption of one's inner mental map, a process which can be extremely disconcerting. We remember King Lear's despairing struggle with his daughters not to restrict him to the most basic human needs, and to allow him to retain his companions.

In the case of death of spouse or friends the 'survivor' will question the value of these lives and subsequently his or her own life. It leads to a growing awareness of the proximity of death and the funeral as a last social statement. As Casanova wrote in his memoirs: 'the greatest misfortune a man can have is to outlive all his friends'.[8]

The confidant – a person to confide in and discuss problems with – becomes increasingly important at this point in the life cycle. He or she serves as a buffer against losses such as retirement, a decrease in social activities, or widowhood. It seems that the maintenance of stable, intimate relationships is extremely important for mental health. Women are somewhat more likely to have confidants than men.[9] These confidants can be spouse, child, or friend, all of whom can play a supportive, emotionally refuelling role, creating a balance between factors of depletion and sources of replenishment in retirement and old age.

THE MANAGEMENT OF RETIREMENT

There exists a large number of theories which try to explain the process of adjustment to retirement. Among the better known ones we can list two: the activity theory and the disengagement theory. Both theories take extreme positions and explain counterbalancing social processes. The prevention of leanings toward isolation, inertia and apathy is the focus of the first theory while the disengagement theory elucidates the reasons which encourage the executive to gradually withdraw from areas of life where expectations can no longer be met.

Activity theory

The activity theory emphasizes the importance of activity for a person's emotional and physical well-being. Compulsory withdrawal from social activities – which retirement often implies – is considered detrimental. Substitutes (such as hobbies or volunteer activities) have to be found in accord with one's past life style and present physical and mental condition. An executive's morale will remain high as long as he or she is able to maintain the same activity level in spite of all the role reductions he or she may experience. The substitutes for lost roles and activities will serve as a new source of identity.[10]

Activity theory is attractive because it suggests a way of preventing increased dependency through the maintenance of vocational interests and recreational activities. These pursuits will make life pleasurable or at least bearable. A main assumption of this theory is that the retired executive will seek and find work substitutes. The leitmotif is that 'busy old people are happy old people', a statement which may be true for some executives.

Disengagement theory

This point of view holds that as a result of physical decline, an inevitable mutual withdrawal process sets in, resulting in decreased interaction of individual and society. Retirement is a natural process of withdrawing from social relationships since, due to physical decline (a predictable outcome of the aging process), the need exists to conserve energies. The work role will simply be left behind without any search for substitutes. The increased psychological preoccupation of executives with themselves and the decreased emotional investments and interests in others makes disengagement a logical and beneficial process of mutual withdrawal. Disengagement can be looked at as both a social and a personal process. On one hand society tries to disengage the older executive from its institutions, on the other hand the executive, unable to keep up with the pace of society, is inclined to withdraw.[11]

A major characteristic of this theory is the movement away from achievement and active involvement, the proposition that the executive wants to withdraw. We can question if this disengagement process can be considered as a 'normal' process or signals the onset of a depression. In addition, disengagement presupposes a process of mutual withdrawal of individual and society. If the executive disengages too early or society disengages before the executive is prepared to decrease his social interaction, the process will be dysfunctional.

The implicit sense of pessimism which this theory disseminates has also a perturbing effect. It discounts or negates man's potential for creative involvement later in life which makes us want to argue that *real* disengagement may only occur at the very end of the life cycle, just before death.

A process of mutual adaptation

Both theories hold extreme points of view, possess elements of truth and explain only part of the emerging phenomena. No real consideration is given to the influence of individual differences and environmental circumstances. In contrast, a combination and integration of the themes developed by these theories will allow for individual differences in adaptation patterns of retirement and will be more in touch with reality.

What we actually observe is how the executive will distribute his or her shrinking energies and resources over fewer but more important activities to conserve effort and to escape demands of lesser interest; in addition, he or she might engage in new activities. This mutual adaptation process necessitates compromise, a sense of personal independence, goal modification, selectivity, and a realistic balance between active engagement and contemplation. It also necessitates a differentiation of roles (apart from the work role) on which to base identity. Some individuals will find themselves at opposite ends of the spectrum, acting according to either the activity theory or the disengagement theory, but for most executives activity and disengagement will occur concurrently and may lead to forms of *re-engagement*.

In accordance with the previously mentioned polarity, integrity and despair, which characterizes the latter part of the life cycle, adaptive behaviour necessitates acceptance of the inevitability of the aging process, requiring confrontation with reality through mature ego processes. Failure of adaptation gives way to a sense of despair and can lead to an acceleration of the aging process. Resilience and patience are other necessities in 'successful' retiring, implying the ability to accept adversity without considering it a personal defeat.

What we notice is that retirement necessitates creative acceptance and congruence between inner mental state and external circumstances which make essential a sense of continuity between past and present and the acknowledgement and acceptance of old age and death.

PATTERNS OF COPING

There are a number of ways in which executives can deal with the last phase of the career life cycle. Some executives handle retirement in a mature way following a pattern of adjustment to their new position; for others retirement is fraught with danger and gives rise to a defensive reaction. In the latter case executives may react to the loss of work that retirement implies through denial, overcompensatory activities, or scapegoating. In this context we should remember that poor adjustment to retirement is usually not a sudden process but, in most cases, suggests a life-long history of characterological problems.

Analogous to the model of dealing with mid-career we suggest a number of ways in which executives can deal with the process of retirement. Again we should keep in mind that in the effort to discern patterns we may occasionally oversimplify or create artificial boundaries. A mixture of styles may very well be applicable to some people.[12]

Adjusted coping styles

The adjusted style can be divided into two groups. As at mid-career the characterization *constructive* can be used for the group of executives who will handle retirement in an extremely mature way. Old age and retirement do not pose any serious problems. Relatively well integrated and free from neurotic conflict, these individuals continue to enjoy life and retain the ability to establish warm, affectionate relationships with other people. They have an optimistic, positive, future-orientated attitude toward the world. And future orientation can usually be viewed among the aged as a sign of physical and psychological adjustment. These executives possess a sense of realism about retirement and find satisfaction in past or new activities and personal relationships. Life is an experience seen without regret for the past or anxiety about the future. Congeniality, personal independence, self-acceptance, co-operation, resilience and patience are among their characteristics. These executives show a sense of satisfaction with past achievements and a sense of anticipation of things to come. Their sense of introspection and their approach to their life review makes for a feeling of integrity and continuity. It also suggests a management history of creativity, innovation, proactivity and career mobility.

For the second group of executives adaptation is a more passive experience and adjustment takes a more *dependent* character. Reichhard and her associates used the term 'rocking chair' people to describe this group of individuals because of their emphasis on dependency and passivity rather than activity and self-sufficiency. These executives welcome the opportunity to be free from the burden of work and enjoy retirement. The new life state is carried on with a sense of general satisfaction with the world and their past careers. They are fairly well adjusted but rely on others for material and emotional support. We observe here that these executives are unambitious but possess insight into their personal strengths and weaknesses. Experimentation and exploration is not their forte. A certain unwillingness exists to get involved in new relationships or activities which will threaten the 'safe' *status quo*. This attitude has also characterized their careers in organizations where 'rocking the boat' is eschewed and conservatism is the norm.

Defensive coping styles

To this group belongs the *hyperactive* executives who use compulsive activities as a way of warding off feelings of anxiety and guilt. Denial of reality and overcompensatory activities become the predominant patterns. Their way of dealing with the coming of age and the threat of encroaching helplessness is to engage in active, ritual-resembling acts and sudden outbursts of activity. These are the original 'workaholics' – individuals addicted to work. They take refuge in habit, routine and frantic action, all ways of handling dreaded dependency and the inactivity which can come with retirement and old age. These executives dislike having nothing to do, have a work history of achievements and social engagement, but lack the spark of creativity and imagination of the constructive group. Under the veneer of work adjustment and compulsive activity rests a deep-seated sense of anxiety. Old age is looked at with pessimism and at the same time ignored through busyness. Preparation for old age is not one of their priorities. Although they seem generally satisfied with their career achievements, the façade of adjustment and activity conceals self doubts and the spectre of depression and other forms of malfunctioning. Little is needed to disturb this delicate equilibrium and to allow for the occurrence of emotional strain; retirement can easily be this catalyst.

The main distinctive feature of the second group, which uses a defensive coping style, is the way that these executives deal with their aggressive impulses. They turn their aggression outward and resort to *distortive* behaviour in interpersonal relationships. Rationalization and scapegoating are used to smooth over dissatisfaction with a 'wasted life' and an unsatisfactory career. They feel bitter over having failed in achieving their often unrealistic life goals and blame circumstances or other people for their disappointments and failures. This group is not only very aggressive and competitive but also provides the incessant complainers in interpersonal encounters. These are the schemers and Machiavellians of organizational life, whose behaviour can be to the detriment of organizational goals, causing a deterioration in organizational climate and performance. As a result of their behaviour, demotion and dismissal is common in their career history. But these executives are self-righteous in order to protect their perception of their past career at the expense of honesty, compassion and self-evaluation. Suspiciousness, pessimism, feelings of failure, depression and a general sense of anxiety are familiar characteristics. They will postpone the day of retirement as long as they can, dreading the thought of becoming inactive and being dependent on other people. Preparation for retirement is avoided or repressed. In the meantime they will terrorize others, creating an atmosphere of anxiety and fear within their organizations. These executives have very little good to say about retirement and old age, particularly since it makes for a sense of despair and a fear of retaliation and death. Actually, for some members of the two previously described groups, the lack of structure (as they are no longer working) that comes with retirement may be so disorientating that it may contribute to a premature death.

Again, the final defensive style is the *depressed*. The behaviour of this group of people has moral masochistic overtones. In this case aggression is turned inward, resulting in self-hate, regret, self-recrimination and low self regard. These executives review their past life with a sense of disappointment and failure; but unlike the distortive group they take responsibility for their actions and blame themselves for their lack of success. This group of executives tends to be rather passive, somewhat depressed, unambitious and lacking in initiative. They are critical of the life they have led and their past career but lack the desire to have another chance. Their career history is often one of work problems and stagnation. Retirement and growing old only underscore their feelings of inadequacy and worthlessness. Although they are able to accept the fact of retirement and aging, they lack an optimistic, constructive attitude. Death is the least of all worries and is viewed as a welcome relief from despair and suffering.

THE ABILITY OF THE AGING EXECUTIVE

The previous discussion indicates how retirement can have a negative impact on social adjustment and can cause mental health problems. The negative effects of retirement, however, may be exaggerated. Adjustment as a pattern among the coping styles, or at least the ability to maintain an emotional equilibrium, seems to be far more prevalent. For example, one researcher, after a review of numerous studies on retirement, even concluded that retirement generally has no adverse effects and, as far as physical health is concerned, tends to improve it. Individuals with poor health after retirement usually had poor health before retirement, which may have been one of the main reasons they retired.[13]

The notion that associates a decrease in mental health with retirement is probably based on conventional wisdom which equates aging with a decrease in mental capacities. Actually, a considerable body of research on aging has cast doubt on the view that mental capacities decline with age. Many symptoms associated with aging may be caused by medical illness, personality variables, or socio-cultural effects.[14]

Apart from the lack of separation between healthy and 'sick' aging populations, another contributing factor to the myth of mental decline has been the predominance of cross-sectional as opposed to longitudinal studies. What this research seems to indicate is that general intellectual decline in old age may be largely a myth. Speed of performance may go down somewhat but not accuracy. Cognitive performance continues to compare favourably with younger groups. Short-term memory may be affected but long-term memory is not. As the Roman statesman Cicero once jokingly said in his very perceptive and accurate treatise on old age: 'I never heard of an old man forgetting where he had buried his money.'[15]

There is evidence that vocabulary, information and knowledge continue to increase with age. Thus, the older executive can perform the job as competently and productively as the younger executive; there seems to be no real decline in learning abilities. He or she certainly has the ability if given sufficient challenge. An additional asset of older executives is their greater experience and maturity in judgement. This, combined with a better record for attendance, safety, reliability and punctuality than younger execu-

173

tives, makes the older executive a very valuable but unfortunately underrated entity.[16]

As we have seen at the mid-career point, it seems to be lack of challenge and opportunities that may lead to rigidity, 'rut' formation and moroseness. Health, education and individual personality differences seem to be more important for mental health and the ability for continued learning than age alone. Of course there remains such a thing as physical aging. But, as can be observed all around us, many individuals have no difficulty in adjusting to age and can be extremely productive and creative later in life. Historians, philosophers and many types of scientists continue to be as productive in their seventies as they were in their forties. In the arts there is usually a decrease in productivity compared to earlier periods in life, but again there are many exceptions.[17] Plato wrote *The Laws* when he was 80 years old. Goethe finished the second part of *Faust* just before his death at 83. Churchill came to power when he was 65 years old. Grandma Moses started painting at the age of 75 when she was past manual labour. She finished her famous painting 'Christmas Eve' when she was 100 years old. Rubinstein at the age of 90 was going strong and performing for capacity audiences.

THE RETIREMENT SYNDROME

All too often retirement has been regarded as the mysterious jump from being young one day to being old the next. The reality is quite different. Physical aging starts in the late twenties and differs from person to person depending on life style and individual predispositions. Chronological and biological age do not necessarily coincide. For some, the slackening of rigid role requirements which some jobs entail, can well have a beneficial effect on mental health due to the disappearance of organizational stress.

Retirement alone does not account for maladjustment. For example, only about 15 per cent of the older population needs mental health services. One study found that only 30 per cent of retired people have significant adjustment problems, and only 7 per cent of them felt that the problems of adjustment were due to missing their job. The remaining 23 per cent attributed the adjustment problems to the conditions under which the retirement role had to be played.[18] Factors such as poor physical health, financial problems, unsatisfactory living conditions, degree of social interaction and differences in psychological make-up contribute considerably.

That is not to say the 'retirement syndrome' is all but a myth. Most of the elderly suffer from one or more chronic illnesses. Of the 65 and older population, it is estimated that 10 to 15 per cent suffers from anxious and depressive symptoms, another 5 per cent are cognitively impaired, and an additional 5 per cent are suffering from personality and other psychiatric disorders. Estimates of psychiatric disorders among the hospitalized elderly range from 40 to 50 per cent. Particularly, the incidence of depression rises with age.[19] Given these statistics it is not surprising that for some executives retirement will come with various psychosomatic disorders such as gastro-intestinal problems, cardio-vascular symptoms and allergy–respiratory irritations. Nausea, headaches, insomnia, irritability, lethargy and generalized anxiety can suddenly occur. Paranoid and obsessional compulsive states can occasionally be observed. Frequently, these disorders will already be noticeable at the pre-retirement stage and are particularly apparent among those executives who resort to the various defensive coping styles. Depression, suicide and hypochondriasis seem to be among the most prevalent disturbances occurring among the retired.

Depression and suicide

The most common disorder of retirement is probably depression, which in some cases requires hospitalization. Reactive depression usually occurs as a consequence of a stressful experience (such as retirement) in a predisposed individual. In some ways it can be viewed as a 'cry for help' and support. It is characterized by feelings of sadness, hopelessness, fatigue, irritability, loss of weight, sleeplessness and lethargy. There is a lack of interest in recreation, family and friends. Feelings of pessimism, negativism and emptiness are rampant, as are feelings of anxiety, guilt and shame. In severe cases depression may lead to suicide.

Suicidal ideas are very common even among individuals suffering from moderate depression, but among the retired we have to take such ideas very seriously, particularly for male retirees. We have indicated before that the risk for women after mid-life is comparatively low.[20] For men, suicide attempts in the over 65 age group are usually successful and, if not, they are very likely to be followed by another successful attempt within a two-year period.

Frustrated dependency, inward-directed hostility, hopelessness and helplessness play a major role in the tragic drama of suicide. These people are often in a state of unbearable despair. Suicide becomes the desperate act of a person who feels trapped, caught in a web of distortive and constricted thought processes somewhat similar to the ones found among individuals with the various defensive coping styles. Men, with their special dependence on work performance and career advancement for self-esteem and identity, are particularly susceptible. Recall Willy Loman's suicide in Arthur Miller's play *Death of a Salesman* soon after his forced 'retirement'.

Hypochondriasis

Hypochondriasis is also a very common condition associated with retirement. It is characterized by inordinate preoccupation and over-concern with the bodily functions without, in many instances, physiological confirmation. Anxiety over the new 'roleless role' which is retirement manifests itself as complaints about somatic problems. The focus on bodily functions is accompanied by the almost complete exclusion of concern for people or objects in the world around them. The body takes on a life of its own. Illness fulfils a psychological function and becomes a legitimation for retirement as the new state in life, and helps to ward off associations of being a failure and being useless.

The symptoms often arise from the person's heightened awareness of body sensations and transformations. Age breeds familiarity with illness, operation and accident, and it is therefore no surprise that this route is taken to express a person's dependency needs and his desire to regain attention, affection and domination. Complaints usually centre around gastro-intestinal dysfunctions and disorders of the heart and circulatory system. Visiting doctors and clinics becomes almost a way of life and makes the retirement experience one of complaints, suffering and meaningless activity.

PREVENTIVE MEASURES

Poor preparation for retirement has been widely recognized as detrimental to mental health. The need for preparation for retirement by the executive, the organization and society is now viewed as essential, but is only beginning to be recognized as a social phenomenon. We are aware that although massive resources have been directed to prepare young people for adult roles, until recently little attention has been given to the preparation process of transition from middle-age to older-age roles.

The role of the person

By and large, we can say that sudden, complete mandatory retirement without preparatory steps can often be detrimental to the emotional and physical well-being of many individuals and should be avoided in favour of a gradual transition. Unfortunately, this preparation does not take place for many executives, who are faced with an abrupt termination of their tenure in their organizations.

The shock of the event of retirement can be eased if the executive prepares him or herself for the change of role and status. As obvious as this might be, it is frequently not the case. For example, one study showed that one quarter of the men and nearly 50 per cent of the women questioned had no idea what to do in retirement (at all socio-economic levels).[21] There exists an attitude of denying and ignoring the inevitable.

The preparatory process needed for retirement is sometimes called anticipatory socialization and involves exploring the new norms and expectations associated with the transition. The purpose is to cushion the transition and facilitate the formulation of realistic life goals as a way to prevent traumatic effects. If the expectations associated with the event are clear and the executive possesses sufficient financial and emotional resources to meet these expectations, crises will be avoided. It is important to realize that an accurate conception of retirement, a favourable pre-retirement attitude, and the existence of plans for retirement will ease the transition and facilitate the retirement process. In addition, it is worth remembering that those executives who, because of poor preparation, are disgruntled and bitter about upcoming retirement can have a damaging psychological impact on the work atmosphere within a company during their last years on the job.

One of the best assurances of good mental health for the older executive comes through active involvement in matters of real and varied interest. But these take time to develop. Without the process of anticipatory socialization the executive is often confused about how to mobilize resources for action. He or she lacks preparation and does not know how to respond. Naturally, anticipatory social-ization necessitates a future orientation, an attitude which some executives find difficult to adopt, given their coping styles. The finding that attitudes toward retirement are usually at their lowest ebb just before retirement aggravates the situation.[22] That these attitudes will improve just after retirement when the 'ills' of retire-ment are better known does not help very much at that point.

The older executive may have to realize the advisability of preparation for retirement many years in advance to ease the process of adjustment. This also implies a consideration of the financial situation after retirement. Early financial measures to facilitate the transition or gradual adoption of a new standard of living can have a beneficial effect.

Anticipation of roles and activities that are attractive to the executive and are available in the family and community (such as volunteer organizations) will help. The development of new inter-ests and roles that may deepen into gratifying leisure pursuits cannot start early enough. This development avoids a dispropor-tionate reliance on career for personal identity. New criteria for self-evaluation and new values and goals may have to be estab-lished. Executives who have skills which are more difficult to adapt to leisure activities are particularly in need of greater diversifica-tion. Executives whose work requires a large number of interpersonal skills, as opposed to work emphasizing technical skills, may have less difficulty in the transition process. A key factor remains a focus on education and intellectual pursuits to facilitate detachment from the organization.

Although senior executives will usually have more time, money and opportunity to prepare for retirement and cultivate alternative interests than lower level employees, their often strong identifica-tion and involvement with the organization may cause neglect of this important area. Most executives do not look forward to retire-ment and they are the ones who regret their exit most. If no precautions are taken the 'organization man' will leave the com-fortable setting of the work environment with poorly defined goals for the future and serious problems of adjustment. This person also tends to retire at a later age in view of his or her interest and greater influence in the organization. We can speculate that it is the middle level employees – those who frequently have less of a career commitment – who may be the least stressed by the transition from pre- to post-retirement. But lower level employees may have financial problems detrimental to adjustment to retirement, often necessitating a frantic search for part-time jobs.

The elimination or reduction of occupational interactions tends to weaken ties of friendship. It will be advisable to enlarge one's circle of friends to replace the ones left behind on the job. The weakening of friendship ties and the loss of occupational identity experienced will be minimized if the executive chooses friends in the same age group. This may result in groups of people retiring together; association can minimize traumatization. However, there are also many positive aspects which accompany possible association with the younger age groups; that way, the older executive may keep involved with contemporary concerns.

Another way of easing the transition to retirement can be by having a 'protégé'. The idea of this concept is that the younger person, guided by the 'sponsor', will gradually assume the older executive's role. The involvement of the retiring executive may allow for a more gentle transition without the sudden cutting down of work with all its frightening and disturbing side effects. The interdependence of careers fosters a sense of similarity and continuity. It allows the retiring executive to make a shift in attitude from a more controlling role to the one of mentor, emphasizing consultation and guidance. Moreover, 'sponsors' will feel that they are leaving a legacy behind, that they are also being missed, and that the occupational identity of the younger executives are very much shaped by their efforts. These perceptions and feelings may strengthen self-esteem, foster a sense of self-worth, and make retirement more acceptable.

The role of the organization

Organizations encourage mandatory retirement practices for a number of reasons. First, the need is expressed for a turnover of senior executives to make room for the younger employee. Second, junior executives are usually less expensive to the organization. Third, the argument is used that a compulsory age for retirement makes for a level of objectivity and is therefore easier to administer. Finally, mandatory retirement eases the process of letting go obsolete or supernumerary employees (due to factors such as changes in information technology or business conditions) and therefore allows for a graceful exit.

In spite of these arguments, mandatory retirement for those

executives who wish to continue working and have the ability represents an incredible waste of management expertise and human resources and may very well be detrimental to the organization's efficient functioning and profitability. Mandatory retirement is also a very arbitrary way of dealing with individual differences, interests and talents in the organization. What seems to be advisable is to base retirement not so much on an arbitrary age limit but on the ability to perform. The best of all worlds would of course be if both parties could have a say in this matter.

Quite a few organizations deal with this problem through the practice of flexible or phased retirement. Flexible or phased retirement may enable the organization to eliminate the deadwood but retain the valued, productive individuals. It will aid in a more orderly transition of responsibilities to the younger executive. The existence of portability in pension rights could be an additional facilitating factor helping to encourage unhappy or obsolete individuals to retire earlier from the job or even change careers. The 'lock-in effect' of non-portable rights, with all its frustration and dissatisfaction, will be prevented.

Flexible or phased retirement usually implies the availability of a period within which one can choose and which enables the executive to delay retirement beyond just a singular cut-off date. This might imply the occurrence of manpower planning problems in the organization which, under a mandatory retirement situation, would be less of an issue, but the effort usually will be well worth it given the increase in human satisfaction, productivity and organizational morale.

We should keep in mind that early retirement has not really been a problem. Actually, most companies allow this practice. For individuals whose knowledge and skills have become obsolete, early retirement may even be a welcome option. They may very well start on a more desired, belated second career. The same may be true for employees working at tedious jobs. And apparently, a large percentage of the labour force takes advantage of the practice of early retirement, most of them giving health reasons as the cause for this choice. Naturally, the present focus on corporate re-engineering or downsizing adds to this practice.

Although there will be a legitimate number of people with serious health problems who welcome early retirement, there is a great discrepancy between the proportion of people who name poor health as the reason for retirement and that proportion of people who – according to health statistics – are still capable of working. There are probably other factors involved. For example, sufficient financial security combined with an unwillingness to continue unappealing work could be a reason. Early retirement because of health can also stand for an honourable way out, serving to circumvent the pressure of younger people jockeying and politicking for the older executive's position. Another reason may be the disappointment of not getting the expected promotion, the reluctance to face the consequences of a demotion, or the inability to keep up with the existing work load. Finally, retirement because of health reasons can frequently be a euphemism for straight out dismissal.

A final point should be made about the role of the organization. Given the rise in second careers, multiple careers, continuation of disrupted careers, or late careers (the latter particularly for women after the child-rearing period has passed), employment of older employees is inevitable. Present research has shed doubt on the myth of mental decline of older executives. Continuous challenge is what is needed to stay mentally alert and prevent 'rut' formation. The second world war demonstrated the ability and usefulness of the older worker; unfortunately, this has been forgotten all too soon. Through second careers, part-time jobs, flexible working hours and advisory roles, retired executives could obtain new outlets for action, stimulation and creativity.

The role of society

Changing attitudes toward the retirement process and practices, and leisure, warrant a few comments about future developments in this domain and the role society can play. Naturally, the most important trend which will affect retirement practices is the decline in birth rate which makes zero population growth an attainable goal in the near future. The decline in birth rate will eventually reduce the supply of people entering the labour market. This trend indicates a need to utilize an increasingly elderly labour force.

Consequently, in countries such as Great Britain, France, Germany, Holland or Sweden, where zero population growth is approaching or has been reached, the existence of mandatory retirement and the trend toward early retirement are seriously questioned. The same thing has been occurring in the United States. What is happening is that the trends towards higher social security payments and early retirement, in combination with a decreasing percentage of people entering the labour market, may lead to a prohibitive rise in taxes to pay for these pension plans. This has started a rethinking process on the question of retirement on the part of government and has resulted in calls for legislation against mandatory retirement plans. Combined pressure by the government and lobbying groups of the elderly is influencing many organizations in various countries to move away from a compulsory retirement age, and may also force unions to change their policies and stop pressuring for increasingly earlier retirement dates.

Unions always have had a rather ambivalent attitude toward the employment of the elderly, partially due to the fear of disruptions on the labour market. In addition, they have held the view that ever earlier retirement ages combined with excellent early retirement schemes are ways of 'delivering the goods' to their constituency. Sufficient pressure which demonstrates the dysfunctional side effects of this policy may reverse this trend. Flexible or phased retirement in various forms might be the pattern of the future, a tendency which can already be discerned in other countries. This trend may have to be accompanied by adjustments of social security practices.

Flexible and phased retirement practices (also allowing for early retirement from a particular job) combined with an increased life span, will make for more people commencing on a second career. This will cause a rise in the number of older people looking for employment.

More attention has to be given to pre-retirement counselling. The government, the unions and employers' organizations probably have to play a more active role here. Through these pre-retirement counselling programmes the rise in discontent among candidate retirees might be prevented or minimized to the benefit of the work climate within the organization.

With this last observation we have now come to the end of our discussion of career. We have observed that retirement for most executives can be something other than a 'terminal state' looked at with an attitude of despair and hopelessness. There are many possibilities for dealing with this phase of the 'career clock' in a creative way. Second careers, new hobbies, sports, travel, volunteer service, educational ventures, new friendships, and involvement with grandchildren are only a few ways of transcending the stage of retirement and adding a new phase to the 'social clock'. These various activities necessitate new values and goals, new criteria for self-evaluation, but also create a new sense of continuity by integrating past with future and thus creating healthy adjustment to the present. Human experience acquired this way with reverence for life will bring acceptance of life and death without despair.

11

METAMORPHOSIS

Just as a cautious businessman avoids tying up all his capital in one concern, so, perhaps, worldly wisdom will advise us not to look for the whole of our satisfaction from a single aspiration. . .[1]

Sigmund Freud

In the story of the Japanese writer Akutagawa 'In a Grove',[2] better known in its film version *Rashomon*, a double crime is depicted: rape and homicide (or possible suicide). The story is told in retrospect by the three participants in the drama: the bandit (supposedly responsible for the warrior's death and the woman's rape), the warrior's wife, and the dead warrior (the latter story narrated through a medium). We are also given a report by a woodcutter who found the body in a grove.

We learn from the testimony given to the High Police Commissioner that the bandit claims to have killed the warrior in honourable combat; the woman claims to have killed her husband in a fit of horror after the rape; the husband claims to have committed hara-kiri out of grief and disgrace.

We are left with an enigma. Even the woodcutter, supposedly a simple disinterested witness, is drawn into the chaos of the incident. The world seems an illusion; each witness is trying to salvage his own sense of reality, pointing at the other as a fraud. Like the king in the introductory chapter, we do not envy the High Police Commissioner in his role as a decision maker. His task is to terminate existing ambiguity and render a formal verdict in this human drama. The nature of the verdict is here not our concern. It is more how he does it, and with what frame of reference in mind. What is the diagnostic process going to be like?

184

With this final paradox we have come full circle. Some of the ways of better understanding individual and organizational dilemmas in the interests of more effective leadership have been outlined in this book. We have noted that the responsibility of leadership becomes the breaking of impasses, providing motivation, career counselling, and giving directions, even in highly paradoxical situations. Leaders are supposed to take an active stand, exercising power and allocating resources. Here we are not talking about abstractions but are referring to contemporary requirements of leadership.

Although we are still fascinated by strong leaders we also look at them with a certain wariness, a fear about the ways in which these people might wield their power. This fear contains a danger since it can lead to an erosion of leadership and organizational mediocrity. Participation might become a disguise for the unwillingness to accept responsibilities, and organizational activities may turn into rituals. Strong leadership, based on a sense of inner conviction and an understanding of one's personal strengths and weaknesses, can make for clarity in organizational roles, instituting trust and a sense of generativity toward subordinates, real participation and delegation, and eventually greater organizational effectiveness.

In leadership the importance of this sense of generativity cannot be emphasized strongly enough. Without empathy toward others there can be no trust, and without trust, organizational learning stops. Absence of empathy changes the leader into an automaton, susceptible to destructive behaviour, and makes for the pathology of leadership. Here we can find the Neros, Caligulas, Hitlers, Stalins and Saddam Husseins.

But early identification of potential intra-psychic dissonance can make for prevention. The dilemmas which leaders have to face first are their own inner conflicts. If we can unravel our own paradoxes and balance the requirements of our inner and outer world, our reality sense will be strengthened and flexible adaptation might be attainable. If we can surmount our developmental tasks we will be able to relate to the objectives and goals of the organization and arrive at a sense of commitment to our choices.

In the previous chapters we have dealt with the vicissitudes of leadership, power and career. We have emphasized the importance of human development, the life stages, and the quality of sustained relationships for effective coping behaviour in organizational life.

We have stressed the need for a certain degree of mastery of the complexities of human motivation. For that purpose we have outlined a number of ways of looking at human interaction to create some understanding of the psychodynamic forces at work. We have suggested that this type of understanding will improve the quality of decision making and sense of commitment to organizations.

The task of executives becomes to transform the theme of conventional rationality and make themselves aware of their limitations, given the pressures of inner fears, anxiety and guilt, as well as affiliative, dependency and aggressive needs. Executives have to come to terms with their own narcissism and thus place limits on potential conflicts between fantasy and reality in their leadership styles. Recourse to fantasy, however, will remain important as a way of mastering disappointments, instead of becoming a way of arresting human development and growth. Healing will come through insight and the establishment of trust in interpersonal relationships.

Many years ago the Austrian writer and poet Stefan Zweig wrote about one man's transformation, an almost mystic experience of sudden personal insight after a long period of lack of vitality and spiritual impotence. After this experience the main character asks himself:

Have I grown younger? All I know is that I have only just begun to live. Oh, I know, too, of the everyday illusion. I know how apt people are to think all their past has been error and preparation. Doubtless it is arrogant to take a cold pen into my warm, living hand, and to write upon the dry paper that at length I am really alive. But even if it be an illusion, it is the first illusion that has made me happy, the first that has warmed my blood and unlocked my sense. If I sketch here the miracle of my awakening, I do it for myself alone, though I know it all better than words can describe. I have not spoken of the matter to any of my friends; they never knew how dead I had become; they will never guess how my life has blossomed afresh. Nor am I perturbed by the thought that death's hand may suddenly be laid upon this living life of mine, and that these lines may be read by other eyes. Those who have never known the magic of such an hour as I have described, will understand just as little as I could have understood six

186

months ago how the fugitive and almost inconsequent hap-
penings of one afternoon and evening could so have touched
my life to flame. The thought of such a reader will not shame
me, for he will understand what I have written. But one who
understands will not judge, and will have no pride. Before
him I shall not be ashamed. Whoever has found himself can
never again lose anything in this world. He who has grasped
the human being in himself understands all mankind.[3]

The author describes here a unique experience. Most instances of
human insight do not offer such a dramatic transformation. But
whatever the intensity of the experience, enrichment will occur
both in personal and organizational life. The willingness which
engagement in this type of dialogue brings, the ability to choose
and learn, will bring humanity back to organizations and will
create a pattern of life that is distinctly our own. Oscar Wilde once
said that 'to regret one's own experiences is to arrest one's own
development. To deny one's own experiences is to put a lie into the
lips of one's own life.'[4] Maybe we should add to this that to
understand one's own experiences makes for a richer, more complex three-dimensional life.

NOTES

PREFACE

1   Marc L. Miringoff, *The Index of Social Health*, Annual Report (Tarry-town, NY: Fordham University Institute for Innovation and Social Policy, 1993); see Gwendolyn Puryear Keita and Steven L. Sauter, *Work and Well-Being: An Agenda for the 1990s* (Washington, DC: American Psychological Association, 1993).

2   See S. M. Weiss, J. E. Fielding and W. B. Baum, *Health at Work* (Hilsdale, NJ: Lawrence Erlbaum Associates, 1990).

1 INTRODUCTION

1   W. H. Auden, *Collected Poems*, E. Mendelson (ed.) (New York: Random House, 1976; London: Faber 1976: 248)

2 THE OBLOMOV THREAT

1   Søren Kierkegaard, *Either/Or*, vol. 1 trans. D. F. Swenson and L. M. Swenson (Princeton: Princeton University Press, 1944: 24).

2   Ivan Goncharov, *Oblomov*, trans. N. Duddington (New York: E. P. Dutton and Co., 1960; London: Dent, 1970).

3   Ivan Goncharov, *Oblomov, see note 2*: 186–7.

4   Ives Hendrick, 'Work and the Pleasure Principle', *Psychoanalytic Quarterly*, 1943, 12: 311–29.

5   Robert W. White, *Lives in Progress*, 2nd edn (New York: Holt, Rinehart & Winston, 1966). See also Robert W. White, *The Enterprise of Living* (New York: Holt, Rinehart & Winston, 1972).

6   Sigmund Freud, 'Inhibitions, Symptoms and Anxiety', *The Standard Edition of the Complete Psychological Works of Sigmund Freud*, vol. 20, James Strachey (ed.) (London: The Hogarth Press and The Institute of Psychoanalysis, 1926: 89). All future references to Freud's works will be designated *Standard Edition*.

7   Erik H. Erikson, *Childhood and Society* (New York: W. W. Norton & Co., 1963: 260; London: The Hogarth Press, 1964).

8 Sigmund Freud, 'Mourning and Melancholia', *The Standard Edition*, vol. 14, 1917. *see note 6.*
9 Gregory Rochlin, *Man's Aggression* (Boston: Gambit, 1973; London: Constable, 1973).
10 For an overview of the various mechanisms of defence see Anna Freud, *The Ego and the Mechanisms of Defense* (London: The Hogarth Press and The Institute of Psychoanalysis, 1937).
11 For an elaboration on narcissism see Otto Kernberg, *Borderline Conditions and Pathological Narcissism* (New York: Jason Aronson, 1975) and Heinz Kohut, *The Analysis of the Self* (New York: International Universities Press, 1975).
12 W. H. Auden, *Collected Poems*, E. Mendelson (ed.) (New York: Random House, 1976; London: Faber, 1976: 227–8).
13 Helen H. Tartakoff, 'The Normal Personality in Our Culture and the Nobel Prize Complex', in R. M. Loewenstein, L. M. Newman, M. Schur and A. J. Solnit (eds) *Psychoanalysis – A General Psychology, Essays in Honor of Heinz Harman* (New York: International Universities Press, 1966: 238–9).
14 Helen H. Tartakoff, 'The Normal Personality in Our Culture and the Nobel Prize Complex': 246–7, *see note 13.*
15 See Sigmund Freud, 'Some Character-Types Met Within Psychoanalytic Work', *The Standard Edition*, vol. 14, 1917, *see note 6.*
16 Erik H. Erikson, *Childhood and Society*: 255–6, *see note 7.*
17 Sigmund Freud, 'Some Character-Types Met Within Psychoanalytic Work', *The Standard Edition*, vol. 14, 1917: 316–32, *see note 6.*
18 Abraham H. Maslow, 'The Jonas Complex', in W. G. Bennis, E. H. Schein, F. I. Steele, D. E. Berlew (eds) *Interpersonal Dynamics* (revised edn) (Homewood, Illinois: The Dorsey Press, 1968).
19 See for example John Bowlby, *Attachment* (New York: Basic Books, 1969; London: The Hogarth Press, 1969) and John Bowlby, *Separation* (New York: Basic Books, 1973; London: The Hogarth Press, 1973). See also Robert W. White, *The Enterprise of Living, see note 5.*
20 Robert W. White, *Lives in Progress, see note 5.*
21 Robert W. White, *Lives in Progress*: 180–1, *see note 5.*
22 Albert Camus, *The Rebel* (New York: Vintage Books, 1956: 22; Harmondsworth: Penguin Books, 1974).
23 Albert Camus, *The Rebel*: 22, *see note 22.*
24 For a more complete analysis of entrepreneurship and the process of change, see Manfred F. R. Kets de Vries, *The Entrepreneur as Catalyst of Economic and Cultural Change*, unpublished doctoral dissertation, Harvard University, Graduate School of Business Administration, 1970.
25 Konrad Lorenz, *On Aggression* (New York: Harcourt, Brace & World, 1966: 72; London: Methuen, 1966).
26 See Johan Huizinga, *Homo Ludens: A Study of the Play Element in Culture* (Boston: Beacon Press, 1955).

3 THE ORGANIZATION OF EMPTINESS

1 Søren Kierkegaard, *Either/Or*, vol. 1, trans. D. F. Swenson and L. M. Swenson (Princeton: Princeton University Press, 1944: 282).
2 Arthur Schopenhauer, *Essays and Aphorisms*, trans. R. J. Hollingsdale (Harmondsworth: Penguin Books, 1970: 43).
3 T. S. Eliot, 'The Love Song of J. Alfred Prufrock', *The Waste Land and Other Poems* (New York: Harcourt, Brace & World, 1962; London: Faber, 1940).
4 Bertolt Brecht, *Jungle of Cities and Other Plays* (New York: Grave Press, 1966: 83; 'In the Jungle of the Cities', in *Collected Plays* vol. 1, London: Methuen, 1970).
5 J. Taviss, 'Changes in the Form of Alienation: the 1900s versus the 1950s', *American Sociological Review* 1969, 27: 65–91.
6 See for example Neal Q. Herrick and Michael Maccoby, 'Humanizing Work: A Priority Goal of the 1970s', in L. E. Davis and A. B. Cherns (eds) *The Quality of Working Life*, vol. 1 (New York: The Free Press, 1975).
7 Karl Marx, 'Economic and Philosophical Manuscripts', trans. T. B. Bottomore, in Erich Fromm, *Marx's Concept of Man* (New York: Frederick Ungar Publishing Co., 1961), trans. R. Livingstone and G. Benton, in *Marx: Early Writings* (Harmondsworth: Penguin Books, 1975).
8 See Emile Durkheim, *La Suicide* (Paris: Alcan, 1897); *Suicide: A Study in Sociology*, (London: Routledge & Kegan Paul, 1950).
9 Ferdinand Tönnies, *Gemeinschaft und Gesellschaft* (Leipzig: Fues's Verlag, 1887).
10 Robert K. Merton, *Social Theory and Social Structure* (New York: The Free Press, 1968: 216).
11 A. Etzioni, 'Basic Human Needs, Alienation, and Inauthenticity', *American Sociological Review* 1968, 33: 870–85.
12 M. Seeman, 'On the Meaning of Alienation', in A. Campbell and P. E. Converse (eds) *The Human Meaning of Social Change* (New York: Russell Sage Foundation, 1972).
13 Eric Josephson and Marie Josephson (eds) *Man Alone: Alienation in Modern Society* (New York: Dell Publishing Company, 1972: 12–13).
14 Søren Kierkegaard, *Fear and Trembling and the Sickness unto Death*, trans. W. Lowrie (Princeton: Princeton University Press, 1968: 148).
15 Karen Horney, *Neurosis and Human Growth* (New York: W. W. Norton, 1950: 157).
16 Erich Fromm, *The Sane Society* (New York: Fawcett Premier Books, 1968: 111; London: Routledge & Kegan Paul, 1956).
17 Erich Fromm, *The Sane Society*: 181, *see note 16*.
18 Rainer Maria Rilke, *The Notebooks of Malte Laurids Brigge*, trans. M. D. Herter Norton (New York: W. W. Norton, 1949: 29; London: The Hogarth Press, 1959).
19 *Diagnostic and Statistical Manual of Mental Disorders* DSM-III-R, third edn (Washington DC: American Psychiatric Association, 1987: 339).
20 *Diagnostic and Statistical Manual of Mental Disorders*: 351–2, *see note 19*.

21 See for example Helen Deutsch, 'Some Forms of Emotional Disturbance and Their Relationship to Schizophrenia', in *Neurosis and Character Types* (New York: International Universities Press, 1965); Ronald W. Fairbairn, *An Object-Relations Theory of the Personality* (New York: Basic Books, 1952); M. Masud and R. Khan, 'Clinical Aspects of the Schizoid Personality: Affects and Technique', *The International Journal of Psychoanalysis* 1960, 41: 430–7; R. D. Laing, *The Divided Self* (London: Tavistock, 1960); Harry Guntrip, *Schizoid Phenomena, Object Relations and the Self* (New York: International Universities Press, 1969; London: The Hogarth Press, 1968).

22 Silvano Arieti, *Interpretation of Schizophrenia* (New York: Basic Books, 1974: 106; London: Crosby Lockwood, 1974).

23 Helen Deutsch, 'Some Forms of Emotional Disturbance and Their Relationship to Schizophrenia': 263, *see note 21*.

24 Harry Guntrip, *Schizoid Phenomena, Object Relations and the Self*: 36, *see note 21*. Guntrip is elaborating on the postulations of Fairbairn, *An Object-Relations Theory of the Personality, see note 21*.

25 Harry Guntrip, *Schizoid Phenomena, Object Relations and the Self*: 24, *see note 21*.

26 R. D. Laing, *The Divided Self*: 93, *see note 21*.

27 Fairbairn, Guntrip, and Arieti discuss at great length the developmental history of the individual predisposed to schizoid behaviour patterns. They dwell on the failure of the schizoid person to establish early object relationships. Compliance (moving toward people), or hostility (moving against people) does not seem to bring satisfaction but causes rejection. Consequently, they argue that the only choice left for a person caught in this dilemma is moving away from people and developing a detached attitude. See Ronald W. Fairbairn, *An Object-Relations Theory of the Personality, see note 21*; Harry Guntrip, *Schizoid Phenomena, Object Relations and the Self, see note 21*; Silvano Arieti, *Interpretation of Schizophrenia, see note 22*.

28 Frank Johnson, 'Psychological Alienation: Isolation and Self-Estrangement', in F. Johnson (ed.) *Alienation: Concept, Term, and Meanings* (New York: Seminar Press, 1973: 64).

29 Harry Guntrip, *Schizoid Phenomena, Object Relations and the Self*: 62, *see note 21*.

30 Thomas Mann, *Confessions of Felix Krull, Confidence Man* (New York: Vintage Books, 1969: Harmondsworth: Penguin Books, 1970).

31 Helen Deutsch, 'Some Forms of Emotional Disturbance and Their Relationship to Schizophrenia', *see note 21*.

32 Erich Fromm, *Man for Himself: An Inquiry into the Psychology of Ethics* (New York: Fawcett Premier Books, 1947: 84; London: Routledge & Kegan Paul, 1971).

33 Harry Guntrip, *Schizoid Phenomena, Object Relations, and the Self*: 47, *see note 21*.

34 Elliott Jaques, 'Social Systems as a Defence Against Persecutory and Depressive Anxiety', in Melanie Klein, Paula Heimann, and Roger Money-Kyrle (eds) *New Directions in Psychoanalysis* (London: Tavistock, 1955: 498).

4 POWER AND HELPLESSNESS

1 John Steinbeck, *The Acts of King Arthur and His Noble Knights* (New York: Ballantine Books, 1976: 58; London: Heinemann, 1977).
2 See for example George L. Engel, 'A Life Setting Conducive to Illness: The Giving-Up-Given-Up Complex', *Bulletin of the Menninger Clinic*, 1968, 32: 355–65; George L. Engel, 'Sudden and Rapid Death During Psychological Stress', *Annals of Internal Medicine*, 1971, 74: 771–87. See also A. H. Schmale, 'Giving Up as a Final Common Pathway to Changes in Health', *Advances in Psychosomatic Medicine*, 1972, 8: 20–40.
3 A. H. Schmale, 'Giving Up as a Final Common Pathway to Changes in Health', *see note 2*.
4 See George L. Engel, 'A Life Setting Conducive to Illness': 360, *see note 2*.
5 For example, T. Kavanagh and R. J. Shepard, 'The Immediate Antecedents of Myocardial Infarction in Active Man', *CMA Journal*, 7 July 1973, 109: 19–22, indicated that an increase in business problems was a predominant antecedent prior to an attack. Stanislav V. Kasl, Susan Gore, and Sidney Cobb, 'The Experience of Losing a Job: Reported Changes in Health, Symptoms and Illness Behaviour', *Psychosomatic Medicine*, March–April 1975, 37(2): 106–22, found a relationship between the anticipation of losing a job and an increase in stress symptoms. A significant association between clusters of social events requiring changes in ongoing life adjustments and time of illness has been indicated by Thomas H. Holmes and Richard H. Rahe, 'The Social Re-adjustment Rating Scale', *Journal of Psychosomatic Research*, August 1967, 11: 213–18. A number of the changes listed in their social re-adjustment scale were found to be work related.
6 Martin E. P. Seligman, Jr, *Helplessness: On Depression, Development, and Death* (San Francisco: W. H. Freeman and Co., 1975).
7 'The Battle over Bureaucracy', *Time*, 6 March 1978: 11–13.
8 See for example, E. Jaques, *The Changing Culture of a Factory* (London: Tavistock, 1951); R. L. Kahn, D. M. Wolfe, R. Q. Quinn, and J. D. Snoek, *Organizational Stress* (New York: Wiley, 1964); Robert D. Caplan *Organizational Stress and Individual Strain: A Social-Psychological Study of Risk Factors in Coronary Heart Disease Among Administrators, Engineers and Scientists*, unpublished doctoral dissertation (Ann Arbor: University of Michigan, 1971); John R. French and Robert D. Caplan, 'Organizational Stress and Individual Strain', in A. J. Marrow (ed.) *The Failure of Success* (Washington: Amacom, 1972); Robert J. House and John R. Rizzo, 'Role Conflict and Ambiguity as Critical Variables in a Model of Organizational Behaviour', *Organizational Behaviour and Human Performance*, 1972, 7: 467–505; Abraham Zaleznik, Manfred F. R. Kets de Vries, and John H. Howard, 'Stress Reactions in Organizations: Syndromes, Causes and Consequences', *Behavioural Science*, 1977, 22: 151–62; C. L. Cooper and R. Payne (eds), *Current Concerns in Occupational Stress* (New York: John Wiley and Sons, 1980).
9 For example Jay M. Weiss, 'Psychological Factors in Stress and Disease', *Scientific American*, June 1972: 104–13 demonstrated that

ulceration differences fluctuate with degree of controllability. More control over the environment through adequate feedback seemed to result in less ulcers.

10 See for example R. A. Champion, 'Studies of Experimentally Induced Disturbance', *Australian Journal of Psychology*, 1950, 2: 90–9 and J. H. Geer, G. C. Davidson, and R. I. Gatchel, 'Reduction of Stress in Humans Through Nonveridical Perceived Control of Aversive Stimulation', *Journal of Personality and Social Psychology*, 1970, 16: 731–8.

11 See A. Zaleznik, Manfred F. R. Kets de Vries, and John H. Howard, 'Stress Reactions in Organizations', *see note 8*. See also Manfred F. R. Kets de Vries, Abraham Zaleznik and John H. Howard, 'Stress Reactions in Organizations: The Minotaur Revisited', McGill University, Faculty of Management Working Paper no. 7530, 1976.

12 Mauk Mulder, *Het Spel om de Macht* (Meppel: Boom, 1972).

5 AN ALTERNATIVE VIEW OF POWER

1 Plato, *The Republic*, in *The Dialogues of Plato*, trans. B. Jowett (Chicago: Encyclopaedia Brittanica, 1952), trans. H. E. P. Lee (Harmondsworth: Penguin Books, 1955: 345).

2 Robert A. Dahl, 'The Concept of Power', *Behavioural Science*, 1957, 3: 201.

3 J. R. P. French and B. Raven, 'The Bases of Social Power', in D. Cartwright (ed.) *Studies in Social Power* (Ann Arbor: University of Michigan, Institute for Social Research, 1959).

4 See for example Michel Crozier, *The Bureaucratic Phenomenon* (Chicago: The University of Chicago Press, 1964) and Andrew M. Pettigrew, 'Toward a Political Theory of Organizational Intervention', *Human Relations*, 1975, 28(3): 191–208.

5 See Bertrand Russell, *On Power* (London: George Allen & Unwin, 1975); Herbert Goldhamer and Edward A. Shils, 'Types of Power and Status', *American Journal of Sociology*, 1939, 45(2): 171–82; J. R. P. French and B. Raven, 'The Bases of Social Power', *see note 3*; Darwin Cartwright, 'Influence, Leadership, Control', in J. G. March (ed.) *Handbook of Organizations* (Chicago: Rand McNally, 1965); Andrew M. Pettigrew, 'Toward a Political Theory of Organizational Intervention', *see note 4*. This type of conceptualization has been particularly proposed by Amatai Etzioni, *A Comparative Analysis of Complex Organizations* (New York: The Free Press, 1975 (revised edn)).

6 See for example R. H. Tawney, *Equality* (London: George Allen & Unwin, 1931); R. Bierstedt, 'An Analysis of Social Power', *American Sociological Review*, 1950, 15: 730–6; Hans Gerth and C. Wright Mills, *Character and Social Structure* (New York: Harcourt, Brace & Co., 1953; London: Routledge & Kegan Paul 1954); Robert A. Dahl, 'Power', in D. L. Sills (ed.) *International Encyclopaedia of the Social Sciences* vol. 12 (New York: MacMillan and The Free Press, 1968).

7 See G. C. Homans, 'Social Behaviour as Exchange', *American Journal of Sociology*, 1958, 63: 597–606; G. C. Homans, *Social Behaviour: Its*

Elementary Forms (New York: Harcourt, Brace & World, 1961; London: Routledge & Kegan Paul, 1973); John W. Thibaut and Harold H. Kelley, *The Social Psychology of Groups* (New York: John Wiley & Sons, 1959); M. Peter Blau, *Exchange and Power in Social Life* (New York: John Wiley & Sons, 1964).

8   For an overview of selected structural, interpersonal, and intra-personal theories of power and an attempt at integration see Manfred F. R. Kets de Vries, 'On Power: Toward a Protean Perspective', McGill University, Faculty of Management Working Paper no. 7626, June 1976.

9   Friedrick Nietzsche, *The Will to Power*, trans. W. Kaufmann and R. J. Hollingdale (New York: Vintage Books, 1968: 366).

10 Bertrand Russell, *On Power*: 8, *see note 5*.

11 Max Weber, in H. H. Gerth and C. Wright Mills (trans. and ed.) *From Max Weber: Essays in Sociology* (New York: Oxford University Press, 1946: 116; London: Routledge & Kegan Paul, 1948).

12 Eduard Spranger, *Lebensformen* (Halle: Max Niemeyer, 1924).

13 Alfred Adler, *Practice and Theory of Individual Psychology* (New York: Harcourt, Brace & Co., 1924; London: Routledge & Kegan Paul, 1929).

14 Karen Horney, *The Neurotic Personality of our Time* (New York: W. W. Norton, 1964: 163).

15 Harold D. Lasswell, *Power and Personality* (New York: The Viking Press, 1967: 39).

16 Harold D. Lasswell, *Psychopathology and Politics* (New York: The Viking Press, 1960).

17 Alexander L. George and Juliette L. George, *Woodrow Wilson and Colonel House* (New York: Dover Publications, 1964).

18 Alexander L. George, 'Power as a Compensatory Value for Political Leaders', *Journal of Social Issues*, 1968, 24: 49.

19 For a suggestion of a model of power as a developmental process see Manfred F. R. Kets de Vries, 'Power and Motivation', *Insead Research Paper Series* no. 114, 1973. See also Abraham Zaleznik and Manfred F. R. Kets de Vries, *Power and the Corporate Mind* (Boston: Houghton Mifflin, 1975).

20 See Sigmund Freud, 'Three Essays on the Theory of Sexuality', *The Standard Edition*, vol. 7, 1905, *see Chapter 2, note 6*.

21 McClelland, influenced by the work of Veroff and supported by an empirical approach to conceptualizing stages of human development, proposes a fairly similar model of intra-psychic power needs. Using a measure of social emotional maturity (as measured by thematic apperception tests) he distinguishes four stages of development (oral, anal, phallic, and generative), each stage with its own unique way of expressing the need for power. He does not try to integrate these ideas with structural and interpersonal theories of power. See David C. McClelland, *Power: The Inner Experience* (New York: Irvington Publisher, 1975). See also J. Veroff, 'Development and Validation of a Projective Measure of Power Motivation', *Journal of Abnormal and Social Psychology*, 1957, 54: 1–8.

22 For a psycho-historical interpretation of Gandhi's life see Erik H.

Erikson, *Gandhi's Truth: On the Origins of Militant Nonviolence* (New York: W. W. Norton and Co., 1966).
23 See William Manchester, *The Arms of Krupp* (New York: Bantam Books, 1970).
24 See Doris Kearne, *Lyndon Johnson and the American Dream* (New York: Harper & Row, 1976).

6 LEADERSHIP AND PARANOIA

1 Plato, 'The Republic', in *The Dialogues of Plato*, trans. B. Jowett (Chicago: Encyclopedia Britannica, 1952: 420), trans. H. D. P. Lee (Harmondsworth: Penguin Books, 1955).
2 Max Weber, *The Theory of Social and Economic Organizations*, trans. A. M. Henderson and Talcott Parsons (New York: Oxford University Press, 1947: 358–9).
3 For a psycho-historical study of the first Henry Ford see Anne Jardim, *The First Henry Ford: A Study in Personality and Business Leadership* (Cambridge, Mass.: The M. I. T. Press, 1970).
4 See Manfred F. R. Kets de Vries, *Prisoners of Leadership* (New York: John Wiley & Sons, 1989).
5 For a discussion of the idealizing and mirroring transference in a leadership context, see Manfred F. R. Kets de Vries, *Leaders, Fools and Impostors* (San Francisco: Jossey Bass, 1993).
6 See John Bowlby, *Attachment* (New York: Basic Books, 1969; London: The Hogarth Press, 1969) and John Bowlby, *Separation* (New York: Basic Books 1973; London: The Hogarth Press, 1973).
7 For a discussion of these group processes see Sigmund Freud, 'Group Psychology and the Analysis of the Ego', *The Standard Edition*, vol.18, 1921, *see Chapter 2, note 6*.
8 Otto Fenichel, *The Psychoanalytic Theory of Neurosis* (New York: W. W. Norton & Co., 1945: 428; London: Routledge & Kegan Paul, 1946).
9 Gustav Bychowski, *Dictators and Disciples* (New York: International Universities Press, 1964: 273). Quotation translated from the German by the author.
10 See Alexander L. George and Juliette L. George, *Woodrow Wilson and Colonel House* (New York: Dover Publications, 1964).
11 See Abraham Zaleznik and Manfred F. R. Kets de Vries, *Power and the Corporate Mind* (Boston: Houghton Mifflin, 1975).
12 See A. A. Rogow, *James Forrestal: A Study of Personality, Politics and Policy* (New York: The MacMillan Co., 1963).
13 Robert Waelder, 'Characteristics of Totalitarianism', in W. Muensterberger and S. Axelrad (eds) *The Psychoanalytic Study of Society* vol. 1 (New York: International Universities Press, 1960).

7 FOLIE À DEUX

1 Erasmus, *Praise of Folly*, trans. B. Radice (Harmondsworth: Penguin Books, 1971: 199).

2 In Hitler's Germany, Bormann was *Reichsleiter*, secretary to the Führer, and eventually party minister, Goebbels was Minister of Propaganda, while Ley was *Reichsleiter* and head of the German Labour Front. Both Goebbels and Ley committed suicide (Goebbels with his family in the bunker). Bormann's fate has been contested.

3 For an excellent description of Hitler's inner circle see Albert Speer, *Inside the Third Reich* (New York: Avon Books, 1971; London: Weidenfeld & Nicolson, 1971).

4 See C. Lasègue and J. Fabret, 'La Folie à Deux ou Folie Communiquée', *Ann. Med. Psychol*, 1877, 5e Série, T.18.

5 For example, Helen Deutsch, 'Folie à Deux', *The Psychoanalytic Quarterly*, 1938, 7: 307–18; A. Gralnick, 'Folie à Deux – The Psychosis of Association: Review of 103 Cases and Entire English Literature With Presentations', part I, *The Psychoanalytic Quarterly*, 1942, 16: 230–63; Part II, 1942, 16: 491–520; Sydney E. Pulver and Manly Y. Brunt, 'Deflection of Hostility in Folie à Deux', *Archives of General Psychiatry*, 1961, 5: 65–73; Berchmans Rioux, 'A Review of Folie à Deux, The Psychosis of Association', *The Psychoanalytic Quarterly*, 1963, 37: 405–28.

6 See Gralnick, 'Folie à Deux – The Psychosis of Association', *see note 5*; also Jesse McNiel, Adrian Verwoerdt, and Daniel Peak, 'Folie à Deux in the Aged: Review and Case Report of Role Reversal', *Journal of the American Geriatrics Society*, 1972, 20 (7): 316–23.

7 See for example Philip Polatin, 'Psychotic Disorders: Paranoid States', in A. M. Freedman, H. I. Kaplan and B. J. Sadock (eds) *Comprehensive Textbook of Psychiatry*, vol. 1, 2nd edn (Baltimore: The Williams & Williams Co., 1975).

8 See K. Dewhurst and J. Todd, 'The Psychosis of Association: Folie à Deux', *Journal of Nervous and Mental Diseases*, 1956, 124: 451–9.

9 This has been suggested by H. Hartman and E. Stengel, 'Studien zur psychologies des induzierten Irreseins', *Jarhbuch Psychait. Neurol*, 1933, 48.

10 Eugene O'Neill, 'Where the Cross is Made', *Seven Plays of the Sea* (New York: Vintage Books, 1972).

11 Thomas Mann, 'The Blood of the Walsungs', *Stories of Three Decades* (New York: Alfred A. Knopf, 1930).

12 Robert Lindner, *The Fifty-Minute Hour* (New York: Bantam Books, 1956).

13 For a discussion of the process of behaviour change see K. Lewin, 'Frontiers in Group Dynamics: Concept, Method, and Reality in Social Science', *Human Relations*, 1974, I: 5–41 and Edgar H. Schein, *Coercive Persuasion* (New York: W. W. Norton and Co., 1961).

14 For example see the work of Solomon Asch, 'Effects of Group Pressure upon the Modification and Distortion of Judgement', in M. H. Guetzkow (ed.) *Groups, Leadership and Men* (Pittsburgh: Carnegie, 1951), also Solomon Asch, 'Studies of Independence and Conformity: A Minority of One Against a Unanimous Majority', *Psychological Monographs*, 1956, 70(9), whole no. 416. See Stanley Schachter, 'Deviation, Rejection and Communication', *Journal of Abnormal and Social Psycho-*

logy, 1951, 46: 190–207. See also Irving L. Janis who, in his book *Victims of Group Think* (Boston: Houghton Mifflin, 1972), describes the process of group think from a slightly different perspective.

15 Stanley Milgram, 'Some Conditions of Obedience and Disobedience to Authority', *Human Relations*, 1954, 18: 57–75.

16 See for example Leon Festinger, 'A Theory of Social Comparison Processes', *Human Relations*, 1954, 7: 117–40.

17 Helene Deutsch, 'Folie à Deux', *see note 5*.

18 This phenomenon has been studied by I. L. Janis, *Psychological Stress* (New York: Wiley & Sons, 1958).

19 For the purpose of our discussion we will follow the example given in most of the literature on this subject and stay with the term folie à deux no matter how many people are involved.

20 Herbert C. Kelman, 'Compliance, Identification, and Internalization: Three Processes of Attitude Change', *Journal of Conflict Resolution*, 1958, 2: 51–60.

21 Psychiatric literature calls this variety folie communiquée, first described in 1881 by Marondon de Montyel, who mentions contagion of ideas but only after the second person has resisted these for a long time. After adoption of these delusions, they will be maintained even after separation.

22 See H. Beckett Lang, 'Simultaneous Psychosis Occurring in Business Partners', *The Psychiatric Quarterly*, 1936, 10: 611–18.

23 See Joseph L. Schott, *No Left Turns* (New York: Praeger Publishers, 1975); 'The Truth About Hoover', *Time*, 22 December 1975: 16–21; Neil J. Welch and David W. Marston, *Inside Hoover's FBI* (Garden City, NY: Doubleday, 1984); and William W. Turner, *Hoover's FBI* (New York: Thunder's Mouth Press, 1993).

24 See Anthony Sampson, *The Sovereign State of ITT* (New York: Stein & Day, 1973; London: Hodder, 1973).

25 See Manfred F. R. Kets de Vries, 'Doing a Maxwell: Or why not to Identify with the Aggressor', *European Management Journal*, 1993, 11 (2): 169–74.

8 THE ENTREPRENEURIAL PERSONALITY

1 Bertolt Brecht, 'Mother Courage and Her Children', In R. Manheim and J. Willett (eds) *Collected Plays* (New York: Vintage Books, 1972: 196; London: Eyre Methuen 1971).

2 See Charles Raw, Bruce Page, and Godfrey Hodgson, *Do You Sincerely Want to be Rich?* (New York: The Viking Press, 1971).

3 Charles C. Kenney, *Riding the Runaway Horse* (Boston: Little Brown, 1992).

4 Joseph A. Schumpeter, *Theorie der Wirtschaftlichen Entwicklung* (Münich and Leipzig: Duncker and Humblat, 1931).

5 Thorstein Veblen, 'Why is Economics Not an Evolutionary Science?', *The Quarterly Journal of Economics*, 1889, 12: (4).

6 As a caveat it may be appropriate to mention two new developments

in the making of entrepreneurs. First, we can observe an increasing number of women who start their own enterprises. A contributing factor is their need to create a structure where they are in control, given the usual unresponsiveness of large businesses to the special needs of working women with children. Since the psychodynamic variables that may explain why, under similar circumstances, some women start their own companies while others don't are still far from clear, I will concentrate on the male entrepreneur in this chapter.

In the case of women entrepreneurs we can speculate, however, on the importance of such factors as a girl's relationship with her father during her childhood, her birth order in the family, the absence of sons, and the importance of strong female role models in the family. In addition (at this point in time, a situation which is changing due to the emergence of female entrepreneurial role models), a woman entrepreneur is likely to have been a tomboy whose father encouraged her to take on untraditional roles and to pursue any career which interested her.

Another less frequent scenario is one in which the young woman observes her father treating her mother as a doormat. He is obviously neither reliable nor a model husband. In spite of her father's inappropriate behaviour patterns, the young woman may feel that she has a privileged relationship with him. However, given what she has experienced during her childhood, she will do anything to avoid finding herself in her mother's position. Her prevailing leitmotif is that she feels she cannot rely on anybody. As a result she may choose a life strategy whereby she does not need to depend on anyone. Creating her own enterprise is often the ideal solution.

The second important development, due to the recent increase in downsizing in organizations, is that many individuals at a later stage in their careers find themselves in a situation with limited options. Consequently, they may feel that they have no choice but to start their own business.

7   William J. Baumol, 'Entrepreneurship in Economic Theory', *The American Economic Review*, 1968, 58(2): 64–71.

8   For a study of the origin of the concept entrepreneur see Fritz Redlich, 'The Origin of the Concepts of Entrepreneur and Creative Entrepreneur', *Explorations in Entrepreneurial History*, 1949, 1: 145–66,

9   Joseph A. Schumpeter, 'Economic Theory and Entrepreneurial History', in H. G. J. Aitken (ed.) *Exploration in Enterprise* (Cambridge, Mass.: Harvard Universities Press, 1965: 51).

10 See Heinz Hartmann, 'Managers and Entrepreneurs: A Useful Distinction', *Administrative Science Quarterly*, 1959, 3: 429–51.

11 Frank H. Knight, *Risk, Uncertainty and Profit* (Boston: Houghton Mifflin, 1940).

12 For a review of studies testing entrepreneurial behaviour patterns see Manfred F. R. Kets de Vries, 'The Entrepreneurial Personality: A Person at the Crossroads', *Journal of Management Studies*, 1977, 14(1): 34–57. For a description of locus of control see Herbert M. Lefcourt, *Locus of Control* (New York: Wiley 1976); see also Manfred F. R. Kets

de Vries, Daphne Zevadi, Alain Noël and Mihkel Tombak, 'Locus of Control and Entrepreneurs: A Three-Country Comparative Study', *INSEAD Working Paper* no. 89/59, 1990.

13 See Norman R. Smith, *The Entrepreneur and his Firm: The Relationship Between Type of Man and Type of Company* (East Lansing: Michigan State University, Graduate School of Business Administration, 1967).

14 See for example Edward B. Roberts and Herbert A. Wainer, 'Some Characteristics of Technical Entrepreneurs', *Research Program on the Management of Science and Technology* (Massachusetts Institute of Technology, 1966: 145–66), and Edward B. Roberts, 'A Basic Study of Innovators: How to Keep and Capitalize on their Talents', *Research Management*, 1968, 11(4). See also Arnold C. Cooper, 'Technical Entrepreneurship: What Do We Know?', *Research and Development Management*, 1973, 3: 59–64.

15 Everett Hagen, *On the Theory of Social Change* (Homewood, Illinois: The Dorsey Press, 1962).

16 The alternative might be the establishment of ghetto areas in cases of extreme hostility in the environment with a normal distribution of vocations within the ghetto.

17 For a review of these studies see Manfred F. R. Kets de Vries, *The Entrepreneur as Catalyst of Economic and Cultural Change*, unpublished doctoral dissertation, Harvard University, Graduate School of Business Administration, 1970.

18 See for example Orvis F. Collins, David G. Moore, and Darab Unwalla, *The Enterprising Man* (East Lansing: Bureau of Business and Economic Research, Graduate School of Business Administration, Michigan State University, 1964). See also Kets de Vries 'The Entrepreneurial Personality', *see note 12.*

19 These polarities have been suggested by for example W. C. Becker, 'Consequences of Different Kinds of Parental Discipline', in M. L. Hoffman and L. S. Hoffman (eds) *Review of Child Development Research*, vol. 1 (New York: Russell Sage Foundation, 1964); and Robert W. White, *The Enterprise of Living* (New York: Holt, Rinehart & Winston, 1972).

20 Robert W. White, *The Enterprise of Living*: 53, *see note 19.*

21 Orvis F. Collins, David G. Moore, and Darab Unwalla, *The Enterprising Man*: 244, *see note 18.*

22 See Anne Jardim, The First Henry Ford: *A Study in Personality and Business Leadership* (Cambridge, Mass.: The M. I. T. Press, 1970); see also Robert Lacey, *Ford: The Men and the Machine* (Boston: Little Brown & Co., 1986).

9 THE MID-CAREER CRISIS: A RENEWED SEARCH FOR IDENTITY

1 Dante Alighieri, *The Inferno*, trans. J. Ciardi (New York: New American Library, 1954: 28).

2 C. G. Jung, *Psychological Reflections: A New Anthology of his Writings*, in

   J. Jacobi (ed.) Bollinger Series 31, (Princeton: Princeton Universities Press, 1973: 136–7; London: Routledge & Kegan Paul 1971).

3 Joseph Heller, *Something Happened* (New York: Alfred A. Knopf, 1974; London: Cape, 1974).

4 Charlotte Bühler, 'The Curve of Life as Studied in Biographies', *Journal of Applied Psychology*, 1935, 19: 405–9.

5 Else Frenkel-Brunswik, 'Adjustments and Reorientation in the Course of the Life Span', in B. Neugarten (ed.) *Middle Age and Aging* (Chicago: University of Chicago Press, 1968).

6 Erik H. Erikson, *Childhood and Society* (New York: W. W. Norton, 1973; London: The Hogarth Press, 1964).

7 Erik H. Erikson, *Childhood and Society*: 267, *see note 6*.

8 Daniel J. Levinson, *The Seasons of Man's Life* (New York: Alfred A. Knopf, 1978). See also Daniel J. Levinson, C. Darrow, E. Klein, M. Levinson and B. McKee, 'The Psychological Development of Men in Early Adulthood and the Mid-Life Transition', in D. F. Hicks, A. Thomas and M. Roff (eds) *Life History Research in Psychopathology*, vol. 3 (Minneapolis: University of Minneapolis Press, 1974); and Daniel J. Levinson, 'A Conception of Adult Development', *American Psychologist*, 1986, 41(1): 3–13. See also Nancy Mayer, *The Male Mid-Life Crisis* (Garden City, NY: Doubleday, 1978).

9 Daniel J. Levinson, C. Darrow, E. Klein, M. Levinson and B. McKee 'The Psychological Development of Men': 254, *see note 8*.

10 Donald E. Super, *The Psychology of Careers* (New York: Harper & Row, 1957).

11 Edgar H. Schein, 'The Individual, the Organization and the Career', *Journal of Applied Behavioral Science*, 1971, 7: 401–26; and Edgar H. Schein, *Career Dynamics: Matching Individual and Organizational Needs*, (Reading, Mass.: Addison Wesley, 1978). See also Jeffrey Sonnenfeld and John Kotter, 'The Maturation of Career Theory', *Human Relations*, 1982, 35: 19–46; Lynn A. Isabella, 'The Effect of Career Stage on the Meaning of Key Organizational Events', *Journal of Organizational Behavior*, 1988, 9: 345–58; David Hall, *Careers in Organizations* (Santa Monica: Goodyear Publishing Company, 1976).

12 This segment of the chapter is heavily influenced by research done by Robert J. Havighurst, 'Middle Age – The New Prime of Life', in C. Tibbitts and W. Donahue (eds) *Aging in Today's Society* (New York: Prentice Hall, 1960); Bernice L. Neugarten (ed.) *Personality in Middle and Late Life* (New York: Atherton Press, 1964); Bernice L. Neugarten 'The Awareness of Middle Age', *Middle Age and Aging* (Chicago: University of Chicago Press, 1968); Roger L. Gould, 'The Phases of Adult Life: A Study in Developmental Psychology', *The American Journal of Psychiatry*, 1972, 129: 521–31; Roger L. Gould, *Transformations* (New York: Simon & Schuster, 1978); George E. Vaillant, *Adaptation to Life* (Boston: Little Brown, 1978); John M. Oldham and Robert S. Liebert (eds), *The Middle Years* (New Haven: Yale University Press, 1989); Robert S. Weiss, *Staying the Course* (New York: The Free Press, 1990).

13 C. G. Jung, 'The Stages of Life', in J. Campbell (ed.) *The Portable Jung* (New York: Viking Press, 1971: 13).

14 Elliott Jaques, 'Death and the Mid-Life Crisis', *International Journal of Psychoanalysis*, 1965, 41(4): 502–14.
15 See for example Harvey C. Lehman, 'The Creative Production Rates of Present Versus Past Generations of Scientists', *Middle Age and Aging see note 5*; Wayne Dennis, 'Creative Productivity Between the Ages of 20 and 80 Years', *Middle Age and Aging see note 5*; Robert S. Weiss, *Staying the Course, see note 12*.
16 See Duane Schultz, 'Managing the Middle-Aged Manager', *Personnel*, 1974, 51: 8–17.
17 Ingmar Bergman, *Scenes from a Marriage* (New York: Bantam Books, 1974: 151; London: Calder, 1974).
18 Ingmar Bergman, *Scenes from a Marriage*: 152, *see note 17*.
19 See for example J. F. Cuber and P. B. Harroff, 'The More Total View: Relationships Among Men and Women of the Upper Middle Class', *Marriage and Family Living*, May 1963. See also Peter C. Pineo, 'Disenchantment in the Later Years of Marriage', *Middle Age and Aging see note 5*; Gould, 'The Phases of Adult Life' *see note 12*, found that satisfaction with marriage reaches rock-bottom around the age of 35.
20 See Marjorie Fiske Lowenthal, Majda Thurner and David Chriboga, *Four Stages of Life* (San Francisco: Jossey Bass, 1975).
21 See Michael Fogarty, *Forty to Sixty: How we Waste the Middle Aged* (London: Centre for Studies of Social Policy, 1975).
22 See Gould, 'The Phases of Adult Life', *see note 12*.
23 See Douglas C. Kimmel, *Adulthood and Aging* (New York: John Wiley and Sons, 1974); also Lowenthal, Thurner and Chriboga, *see note 20*.
24 See Neugarten, 'The Awareness of Middle Age', and David Gutmann, 'Parenthood: A Key to the Comparative Study of the Life Cycle', in N. Datan and L. H. Ginsberg (eds) *Life Span Developmental Psychology* (New York: Academic Press, 1975); see also Kenneth Soddy and Mary C. Kidson, *Men in Middle Life* (London: Tavistock Publications, 1967 Philadelphia: J. P. Lippincott Co., 1967).
25 Cyril Sofer, *Men in Mid-Career* (Cambridge: Cambridge University Press, 1970: 271).
26 See for example Raymond G. Kuhlen, 'Developmental Changes in Motivation During the Adult Years', *Middle Age and Aging see note 5*; and Kimmel, *Adulthood and Aging, see note 23*.
27 See Lowenthal, Thurnher, and Chriboga, *Four Stages of Life, see note 20*.
28 Meyer Friedman and Ray H. Rosenman, *Type A Behavior and Your Heart* (New York: Alfred A. Knopf, 1974)
29 See Peter Sainsbury, 'Social and Epidemiological Aspects of Suicide with Special Reference to the Aged', in R. H. Williams, C. Tibbitts and W. Donahue (eds) *Processes of Aging*, vol. 2 (New York: Atherton Press, 1964). See also Robert M. Butler, 'Psychosocial Aspects of Aging', in H. I. Kaplan and B. J. Sadock (eds) *Comprehensive Textbook of Psychiatry*, vol. 2, fifth edition (Baltimore: The Williams & Wilkins Company, 1989).
30 US National Center for Health Statistics, *Vital Statistics for the United States*, Annual 1992, Washington DC: 83.

31 Goethe, *Faust*, Part 1, trans. F. Wayne (Harmondsworth: Penguin Books, 1972: 43).
32 Herschel B. Chipp, *Theories of Modern Art* (Berkeley: University of California Press, 1968: 79).
33 Jaroslav Hašek, *The Good Soldier Svejk*, trans. C. Parrott (New York: Thomas Y. Crowell Co., 1974; London: Heinemann, 1973).
34 Jaroslav Hašek, *The Good Soldier Svejk*: 76, see note 33.
35 Ingmar Bergman, *Scenes from a Marriage*: 154, see note 17.
36 Ingmar Bergman, *Face to Face* (New York: Pantheon Books, 1976: 64–5; London: M. Boyars 1976).
37 Douglas T. Hall, *Careers in Organizations* (Pacific Palisades: Goodyear Publishing Co., 1976).

10 IS THERE LIFE AT RETIREMENT?

1 Dylan Thomas, *Collected Poems 1934–1952* (London: J. M. Dent & Sons Ltd, 1952: 159).
2 See Robert N. Butler, *Why Survive? Being Old in America* (New York: Harper & Row, 1975: 68). See also Lissy F. Janvik and Gary W. Small, 'Geriatric Psychiatry: Introduction and Overview', *Comprehensive Textbook of Psychiatry*, vol. 2, see Chapter 9, note 29.
3 Winston L. S. Churchill, *The Second World War*, *vol. 1*, *The Gathering Storm* (Boston: Houghton Mifflin, 1948: 526; London: Cassell, 1948).
4 As quoted in Simone de Beauvoir, *The Coming of Age*, trans. P. O'Brien (New York: G. P. Putnam's Sons, 1972: 430).
5 See Marjorie Fisk Lowenthal, Majda Thurner, and David Chriboga, *Four Stages of Life* (San Francisco: Jossey Bass, 1975).
6 Erik H. Erikson, *Childhood and Society*, see Chapter 9, note 6.
7 Carl G. Jung, 'The Stages of Life', in J. Campbell (ed.) *The Portable Jung*, see Chapter 9, note 13.
8 As quoted in Simone de Beauvoir, *The Coming of Age*: 435–6, see note 4.
9 See Douglas C. Kimmel, *Adulthood and Aging* (New York: John Wiley & Sons, 1974).
10 See for example Eugene Friedmann and Robert J. Havighurst (eds) *The Meaning of Work and Retirement* (Chicago: University of Chicago Press, 1954), and Stephen J. Miller, 'The Social Dilemma of the Aging Leisure Participant', in A. M. Rose and W. A. Peterson (eds) *Older People and their Social World* (Philadelphia: F. A. David, 1965).
11 See for example Elaine Cummings and William E. Henry, *Growing Old: The Process of Disengagement* (New York: Basic Books, 1961).
12 The five suggested styles are to a large extent based on an empirical study by Suzanne Reichard, Florine Livson and P. G. Peterson, *Aging and Personality: A Study of Eighty-Seven Older Men* (New York: John Wiley, 1962). The study by Bernice L. Neugarten, William J. Crolty and Sheldon S. Tobin, 'Personality Types in an Aged Population', in B. L. Neugarten (ed.) *Personality in Middle and Late Life*, (New York: Atherton Press, 1964) was also of some influence. Many of the conclusions of

these two studies concur with the author's personal findings in studying retiring or retired executives.

13 See Robert C. Atchey, *The Sociology of Retirement* (New York: Schenkman Publishing Company, 1976). See also W. E. Thompson and G. Streib, 'Situational Determinants: Health and Economic Deprivation in Retirement', *Journal of Social Issues*, 1958, 14: 18–34; A. W. Pollman, 'Health as an Early Retirement Factor', *Journal of Gerontology*, 1971, 26; and Marion P. Crawford, 'Retirement as a Psycho-social Crisis', *Journal of Psychosomatic Research*, 1972, 16: 375–80.

14 For example, it remains open to question if reduction in speed is a consequence of aging or caused by factors such as health status, environmental deficits, arterial blood pressure, or depression. More rigorous research seems to be needed whereby the dysfunctional effects of disease are separated from aging. See Robert N. Butler, 'The Façade of Chronological Age: An Interpretative Summary', in B. L. Neugarten (ed.) *Middle Age and Aging* (Chicago: University of Chicago Press, 1968); see also Robert N. Butler, 'Psychosocial Aspects of Aging', *Comprehensive Textbook of Psychiatry*, *see Chapter 9, note 29*.

15 Cicero, *Selected Works*, trans. M. Grant (Harmondsworth: Penguin Books, 1971: 221).

16 See National Council on the Aging, *Utilization of Older Professionals and Scientific Workers*, May 1961; Roger O'Meara, 'Retirement', *Across the Board*, January 1977: 4–8; *Aging America*, 1987–88 edn, prepared by US Special Committee on Aging, American Association of Retired Persons, Federal Council on Aging, US Administration on Aging, US Department of Health and Human Services, Washington, DC, 1987; D. Gutmann, *Reclaimed Powers: Toward a New Psychology of Men and Women in Later Life* (New York: Basic Books, 1987).

17 See Wayne Dennis, 'Creative Productivity Between the Ages of 20 and 80 Years', in B. L. Neugarten (ed.) *Middle Age and Aging*, *see note 14*.

18 See Atchey, *The Sociology of Retirement*: 110, *see note 13*. See also Butler, 'Psychosocial Aspects of Aging', *see note 14*.

19 See Butler, *Middle Age and Aging*: 227–8, *see note 14*. See also M. Berenger (ed.) *Psychogeriatrics: An International Handbook* (New York: Springer Verlag, 1987).

20 See Peter Sainsbury, 'Social and Epidemiological Aspects of Suicide with Special Reference to the Aged', *see Chapter 9 note 29*; and National Center for Health Statistics, *Vital and Health Statistics Series* (Washington DC: US Government Printing Office, 1967, 20: 5).

21 See Marion P. Crawford, 'Retirement and Disengagement', *Human Relations*, 1971, 24(3): 271.

22 Atchey, *The Sociology of Retirement*, *see note 13*.

11 METAMORPHOSIS

1 Sigmund Freud, 'Civilization and its Discontents', *The Standard Edition*, vol. 21, 1930: 85, *see Chapter 2, note 6*.

NOTES

2 Ryunosuke Akutagawa, *Rashomon and Other Stories* (New York: Liveright, 1952).
3 Stefan Zweig, 'Transfiguration', *Kaleidoscope*, trans. E. and C. Paul (New York: The Viking Press, 1934: 153–4).
4 Oscar Wilde, *De Profundis and Other Writings* (Harmondsworth: Penguin Books, 1954: 156).

Index

205